Studies in Modern History

General Editor: **J. C. D. Clark**, Joyce and Elizabeth Hall Distinguished Professor
of British History, University of Kansas

Titles include:

Bernard Cottret (*editor*)
BOLINGBROKE'S POLITICAL WRITINGS
The Conservative Enlightenment

Richard R. Follett
EVANGELICALISM, PENAL THEORY AND THE POLITICS OF CRIMINAL LAW
REFORM IN ENGLAND, 1808–30

Philip Hicks
NEOCLASSICAL HISTORY AND ENGLISH CULTURE
From Clarendon to Hume

William M. Kuhn
DEMOCRATIC ROYALISM
The Transformation of the British Monarchy, 1861–1914

Kim Lawes
PATERNALISM AND POLITICS
The Revival of Paternalism in Early Nineteenth-Century Britain

Nancy D. LoPatin
POLITICAL UNIONS, POPULAR POLITICS AND THE GREAT REFORM ACT OF
1832

Marjorie Morgan
NATIONAL IDENTITIES AND TRAVEL IN VICTORIAN BRITAIN

James Muldoon
EMPIRE AND ORDER
The Concept of Empire, 800–1800

W. D. Rubinstein and Hilary Rubinstein
PHILOSEMITISM
Admiration and Support for Jews in the English-Speaking World, 1840–1939

Lynne Taylor
BETWEEN RESISTANCE AND COLLABORATION
Popular Protest in Northern France, 1940–45

Studies in Modern History
Series Standing Order ISBN 0–333–79328–5
(*outside North America only*)

You can receive future titles in this series as they are published by placing a standing order
Please contact your bookseller or, in case of difficulty, write to us at the address below with
your name and address, the title of the series and the ISBN quoted above

Customer Services Department, Macmillan Distribution Ltd, Houndmills, Basingstoke,
Hampshire RG21 6XS, England

Evangelicalism, Penal Theory and the Politics of Criminal Law Reform in England, 1808–30

Richard R. Follett

palgrave

First published 2001 by
PALGRAVE
Houndmills, Basingstoke, Hampshire RG21 6XS and
175 Fifth Avenue, New York, N. Y. 10010
Companies and representatives throughout the world

PALGRAVE is the new global academic imprint of
St. Martin's Press LLC Scholarly and Reference Division and
Palgrave Publishers Ltd (formerly Macmillan Press Ltd)

ISBN 0–333–80388–4

This book is printed on paper suitable for recycling and
made from fully managed and sustained forest sources.

A catalogue record for this book is available
from the British Library.

Library of Congress Cataloging-in-Publication Data
Follett, Richard R., 1963–
     Evangelicalism, penal theory, and the politics of criminal law reform in
     England, 1808–30 / Richard R. Follett.
         p cm. — (Studies in modern history)
     Includes bibliographical references and index.
     ISBN 0–333–80388–4
     1. Criminal justice, Administration of—England—History—19th
     century. 2. Criminal law—England—History—19th century 3. Great
     Britain—Politics and government—1800–1837. 4 Social reformers-
     –England—History—19th century. 5. Evangelicalism—England–
     –History—19th century. I. Title. II. Studies in modern history (St.
     Martin's Press)

HV9960.G72 E544 2000
364 942'09'034—dc21
                                                          00–059151

10   9   8   7   6   5   4   3   2   1
10   09 08 07 06 05 04 03 02 01

Printed and bound in Great Britain by
Antony Rowe Ltd, Chippenham, Wiltshire

Contents

List of Abbreviations

CPS   The Capital Punishment Society (The Society for Diffusing Information on the Subject of the Punishment of Death)
LSF   Library of the Society of Friends
PDS   Prison Discipline Society

Preface and Acknowledgements

On a dreary January day in 1817, Thomas Fowell Buxton went to visit Newgate Prison with two fellow members of the Prison Discipline Society. The jail was a little less filthy than it had been when he had first gone there in 1816, when the Society had begun its efforts to improve England's prisons and reach out to the juvenile offenders that often crowded their cells. He saw 44 'little wretches collected together', some under sentence of death, but, he wrote his wife, 'the certainty that none of them will be executed, rather took off the awfulness of their situation'.[1] Their plight, that is their destitution and questionable future, and their seemingly wilful obliviousness to it, distressed Buxton; but the condition of four other young men, whose sentence of death was to be carried out the following week, moved him even more deeply. He could not get near enough to speak to them, but the sight was sadness 'sufficient for that day'. Recalling the scene, he wrote that it made him desire to do something, that his 'life may not pass quite uselessly – but that in some shape or other I may assist in checking and diminishing crime and its consequent misery'. If all had an obligation to do some good, then surely he had a responsibility to use his talents to do as much as he could. He had come to a crossroads, where he must choose a direction. He could go on in his private business, 'not absolutely forgetful of futurity, nor absolutely devoted to it – I may get riches & repute & gratify my ambition & do some good ... and at length I shall find all my time on earth expended – & in retracing my life I shall see little but occasions lost and capacities misapplied'. The other path promised more labour, and less self indulgence: 'I may become a real soldier of Christ, I may feel that I have no business on earth but to do his will & to walk in his ways – & I may direct every energy I have to the service of others.' He believed he knew which of these paths he would most gladly choose, but, he wrote on, ' "what I would that I do not, but what I hate, that do I", – in short the cares & the pleasures, & the business of this world check the good seed – & we are perpetually deceived, we would sow to the Spirit, & we sow to the flesh – we desire heaven, & we are chained to the earth'.

---

[1] Letter to Hannah Buxton, 5 January 1817, Buxton Papers, Rhodes House, MSS Brit. Emp. s. 444, v. 1, ff. 195–8.

Encountering this letter for the first time, I was struck by its tone of struggle, hope, and self-criticism. It spoke of an intent many shades brighter than the dim picture of penal reform in such works as Michel Foucault's *Discipline and Punish*, Michael Ignatieff's *A Just Measure of Pain* or V. A. C. Gatrell's *Hanging Tree*. As I dug into the materials on criminal law and prison reform, I found a very human mix of motives and intentions, some as personal and promising as Buxton's, some calculating, rational and enlightened, and a few that were harsher, more vengeful, perhaps even sinister. What I could not find was a dominant mode or argument that in any way spoke for the whole movement of reform in the early nineteenth century. Given the dominance Jeremy Bentham has had in the histories of penal law reform, this surprised me; perhaps he was not the shaker and mover he had been portrayed to be? I was also initially puzzled at the marked presence of Evangelical politicians and social leaders, who interacted with the 'utilitarian' reformers as if nothing separated them but a vague word or two. As it became clear that the support of the famous 'Saints' around Wilberforce helped make criminal law reform a parliamentary issue, I realized I needed both to understand how they fitted into the picture in a way previous histories had not accounted for, and also to come to grips with how penal reform fitted with their Evangelical outlook on politics and society.

This study is the result of these queries, and it is intended to be a mild revision, or perhaps a rerevision. For though one can never again write the history of criminal law with the untroubled optimism and faith in the ultimate triumph of humanitarian principles as Leon Radzinowicz did, one must also face the fact that what we value as civilized and humane at the beginning of the twenty-first century, was very much shaped by the debates and reforms of the early nineteenth. I do not intend to describe a simple picture, nor one held together by one strong theoretical perspective; I simply could not fit the story into any particular mold.[2] What follows is instead a complex and sometimes 'thick' description of the actors and acts, and the texts and contexts that surrounded and created the criminal law reforms of early-nineteenth-century England. I doubt it will be the last word on the matter; I only hope it will be a good and solid one.

[2] Though I do find an affinity with some of the assertions of George M. Thomas, *Revivalism and Cultural Change: Christianity, Nation Building, and the Market in the Nineteenth-Century United States* (Chicago: University of Chicago Press, 1989), particularly his view that religious movements, as carriers of a particular world-view or ontology, attempt 'to construct a new social order... in their specific claims and demands', p 14.

One person's name appears as the author of this study, but its completion was dependent on the support and efforts of many others. I am first grateful to my graduate advisor, Professor Richard W. Davis, for having steered me through the historiography on British politics and Evangelicalism; in a similar way I am thankful for the instruction in Anglo-American legal history provided by Professor David Konig. Professor Gregory Claeys, now of the Royal Holloway College, University of London, provided me both aid in formulating the ideas for the dissertation which led to this book, and practical assistance during my stay in Britain. The fellowship grant and year-long support provided by the British Fulbright Commission and staff allowed me to move about from one British archive to another while gathering the 'raw' material needed for this work. I am indebted to both the staff and my fellow guests at William Goodenough and London Houses in Mecklenburgh Square, for their high standards and warm camaraderie during my stay there. I must also thank the librarians and staff of the British Library, of the Western Manuscripts Room of the Bodleian Library, of the Rhodes House Library at Oxford University, and of the Cambridge University Library. The Library of the Society of Friends, Friends House, London, provided invaluable service and resources on the Quakers and their involvement in British politics in the early nineteenth century. The staff of the Public Records Office, both at Kew and at the old Chancery Lane facility, were very helpful in tracing down obscure references. A special thanks is due to Lincoln's Inn and its Librarian for allowing me to examine the Sir Samuel Romilly Manuscript in their very comfortable reading room. I am also grateful for the advice and support given by several historians in Britain, including David Bebbington, V. A. C. Gatrell, Boyd Hilton, and Ian Remmie, who was visiting Cambridge while I was there. Back in the USA, I would have floundered without the aid of the Washington University librarians who provided ideas on where to find things along the way. I owe a special thanks to R. K. Webb, who read over an early chapter of this study and gave me timely guidance and encouragement, and to Victor Bailey, whose sage advice helped me edit the manuscript sensibly. Tim Baldwin, a friend and teacher, provided well-formed criticism that has made this work far more readable. Finally, I thank J. C. D. Clark for his initial interest in this study, which motivated me to make something of it, Aruna Vasudevan for her guidance through the publishing process, and Alison Black for her gentle editing of the manuscript. These have all helped to make this work better; whatever errors remain are my own.

Several others provided good cheer and encouragement in the process of completing this study, especially my friends and colleagues Padraic

Kennedy, Derek Blakeley, and Catherine Forslund. Beyond the walls of the academy I am especially grateful to Bill and Christy Keating for their help and support, that I might 'pursue my calling'. I feel a singular appreciation to Gene Allen and the employees of Missouri Petroleum Products Company, who have put up with me these past few years while I finished this work.

Of all those who have made my research possible, I am most thankful for my wife, Altha, and my daughters, Kate and Molly, who have suffered much neglect in the process of my completing this book. It is dedicated to them for their perseverance and love toward one whose mind has often been miles and centuries away from home.

1
Mitigating the 'Bloody Code': an Introduction

Between 1808 and 1830, the British parliament debated the amelioration of England's 'Bloody Code' of criminal statutes. Before 1808, the few attempts to challenge England's expanding list of capital statutes had generated little sustained discussion. After 1830, the matter gained enough public attention to warrant professional and royal commission investigations. 'Amelioration' initially meant simply the repeal or amendment of statutes which made crimes as minor as pick-pocketing and shoplifting punishable by death. In the late 1760s William Blackstone counted 160 crimes that might lead a convict to the scaffold, and by 1819 Thomas Fowell Buxton could specify 223. In practice, relatively few offenders were hanged, but to reformers that fact, combined with the apparently random selection of those who were, proved that the existing laws were inappropriate. The repeal of capital statutes goes hand-in-hand with the reform and expansion of the prison system in Britain. But unlike the question of prisons, amendment of the Bloody Code raised cries of 'innovation' in the structure of the English law and constitution. The members of Parliament who led the reform effort were of eminently respectable backgrounds and social position, eschewing radical causes and rhetoric which might have inflamed the democratic elements in the population. Yet one could not deny that the assault upon the vast number of laws dealing with property challenged assumptions about the limits of government authority as well as the nature of criminal jurisprudence. A shift was occurring in these assumptions which found expression in the politics surrounding the amendment of the criminal statutes.

This change in perspective makes the debates and public discourse on penal reform fertile ground for examining the interrelated concerns and pressures at work in early nineteenth-century Britain. Religious revival, enlightenment humanitarianism, legal utilitarianism, and the optimism of commercial expansion all fed into the image of a civil society in which the death penalty would be reserved for only the most heinous of crimes against the person. But what does it mean to say that the Evangelical revival affected the age, and how did humanitarianism influence political perspectives? Such terms have been used so often and with such ambiguity that they demand fresh definition and clear illustration if they are to signify at all, especially when one turns to their impact on the changes in England's law of sanctions.

The early view of this era of reform portrayed it as a time of hopeful progress, when the foundations of the modern welfare state were being laid down. Conditions in the last third of the twentieth century have caused historians to question this optimistic view, and some have characterized penal reform as simply a shift in the mechanisms of social control. Others, more subtly, have argued that it was all a change in the language and conception of punishment, perhaps made necessary by the expanded population, which nonetheless helped preserve the existing power structures and political elite. By examining the politics of criminal law reform between 1808 and 1830, this study clarifies the components of political discourse and the processes which made reform possible. That social control was always a concern for reformers and conservatives alike is not in dispute, but a balance must be struck between this obvious concern for public order and the protection of persons and property, and the real desire on the part of reformers for a less bloody, fairer and more transparent administration of law and punishment. Readjusting the balance suggests that the shift in assumptions about punishment and government authority was neither a simplistic march of progress, nor a sinister play of language to retain social control and power. Those involved in reform sought substantive changes that would bring existing institutions more into line with their basic conceptions of justice, mercy, and how legal practice should reflect the most deeply held beliefs of a people. Some of those beliefs were indeed about order; others were about religious truth and expedient government. And while not perfectly successful in their own day, politicians like Romilly, Mackintosh, and Buxton significantly furthered the dialog that made the content of a society's law of sanctions a measure of its civilization – a criterion of judgment alive today in both international discussions of human rights and domestic debates on social policy. For better, or for worse, we are the heirs of these early nineteenth-century debates.

A particular focus in this book is to ascertain and illustrate the role played by Evangelicals, in and out of Parliament, in promoting and shaping alterations traditionally viewed as based in utilitarianism. The role of religious belief in shaping the law is of particular interest, since it has been argued that by the end of the eighteenth century, religion was largely superfluous to legal thought. Though few deny the importance of Evangelicalism to the early nineteenth century, rare is the attempt to specify how religious language or political action actually changed the nature of the politics and discourse in the era. One usually finds only vague generalizations about the new importance placed on morality in public matters. What this morality was, how it connected with utilitarian emphases, and why it mattered in criminal law reform are themes this book will explore. Specifically, the evidence gathered here will illustrate that Evangelicalism affected penal law reform in two fundamental ways. First, Evangelical MPs cast the key votes that committed the House of Commons to criminal law reforms over Government objections, and their activism helped bring others around to the reformers' view. Second, because of their involvement, the Evangelicals affected the discourse on punishments and shaped the options for reform.

This first chapter provides an overview of the historiography of English penal law and its alteration, and it must begin with examination of the great myth that Jeremy Bentham was the progenitor of English law reform. One can hardly exaggerate the contribution that earlier historians have attributed to Bentham. While utilitarianism and Bentham cannot be left out of the story, their place in it must become less if other elements are to be understood properly. The chapter also introduces the literature on the Evangelical revivals in Britain. Chapter 2 launches us into the politics of reform as Sir Samuel Romilly initiated his campaign to amend the laws. Chapter 3 provides a close examination of Romilly's background and thought about the criminal laws, establishing him as a figure independent of Bentham, though he was a friend to the philosopher of utility. Chapter 4 takes a closer look at Evangelical ideas about politics, laws, and punishments, and shows not only how penal reforms connected to their theological beliefs, but how these beliefs connected to language more commonly associated with utilitarianism. Chapter 5 furthers the examination of the Evangelicals by looking in detail at how two of the parliamentary leaders, William Wilberforce and Fowell Buxton, came to support and pursue penal reforms. Chapter 6 provides a needed look at the arguments and motives of the conservative opposition, to recapture their worldview and show why the Bloody Code could last so long, in so 'civilized' a nation as England. Chapters 7 and 8 then follow the political clash and confluence of these forces, exploring how public support for criminal law reform grew and eventually came to dominate the Commons. Finally, chapter 9 examines what happened when the Government took up reform and the public reaction when Sir Robert Peel's measures were viewed as insufficient; its conclusion then summarizes the significance of Evangelicalism to the politics of criminal law reform.

Of the myth of Bentham and the language of Blackstone

Jeremy Bentham was called to the bar in 1769, but he practiced law for only a few years and never argued a case in court. He was never appointed a judge or even a justice of the peace. Neither did he serve in Parliament. Yet Bentham has been called the 'greatest of English law reformers' and 'legislator of the world'. No historian of nineteenth-century English law is without an opinion on Bentham's influence. Many have been downright effusive in their praise, most often of the particulars of Benthamic reform,[1] of mitigation of the criminal sanctions or of creation of a local court system, for instance, but also of the systematic thinking which stood behind them. At the same time, however, these legal historians have often been aware of the gap between what Bentham desired to see in a legal system and what actually came to be in the course of the century. Bentham's despised 'judge-made' common law remained dominant, although its hold on the English system was loosened by reforms in the 1870s. Lawyers continued to use a specialized language beyond the reach of most people not initiated into its usage. And the principle of utility, though in some ways practically operative in British political and social considerations well before Bentham, was never formally acknowledged as a basis for law-making or reform.

Given these obvious gaps, some assessment of Bentham's reputed and actual impact is necessary. Bentham's writings on jurisprudence filled many volumes, many not published until this century.[2] His notions of penal law are succinctly put in his *Introduction to the Principles of Morals and Legislation*, first printed in 1780, but not released until 1789. It was almost universally ignored at that time and received wider recognition only after republication in 1823. By then Bentham had become better known as the author of *Panopticon; or the Inspection House* (1790), in which he described his model prison/factory. The *Introduction* defined Bentham's now famous principle of utility, by which any action 'whatsoever' was approved or disapproved, according to its tendency to 'augment or diminish the happiness of the party whose interest is in question'.[3] Generalizing from the individual to the community,

Bentham's utilitarianism sought to promote the greatest happiness of the greatest number and delineated criminal offences which disrupted or threatened the happiness of the community. His ideas were made famous on the continent by the 1802 publication in Paris of the *Traités de législation civile et pénale*, a work that owed much of its coherence to the editor, Etienne Dumont.[4] Bentham's later publications never really extended the penology addressed in these works, which basically argued that criminal behavior could and should be molded by applying specific degrees of pain or suffering, according to the gravity of the offense. The difficulty lay both in determining how to judge this gravity and in devising a means for meting out punishment.

Bentham's writings never quite surmounted this difficulty of finding appropriate applications, and one is at first hard pressed to account for the greatness of his reputation. Indeed, many of Bentham's contemporaries were less than friendly. Francis Horner, a barrister, MP, and contributor to the *Edinburgh Review*, wrote for many when he commented in 1803 that 'Bentham's name is repulsive'.[5] He had found even Dumont's edited version of Bentham's writing hard going. Romilly, who genuinely liked Bentham, nonetheless found his approach to law and social criticism impractical and sometimes libelous.[6] From the beginning, however, the person most responsible for Bentham's reputation as a law reformer was Bentham himself. At the age of twenty, while reading Helvetius, he asked himself, 'And have I indeed a genius for legislation? I gave myself the answer, fearfully and tremblingly – Yes!'[7] In pursuit of applying this genius he wrote many thousands of sheets, and sent hundreds of letters to monarchs and statesman all over the world. He offered to create a code of laws for Russia, for the United States, and for many of the emerging states in Latin America. Most of these sent him polite but negative replies, though some took his specific suggestions seriously.[8] In his own country, he cultivated relationships with men whom he supposed might implement his ideas. The list included Romilly, James Mackintosh, Francis Place, Basil Montagu, James and John Stuart Mill, as well as many attached to the *Edinburgh Review* and anyone connected with the more radical *Westminster Review*. One of these associates was Henry Brougham, who became the Lord Chancellor in 1830, two years after he had launched a campaign to reform the common law courts in England. In a much quoted passage introducing his own speeches on law reform, Brougham declared,

The age of Law Reform and the age of Jeremy Bentham are one and the same.... No one before him had ever seriously thought of exposing the defects in our English system of Jurisprudence.... None ever before Mr. Bentham took in the whole departments of legislation. None before him can be said to have treated it as a science, and by so treating, made it one.[9]

Brougham clearly admired Bentham's analysis of the law and concluded that all the improvements in jurisprudence he had observed had been advocated by Bentham or his school. His subsequent remarks, however, contained more than a little criticism of Bentham's ideas and style, but many historians have quoted Brougham's opening lines and ignored the rest.

John Stuart Mill was the most important promoter of Bentham's ideas after Bentham himself. Mill's father James became a close friend of Bentham, and the younger Mill's whole childhood was influenced by the philosopher's ideas. While Mill's writings might not have been as prolific as Bentham's, Mill's were without doubt more popular and more widely read by his contemporaries. In an 1838 article in the *London and Westminster Review*, Mill called Bentham a 'teacher of teachers' and gave him the credit for initiating the spirit of inquiry into the laws that led to the reforming commissions of the 1830s.[10] Other of Mill's writings, such as his essay 'Utilitarianism', made the system of thought associated with Bentham accessible to a mass of readers who would not otherwise have taken the time to wade through Bentham's own prose. Without Mill, who also edited his work on the rules of evidence, Bentham might well have been set aside like so many other theorists of the early nineteenth century. As one legal historian has observed of Bentham's contemporaries, 'The legal profession to a man ignored Bentham and all his works; they regarded him merely as an elderly gentleman full of visionary schemes which he dimly expounded in very bad English.'[11] Mill would not have disagreed, for he readily acknowledged that Bentham's sway was indirect. The assault on England's established institutions was carried out not through the philosopher's own writings, but 'through the minds and pens which those writings fed – through the men in more direct contact with the world, into whom his spirit passed'.[12] Mill's *Autobiography* did much to establish the perception of the potency of these men, the philosophical radicals.

The next step in the growth of Bentham's reputation was taken by the distinguished historians of English law in the later nineteenth century. Sir James Fitzjames Stephen and Sir Henry Maine both praised the rationality of Bentham's system and asserted its impact on their own time.[13] Early in the twentieth century A. V. Dicey also boosted Bentham's fame, calling the era from 1825–70 the 'period of Benthamism or Individualism' and declaring that during this time, 'legislation was governed by the body of opinion, popularly, and on the whole rightly, connected with the name of Bentham'.[14] He blurred numerous distinctions by equating Benthamism and individualism, emphasizing those aspects of government and social action which he thought supported individual freedom, but which were often outside or even contrary to Bentham's approach and writings.

Elie Halévy took Bentham's legacy beyond legal history.[15] Halévy's more subtle account of Bentham's influence on nineteenth-century England lacked Dicey's ideological concern with individualism versus collectivism. Rather than portraying Benthamism as an optimum English individualism, he defined utilitarianism as 'nothing but an attempt to apply the principles of Newton to the affairs of politics and of morals', placing Bentham cleanly in line with the Enlightenment. Bentham's achievement with regard to crime was to show that the 'problem for the statesman was to define obligations and punishments in such a way that private interests shall be brought by artificial means to coincide with the public interest'.[16]

In the standard work on the history of English criminal law, Leon Radzinowicz completed the picture of Bentham as the 'greatest of English legal reformers'.[17] Like many other legal historians, Radzinowicz was careful to maintain that 'the fundamental tenets of [Bentham's] doctrine have by no means been universally adopted', but while such writings as the *Table of the Springs of Action* and *Felicific Calculus* are full of artificial conceptions, Bentham's 'projected changes in the law have become an integral part of the legal system' in England.[18]

Radzinowicz's portrayal may be called the high point of Bentham's reputation, as the early nineteenth-century doubts about his influence found new expression by the late 1950s. Bentham's impact was first challenged in regard to administrative reform.[19] D. J. Manning's study, *The Mind of Jeremy Bentham*, focused on the political implications of Bentham's theory. If Dicey's Bentham was bedecked as the penultimate liberal, then Manning's portrayal put him in the guise of the proto-totalitarian, because Bentham failed to place any clear limits on the power of his sovereign legislature. Of Bentham's practical influence, Manning was skeptical; he thought it likely that Bentham's proposals corresponded to later changes only to the extent that they were common sense notions inspired by a 'feeling for rectifying inconsistencies in an established way of life'.[20] Even the legal philosopher H. L. A. Hart, who was far more partial to the utilitarian's creed than Manning, had to agree with Sydney Smith's comment that Bentham needed a middle-man to make him presentable to the people.[21] Hart considered Bentham a powerful thinker, but did not belabor his influence on others or on later events. In William Thomas's 1979 study, *The Philosophical Radicals*, even the effectiveness of Bentham's followers came under fire. Contrary to the inherited notion that the Benthamites were organized and politically effective, Thomas found that 'the Philosophical Radicals ignored or misread many of the signs of the times, were far from united, and preached a doctrine which was in many ways perplexed and contradictory'.[22] Or as Helen Beynon observed, though 'Bentham dreamt at night ... of having a band of disciples, ... those of Benthamite persuasion – and it was persuasion, Bentham did assiduously cultivate these people – were apt to be very wayward disciples'.[23]

Despite growing dissatisfaction with Bentham's traditional reputation, it has remained strong in the historiography of criminal law. In a 1983 article on the 'revisionist' history of crime in Britain, David Philips still concluded that to cope with the social flux and unrest of the early industrial revolution, 'the governing class had to take up, however reluctantly, the types of solutions proposed by Jeremy Bentham and his utilitarian disciples'.[24] He hedged by noting that Bentham's proposals 'were not necessarily the direct source of the reforms finally implemented', but one gets the impression that Bentham's was the only show playing for legal and bureaucratic reform. Randall McGowen, in an otherwise insightful article on the political debates on English criminal law, also appealed to Bentham as 'the fountain from which reform drew its strength'.[25] Even a recent legal history by W. R. Cornish and G. de N. Clark, which provides a useful perspective on the changes in English law between 1750 and 1950, still shows Bentham as the chief theoretical spokesman for penal law reform in England.[26] The many individuals and interests involved in the reforms are all melted down under the evidently all-encompassing label 'Benthamites'.[27]

The language of the arguments in Parliament calls the myth of Bentham's influence most seriously into question. In the period under consideration in this study, 1808–30, one seldom hears an appeal to the 'principle of utility' in the halls of Westminster, even by those who have been classed as 'Benthamites'. One might hear an appeal for practical measures of reform, or a question as to the utility of a specific measure, but these often came from conservative politicians challenging the wisdom of proposed changes to established laws. The writer most cited by those earnest to press criminal law reforms was William Blackstone. The fourth volume of the *Commentaries on the Laws of England*, which dealt with the criminal law, first appeared in 1769. At the beginning of this volume Blackstone expressed satisfaction with Cesare Beccaria's thoughts on the nature of punishment in *Dei Delitta e delle Pene*, published in 1764 in Italian and in English in 1767.[28] Blackstone did not simply mimic Beccaria's ideas, however, but rather took those he found applicable and adapted them to the tradition of the common law. He did not adopt a rigidly rationalistic approach, which Bentham later pursued, but Blackstone did suggest many penal reforms.

With regard to the capital statutes specifically, one argument from Blackstone appeared again and again in pamphlet and parliamentary debate. The famed commentator found much wisdom in the English legal system, but he also found the 160 statutes that made specific crimes punishable by death difficult to justify:

> So dreadful a list, instead of diminishing, increases the number of offenders. The injured, through compassion, will often forbear to prosecute: juries, through compassion, will sometimes forget their oaths, and either acquit the guilty or mitigate the nature of the offence: and judges, through compassion, will respite one half of the convicts, and recommend them to the royal mercy. Among so many chances of escaping, the needy or hardened offender overlooks the multitude that suffer; he boldly engages in some desperate attempt, to relieve his wants or supply his vices; and, if unexpectedly the hand of justice overtakes him, he deems himself peculiarly unfortunate, in falling at last a sacrifice to those laws, which long impunity has taught him to contemn.[29]

With only slight variation, this argument found its way into almost every speech in favor of mitigating the penal laws, and against it the conservative ministers and judges could only assert an increasingly unconvincing argument for the ancient wisdom of the law and the supposed deterrent effect of the terror of the threat of death. Reformers also looked to Blackstone for his specific recommendations and his general principles with regard to capital punishment. Since Blackstone also praised the ancient wisdom of the common law, he was a useful foil against the conservatives. The language of Blackstone rather than of Bentham prevailed in the early decades of criminal law reform.

Of crime, criminal justice and the claims of humanitarian reform

The rise and fall of Bentham's reputation exemplifies a trend in the broader historiography of nineteenth-century England. Martin Wiener has shown that 'the disillusionment with both the virtue and efficacy of the state that came to permeate political and social discourse in the 1970s and 1980s was also taking place within the writing of the history of modern Britain'.[30] By 1960, Wiener argues, a '"Fabian" consensus historiography had crystallized' in which 'historical writing projected a highly positive view of the capabilities and beneficence of the state, along with a strongly evolutionary outlook'. But this Fabian vision ran aground on social and political frustrations in the 1960s and 1970s, giving rise to new interpretations of the history of the state on both the Right and the Left. From both directions, the new historiography challenged the moral status of state intervention and tended to portray past reforms as the application of new methods of social control instead of humanitarian improvements. Wiener does not mean that because much British historiography has also been part of recent political debate, its validity as history should be dismissed; rather, while warning us of the inspiration and bias of this revisionism, he contends that it has opened new areas of inquiry. Of particular concern for this study, revisionism has raised new questions about the history of criminal justice. The old picture of benign humanitarian progress has been replaced with an image much more complex and influenced by the darker sources of human motivation. The literature of crime and the law is vast and expanding; this review addresses those parts which have most affected our understanding of criminal law reform.[31]

Radzinowicz's first volume of his *History of the English Criminal Law*, published in 1948, perfectly fits Wiener's description of the 'Fabian consensus historiography', both in its unrelenting positive regard for criminal law reforms and in its emphasis on Bentham. Radzinowicz explored the implications of Enlightenment penal philosophy for the reform of English criminal laws, and his description is very much a story of the slow permeation of new ideas into formal social institutions. Although he overemphasized the Beccarian and Benthamic elements in the reforms, Radzinowicz has provided an enduring account of the parliamentary action.

One able challenge to Radzinowicz's approach came from Douglas Hay and E. P. Thompson in their studies of law in the eighteenth century. Hay argued that what appears to us as a wildly irrational expansion of capital statutes in the eighteenth century actually served the purposes of the ruling classes rather well, emphasizing their power and authority, by allowing them to bend the letter of the law for the sake of a manipulative mercy.[32] Thompson's detailed study of the origins and consequences of the Waltham Black Act of 1723 provided more evidence of the utility of the law in supporting particular class interests, but he tried to go beyond the simple social-control models. There was no doubt that the criminal law was about social control. But to say, 'Look, see how these corrupt Whig politicians used the law to enforce their sense of order on the lower classes', seemed to Thompson neither surprising nor particularly insightful. What struck him was that while the law could 'be seen instrumentally as mediating and reinforcing existent class relations' and providing these with ideological legitimation, one had also to recognize that these 'class relations were expressed, not in any way one likes, but *through the forms of the law*', and the law, like other institutions, had its own characteristics and to some extent its own independent history and logic of evolution.[33] This meant that the law might be laid down by the ruling elite to serve their own purpose, but once the rules of the game were set, 'they could not break those rules or the whole game would be thrown away'. Furthermore, rather than treating the rhetoric about order as hypocrisy, the lower classes used it for their own purposes. The upper and middle classes may have appeared more often in court to prosecute property offenses than did the lower orders, but the poor were not strangers to the role of plaintiff.[34] The law laid down a basis for universality and regularity of treatment which did indeed serve to legitimate the ruling power. At the same time, it placed that power under specific constitutional limits. The so-called rule of law had to be treated differently from the exercise of arbitrary power. Thompson believed more traditional Marxists had failed to recognize that the inhibitions on power were real.

Thompson's and Hay's neo-Marxist approach did much to push the discussion of law and society away from a simplistic functionalism. Another challenge to the old history of criminal law has come from historians concerned with issues of language and society. Perhaps the most seminal of these has been Michel Foucault, who desired to show the change in the discourse on punishment as a shift from punishing the body to punishing the mind.[35] Foucault's account was somewhat forced, and ran aground on his example of Bentham's Panopticon as the ultimate expression of this phenomenon – he conveniently ignored the fact that the British Parliament chose not to follow Bentham's model. Michael Ignatieff did more to identify sources for the new discourse on punishment in Britain, including those originating in notions of political economy or Evangelical reformation, though he also accorded Bentham a symbolic significance as the ultimate expression of the age.[36] Both these historians were interested in language as a means to power: the changing discourse on punishment, while advertised as increased humanitarianism, in fact merely altered the technology of social control. The alteration in the dominant discourse necessitated change in the laws, but in terms of power, legal and penal reform really changed nothing.

The new emphasis on the relationship between power and language opened other possibilities for inquiry. One attempt to apply this version of structuralism to the history of criminal law has appeared in Randall McGowen's articles. In 'The Image of Justice', McGowen made a closer examination of the Parliamentary debates and concluded that the issue in dispute was not the humanity of the law, nor even its efficiency, 'but how to present a more pleasing image of justice' so that the law would have greater legitimacy, and hence could be made more efficient.[37] The reformers pushed an image of 'the impersonal and impartial rule of law' and of greater 'formal equality', in contrast to the conservatives' hierarchical and deferential vision of society, which had the double-edged characteristics of flexibility and personal involvement. The reformers succeeded because they were able to impose a discourse in which discretion was viewed as an evil because it caused the law to be uncertain. By taking seriously the shift of language about the nature of criminal law, McGowen has succeeded in showing both that class interest was not so simple as cruder descriptions of social control made out and that ideas did matter. He also suggested links between religious opinions and penal philosophy, which provides a background for the discussion of Evangelical views of the matter.[38]

One weak element in the structuralist interpretation is the lack of compelling explanation of why the discourse changed at all, of why the appeal to certainty and humanity should have become more compelling than appeals to discretion and mercy. One finds an assumption that the social changes of a market-oriented, early industrial society made new formulations of human values more acceptable, without a clear explanation why those formulations – the appeal to humanity, the demand for greater certainty – should have been more plausible to that society, or of why the up-and-coming class advocated the formulation. Thomas Haskell's essays on capitalism and humanitarian sensibility have provided one suggestive framework.[39] Haskell willingly accepted that humanitarian reformers were not as altruistic as they made themselves out to be and was not convinced that explanation of their efforts required belief in moral progress: 'Whatever influence the rise of capitalism may have had generally on ideas and values through the medium of class interest, it had a more telling influence on the origins of humanitarianism through changes that the market wrought in *perception* or *cognitive style*'.[40] Involvement in a market economy 'gave rise to new habits of causal attribution that set the stage for humanitarianism'.[41] People learned two interconnected lessons from the market place: (1) Keep your promises, and (2) Attend to the long-term or remote consequences of your actions – realize, for instance, that failure to aid a suffering stranger may be an opportunity lost. The market economy enabled people to think more efficiently about the impact of their actions on society, and of the impact of existing laws and practices as well. Out of this came stronger concern and compassion for those less fortunate, who suffered under the existing institutions. Haskell understood that concern for others was not new: eighteenth-century writers saw this as part of their Christian tradition. But Haskell argued that in the market-oriented society, the inherent if hidden appeal to self-interest affected more people, *and* 'inspired people's confidence in their power to intervene'.

Another problem of the structuralist accounts of criminal law has been the politicization of all relationships in society, as if everything one did was necessarily aimed at coercion and domination. As David Sugarman has pointed out, these accounts have taken too seriously the view that the state in the modern world has a monopoly on legitimate violence and is solely responsible for providing social order.[42] Confronted by these concerns, Ignatieff reevaluated his earlier views on penal reforms and decided that more was happening than the reproduction of power relations. He went so far as to criticize Foucault for having neglected 'large aspects of human sociability, in the family and in civil society generally, which are conducted by the norms of cooperation, reciprocity and the "gift relationship"'.[43] These references to civil society reopened discourses in the eighteenth and early nineteenth centuries that had often been ignored. Ignatieff directed attention to consideration of Adam Smith's notions of sympathy to get beyond thinking of social order only in the language of power, an effort begun by Norman Fiering, and then taken up by Randall McGowen and more recently by V. A. C. Gatrell.[44]

Understandings of civil society were intimately connected with notions of manners and the progress of civilization; we might therefore talk about the importance of ideas in prompting or shaping reforms, while linking those ideas to social and economic changes, which was Haskell's goal. These revisions have opened the way for more constructive exploration of arguments that claimed a spiritual, as well as a material, basis for the criminal law. In considering religion and criminal law reform, one confronts Hay's declaration that law replaced religion as the legitimating ideology of English society. Religion is more than ideology in the way he used that word, but Hay's assessment proves inadequate, for it ignores the deployment of language in criminal law debates derived from and appealing to the values and teachings of Christianity, both to *de*legitimate the capital statutes and their administration, *and* to legitimate the reformers' alternative proposals.[45] An understanding, then, of the impact of religion on penal law reform becomes a necessity.

Of Evangelicals and their impact

Among the most conspicuous supporters of penal reform who have never been called Benthamites were William Wilberforce and the group of Evangelical politicians called the Saints, or sometimes the Clapham Sect, after the village of Clapham, where a core of the members lived. While Wilberforce maintained a good relationship with Bentham, one might assume that their reasons for supporting penal reform differed. As Brougham noted, Bentham's ideas included a 'scientific' or rationalistic criticism of the system, implying the need for great structural change. These views, among others, justly earned Bentham a reputation as a radical among his contemporaries. The Evangelicals generally, and Wilberforce particularly, eschewed radicalism and most efforts that bore that name. Chapters 4 and 5 below explore the 'radical' content of Evangelicalism with regard to penal theory, but some of the more general historiography on the social influence of religious belief is also necessary to situate the scope and reason for this study.

'Evangelical' can be defined broadly or narrowly, but most often it is employed imprecisely. In this study, 'Evangelical' in the uppercase, whether used as a proper noun or adjective, denotes individuals, groups and trends which stemmed from the Evangelical revival of the eighteenth and early nineteenth centuries in Britain and America. The uppercase seems justified because the people involved and the movement more generally constituted an identifiable subgroup in the religious, social and intellectual history of the period. It can refer both to members of the Established Church and to orthodox Dissent affected by the revivals. The word 'evangelical' itself comes from the ancient Greek, *euangelia*, which means simply 'good news'. 'Gospel' has the same root meaning and has become the standard English translation of the Greek, the four gospels of the New Testament being literally the *euangelia* according to Matthew, Mark, Luke and John. The Christian use of the phrase finds earliest expression in the letters of St. Paul, where he speaks of the good news of God's grace toward human beings through Jesus Christ.[46] In this sense, any group which claims to follow the teachings of Jesus and the Apostles could be described as 'evangelical', and the word has often been appropriated by groups pressing for reforms in existing church institutions; hence, the Protestant church in Germany has called itself the 'Evangelische Kirche' from the sixteenth century to the present. In Britain, however, the term has a specific reference to the Methodist revival that began in the fourth decade of the eighteenth century, most often associated with ministries of John Wesley and George Whitefield. The movement diversified in the nineteenth century but has continued to be an identifiable and vocal party in anglophone Christianity to the present.

The best description of the tenets and history of that movement has come from David Bebbington's history, *Evangelicalism in Modern Britain*. Evangelicals themselves have often claimed merely to be conveying the beliefs of the primitive Church and the Reformation, but Bebbington identified particular attributes of the eighteenth-century movement which have typified Evangelicalism to the present. He set out four defining characteristics.[47] The first he terms 'conversionism', the emphasis on the conscious, personal, and emotional process of recognizing one's sinfulness, repenting of it, and placing one's faith in Christ for salvation. One's whole life must be made anew, evidenced by outward changes which are more dramatic for some than for others. While Evangelicals have responded to biblical criticism in various ways, accepting greater or lesser amounts of questioning, they have always affirmed a high view of the Bible as the revelation of God's will toward human beings. This emphasis on divine revelation Bebbington called 'Biblicism'. For Evangelicals, the central tenet taught in the Bible, the doctrine which holds the rest together, was the death of Jesus Christ on the cross for the forgiveness of human sinfulness. Bebbington gave this idea of the centrality of the Cross the technical title of 'crucicentrism'. One might question much in doctrine and practice, but to deny the atoning death of Jesus put one beyond the Evangelical pale. The final characteristic, 'activism', could be seen as the logical extension of taking one's conversion and theology seriously. If the Bible said to go and make disciples, then that was what it meant: and Evangelicals have accordingly always laid great stress on preaching and instruction for conversion and for the spiritual growth and well-being of believers. Bebbington noted that even unsympathetic observers admitted that Evangelical clergy set high standards of missionary zeal and service to their congregations.[48] Love of one's neighbor, however, meant not only concern for his eternal soul, but for his present suffering also. Besides the host of missionary enterprises, Evangelicals undertook many projects of charity and social improvement through a multitude of voluntary societies and associations. The campaign against slavery was but the most famous effort to bring Christian ethics to bear on public policy. Any one of these four characteristics might be claimed beyond Evangelical circles; Bebbington would argue that the concurrence of all four meant the Christian was moving into the Evangelical camp.

1)   The Clapham Sect and early nineteenth century politics

It is an oft repeated claim that Evangelicals focused on the salvation and reform of individuals and avoided criticism of the larger structures of society. Yet in criminal law reform, as in antislavery, the Saints tackled large institutions, and worked for reforms that required changes in both the operation and the understanding of law in English society. Indeed, opponents construed reform as an attack upon the constitution and the venerable tradition of the common law. In supporting curtailment of the hanging statutes, Evangelicals also found themselves in opposition to much of the Anglican Church hierarchy, at least in the first decades of the parliamentary reform effort.[49] How Evangelicals perceived their political role requires some explanation.

The later nineteenth-century image of the Evangelical as a self-righteous prude, socially inept, exaggeratedly deferential to superiors, condescending toward inferiors, and more prone to hypocrisy than to good works, derived more from the fiction of writers like Dickens and Thackeray than from careful historical investigation. That nineteenth-century Evangelicals were of unusually serious bearing is not to be denied, but recollections like those of Sir James Stephen on the Clapham Sect, or E. M. Forster's biography of his great aunt Marianne Thornton, suggest that, for all their earnestness, they deeply enjoyed life.[50] If morality was important, it was secondary to love. Still, the public image of Wilberforce and his allies has emphasized probity and sobriety, and one doubts they would have been displeased by this.

Twentieth-century interpretations of Evangelical involvement in political and social reform have varied considerably. E. M. Howse presented the Saints as 'this-worldly-minded' reformers motivated by ethical considerations derived from their religious convictions.[51] Ford K. Brown, on the other extreme, portrayed the Evangelicals in the 'age of Wilberforce' as heavenly-minded revivalists who used abolition of the slave trade and philanthropy simply to grab public attention and gain a hearing for their version of Christian piety.[52] In doing so, Brown insinuated, they laid the foundation of Victorian repressiveness. Other historians have followed Elie Halévy's suggestion that the Evangelical revivals served as an antidote both to upper-class selfishness, on the one hand, and to revolutionary enthusiasm on the part of the masses on the other.[53]

One problem common to these approaches is the tendency to treat Evangelicalism out of context and in terms other than its own; they evaluate the movement solely by its impact on matters which it may or may not have been aiming to affect. After all, the Evangelicals were not the only group in society working for social order. Disentangling Evangelical intentions is admittedly as difficult as unravelling any in historical analysis, but reinterpretations have often begun with closer scrutiny of their opinions and behaviors.[54] Ian Bradley followed this plan, making careful study of Evangelical actions and beliefs in politics before drawing conclusions about their supposed impact on society at large. He clarified the groupings of Evangelicals in Parliament, finding that the Saints formed an active and vocal minority, whose attitudes and activities were 'very much more liberal' than most historians had previously acknowledged.[55] By showing the Saints to be a group distinguishable from Evangelical MPs more closely associated with one party or the other, Bradley effectively separated them from criticism applicable only to Tories. Bradley's study restored to the Saints an independence of mind and political action which had been missed in earlier evaluations. The attitudes of public and private probity, diligence in the discharge of public duties, and the commitment to be true to one's conscience, all part of an Evangelical approach most manifest in the efforts of the Saints, shaped the culture of England in the decades to come. Bradley named this mindset a 'call to seriousness', which prevailed in part because it was successful at getting things done. Bradley further observed,

> Their achievements probably go a long way towards explaining the Victorians' optimism about the ease with which the world could be changed and their tendency to feel that once a society was established to attack a particular problem, that problem was already as good as solved.[56]

The Evangelicals therefore gave optimism, as much as sobriety, to the age which followed.

The Evangelicals brought to British politics a standard of personal and public behavior which would have baffled many in the eighteenth century. The standard made good political sense, however, recognizing the demands of radical agitators for eliminating corruption in government while assuring the ruling classes that moderate reforms need not lead to social upheaval. In criminal law reform Evangelicals achieved this effect by combining rationalistic arguments for proportionality and certainty in punishment with religiously-based notions of justice and mercy. This combination dampened the more extreme rhetoric on both sides of the penal reform question while providing a moral argument that was difficult to refute in the existing culture.

2) Of Evangelicalism and utilitarianism

The links between Evangelicalism and utilitarianism have tended to perplex historians, because the two movements have generally been conceived as antithetical. This proposition was developed by Elie Halévy, who believed that the rapid spread of utilitarian principles in an environment saturated with Evangelical religion presented a paradox to one trying to understand nineteenth-century England.[57] Theoretically the two approaches appeared hostile. The one emphasized the need, both personal and social, for strong Christian faith and morals. The other grew more and more anti-religious in the early decades of the nineteenth century and came to concentrate on a wholly secular, or in Bentham's terms 'rational', comprehension of society and the individual. Nonetheless, in terms of working out their beliefs, Halévy found much agreement between Evangelicals and utilitarians; for instance both preferred voluntary associations to government in shaping philanthropy and addressing social needs. Both movements sought reforms in government when laws or administrative practice hindered individual responsibility or improvement. When assessing British individualism, Halévy found in it 'a mixture whose constituents are often mingled beyond the possibility of analysis, a compound of Evangelicalism and Utilitarianism'. Halévy could not get beyond certain assumptions, however. He could not, for instance, view benevolence as something intrinsic to Evangelical piety. When discussing Wilberforce's support for Sir Francis Burdett's motion to abolish flogging in the army, Halévy wondered how it was that the Evangelicals came 'to temper their austere code with so much mercy? Had they been influenced unconsciously by humanitarian Liberalism?' That humanitarian liberalism might have the same roots as

Evangelicalism was not among Halévy's conceptual options, though Evangelicals themselves believed that religion provided the only secure foundation for benevolence and philanthropic endeavor, which otherwise would waver and collapse in the face of social opposition and changing fashion.[58]

Attempting to get beyond Halévy's formulations, Boyd Hilton has argued in *The Age of Atonement* that the spread of liberal economic and social ideals in the first half of the nineteenth century owed more to Evangelical notions of the efficacy of suffering and striving for spiritual regeneration, which he claimed were stirred by the doctrine of Atonement, than to either philosophical radicalism or the gradual dispersion of Adam Smith's political economy. Hilton recognized that in the early nineteenth century many Christian writers, especially Evangelicals, developed economic views 'in conscious opposition to utilitarian or classical economics', but asserted that despite this, they led to identical policy recommendations because at base they were more similar than has generally been acknowledged.[59] Hilton observed that despite its foundation in hedonistic egoism, utilitarianism took self-denial to be a personal value as much as did Evangelicalism. For the utilitarian political economist, self-denial now was for the hope of gain or greater security later in life. Evangelicals simply prolonged this anticipation into eternity: this life was short, and any trouble here would be incomparable to the joys in the life to come. At the same time it may be said that Evangelicals readily endorsed trade and commerce, albeit with concern that one not become too enamored of money-making.

One may find much in Hilton's study with which to argue, but his general description of the 'utilitarian' values espoused by Evangelicalism has helped to uncover the common Enlightenment heritage of both utilitarianism and Evangelicalism. This assertion rubs against a common bias – most historians describe the Enlightenment as at least anti-clerical, if not downright anti-Christian (though this popular generalization applies consistently only to the Enlightenment in France)[60] and often assume that religious revival was simply an emotional reaction to eighteenth-century rationalism, at best a harbinger of the Romantic movement, at worst an attempt to hold on to outdated doctrines by ignoring or condemning the intellectual developments of the period. While Evangelicals did write critically of Enlightenment figures such as Hume and Voltaire, their censure was reserved for writings against Christian beliefs. Other aspects of Enlightenment thought, like Hume's empiricism, were much accepted among the leaders of the eighteenth-century revivalists. Roger Anstey, in his study of the British abolition of the slave trade, has shown that the Enlightenment values of liberty, benevolence, and happiness all have Evangelical versions, some of which generated socially more powerful rhetoric than anything written by more secular philosophers.[61] But even Evangelical theology owed something to Enlightenment thought. As W. R. Ward observed,

> The famous free-for-alls which arose from the self conscious return to the past have disguised the degree to which the Evangelicals shared in the assumptions of the enlightenment, and constituted the second channel of its influence.... For the Evangelicals conceived that they were applying the inductive method in the field of religion, while the polemical backwoodsman was sacrificing the truth to system.[62]

Bebbington has further identified 'vital Christianity' (an Evangelical self-description) as the result of a self-conscious movement toward 'experimental religion'. In this regard, it had a distinctively anti-metaphysical bent, like utilitarianism. Even more like Bentham and his friends, 'Evangelicals elevated happiness into the primary place among human objectives. In seeing vital Christianity as the way to achieve it, they were differing from the Utilitarians about means, not ends'.[63]

To describe Evangelicalism as positively connected with the Enlightenment is not to claim for it any greater legitimacy. Rather, only by recognizing that Evangelicals employed Enlightenment ideas as their own can we understand their involvement in criminal law reform with any coherence. This study will make clearer the extent of the shared vision between utilitarianism, seen traditionally and uncontentiously as an Enlightenment product, and Evangelicalism, and how that vision was manifested in a certain perspective on civil society.

For all the talk of movements and trends, of social changes and the press of numbers on institutions, the political campaign for criminal law reform began as a lonely crusade by one compassionate lawyer with a strong conscience and a steadfast will. The story begins with Sir Samuel Romilly's endeavour to leave the laws better than he had found them.

2
Raising the Hue and Cry, 1808–10

The very structure and assumptions of English criminal law seemed to encourage the proliferation of capital statutes in the eighteenth century. The great majority of these crimes related to the taking or damaging of property. Sometimes a single act generated a number of crimes, as in the case of the Waltham Black Act. Passed in 1723, the 'Black Act' originally outlawed poaching in disguise or in 'blacked' face, but judicial interpretations soon divorced its various provisions from their original context, leading to a list of fifty or more crimes punishable by death.[1] English legal expectations were shaped by the common law, an uncodified tradition refined over the centuries by the interpretation of the judges. The common law specified certain broad categories of offenses, such as murder and larceny. When William Blackstone described the offense of murder, he did not draw upon a positive statute, but upon a description given by Sir Edward Coke, Lord Chief Justice during the reign of James VI/I.[2] Blackstone upheld the myth that the common law was handed down from time immemorial: a judge (or commentator) could never be declared to have 'defined' some part of it; at best he could be said to describe or discover it.

Blackstone grouped larceny with 'malicious mischief' and the many types of forgery under the general heading 'crimes against private property'. Varieties of each of these offenses were capital. In the case of larceny, the common law recognized two basic subdivisions, simple larceny (further divided into petit and grand larceny), and compound larceny, which was an aggravated robbery, implying some physical threat to the person robbed. By ancient tradition, theft was punishable by death when the value of goods exceeded twelve pence (the value defining grand larceny). This value had not changed in centuries, but the way of handling larceny had. By a statute passed in the reign of Queen Anne, any offender declared guilty of simple larceny was given 'benefit of clergy'.[3] This 'benefit of clergy' was another of the oddities of English law. Dating back to the medieval quarrels between the Church and the Crown, benefit of clergy originally applied only to those who belonged to an order of the Church, which meant that the King and his minions could not punish the priest, friar or nun in the same way as other subjects. To discover if one qualified for benefit of clergy prior to the statute of Queen Anne, a reading test was administered, on the grounds that only the clergy were likely to be able to read. The test usually took the opening lines from Psalm 51, which meant that anyone with any wit could memorize them. Benefit of clergy did not get one off completely, however: offenders were branded or whipped, sometimes both, and by statutes passed in the early years of George I, convicts were also liable to transportation to America.[4] After the American War of Independence, this penalty was replaced with imprisonment or transportation to Australia. The benefit of clergy applied to most felonies, though the common law denied it to those convicted of arson, highway robbery and a few other offenses. It never applied to high treason or misdemeanors. This privilege of the law partly explains the ease with which new capital statutes were created in the 1700s. Rather than create a whole new offense, a statute would simply remove the benefit of clergy from a crime already recognized as capital under the ancient common law. If an explanation had to be offered, some reference might be made to aggravation of the simple crime which made it more pernicious or more difficult to detect and prosecute the offender.

Before the nineteenth century, attempts to reform England's criminal laws had been few and far between. Outside Parliament many had expressed doubts about the efficacy of the hanging statutes, but within the Palace of Westminster the number of inquiries into the capital punishment could be counted on one hand. A Committee of the House of Commons appointed in 1750 put forward proposals, but all those which would have restricted the punishment of death were defeated in the House of Lords.[5] A second inquiry committee was appointed in 1770 and renewed in 1772. They proposed the repeal of eight capital statutes, on six of which the Commons agreed. Significantly, none of these statutes dealt with crimes against property. The 'penal laws bill' was lost in the Lords when Parliament was prorogued. The only other bid to investigate and perhaps mitigate the penal code came in 1787, but the motion for the appointment of a commission was withdrawn after William Pitt, then prime minister, spoke strongly against it.[6] Pitt put criminal law reform in a double-bind by arguing first that changes ought to take place according to settled principles, while at the same time avoiding any parliamentary discussion which might have led to such principles by a second stipulation that changes ought first to be discussed and approved by the judges. In practice it meant that one could more easily pass new capital statutes than even raise the topic of the severity of the English laws.

Pitt's government aided criminal law reform indirectly, however. He undertook several administrative reforms, especially in the area of finance, but the principles went much further. The confused condition of the statute book prompted Charles Abbott (later Lord Colchester), with Pitt's approval, to engage in a review and reorganization of the laws in 1796 and 1799. This resulted in a more complete and authoritative edition of the English statutes in the first decade of the 19th century.[7] One could see penal reform as a natural extension of this movement toward administrative rationalization. The response of conservatives like Lord Ellenborough and Lord Eldon, however, indicated that attempts to amend the system governing punishment struck at deeply held assumptions about the nature of authority in English government that had not been disturbed by the previous bureaucratic and procedural changes. Theories, 'sensibilities', and legal practice had all been shifting quietly for decades; the politics of criminal law reform forced the conflicts into the public light.

Getting started

The parliamentary effort to reform the criminal laws of England began without fanfare or public outcry. In early 1808, the late Solicitor General Sir Samuel Romilly gave notice in the House of Commons that he intended to introduce a bill to amend the criminal law of England. A reserved and highly competent barrister, Romilly was responding to no pressure group nor appeasing any constituency. The attempt to ameliorate England's laws was Romilly's personal initiative, and he realized that it lacked popularity. Indeed, as he addressed the Commons he remarked that in bringing forward an amendment to the criminal law, he knew that from that part of the public 'whose opinion may be supposed to have most influence on my conduct, instead of expecting praise, I must be satisfied with escaping censure'.[8] But he did not take up the matter suddenly or lightly; he had been considering it for some years. He had promised himself long before, that if ever he sat in the Commons, he would bring forward measures for reforming the criminal code, and he apologized for delaying a proposal.

During the previous year Romilly had gone back and forth on his intention to pursue criminal law reform, in part because of the precariousness of his political situation after the fall of the Ministry of All the Talents in spring 1807. Only by the invitation of Charles James Fox had Romilly entered Parliament at all. Until 1806 he had been a private lawyer whose practice in the Court of Chancery had increased steadily, until he sat at the front of the bar, second only to the Lord Chancellor Eldon in authority in that court. Romilly was on good terms with public men of various allegiances, but had long admired Fox's politics. He had no qualms about accepting the position of Solicitor General when offered it in the Fox–Grenville coalition, though he had turned down previous offers to enter Parliament. Both the first Marquis of Lansdowne and the Prince of Wales had offered him seats, but citing a desire to enter on his own, Romilly had politely, though firmly, declined their invitations.[9] The difference in this case was that he had no objection to serving in the ministry of Fox and Grenville, as he was already a supporter. To accept a parliamentary seat added no new obligation. Fox arranged for a seat at Queensborough, a borough very much under the influence of the Ministry.

The significant but short-lived Ministry of All the Talents foundered on the issue of extending the rights of Roman Catholics and Protestant Dissenters in late March 1807. Perhaps its greatest claim to fame was the abolition of the slave trade, which William Wilberforce and his allies had been pressing for twenty years. Romilly had spoken strongly in favor of abolition in February, leading the Commons in three cheers for Wilberforce.[10] Little time remained to the Ministry after that. Romilly stayed on as Solicitor General into April, when Thomas Plumer succeeded him. On 27 April, Parliament was prorogued and new elections called. Romilly intended to procure another seat, since he now had no hope of retaining Queensborough. His main problem was that seats which had been going for £2000–£4000 in previous general elections were selling at much higher rates because of the King's eagerness to secure a steady majority for his new Government. Romilly detested the buying of seats, but had to admit that it was 'almost the only way in which one ... who is resolved to be an independent man, can get into Parliament'.[11] After nearly despairing, he was told by his former Attorney General, Arthur Piggott, that the Duke of Norfolk had consented to bring him in for Horsham, but it was a precarious seat at best. He had no doubt of winning in the first instance, but efforts would be made to have the returns declared invalid. Romilly accepted the offer.

While Solicitor General, Romilly had had little time for law reform, though he did introduce a measure to alter the laws concerning bankruptcies and certain kinds of debt.[12] On holiday in August 1807, Romilly reflected on the previous year. During his meditations he recalled an earlier desire, inspired by 'instances of judicial injustice' observed while he was on circuit, to attempt some reform of criminal laws and their administration, if ever he gained the opportunity.[13] He resolved to try something, however small, rather than never be heard. He considered first a bill that would authorize a court to pay the expenses of a man imprisoned under an accusation of a felony, but later acquitted at the trial. Imprisonment meant ruin for most people, since one could not work in jail, and in the first decades of the nineteenth century one still had to pay the jail-keeper for provisions. Since an acquittal was supposed, in theory, to restore a man to his reputation, Romilly felt it only fair to restore him to fortune as well, though he readily admitted the need for discretion as to when and how large a provision should be made. He believed a precedent had been set for paying such expenses in an Act from the reign of George II, which gave expenses to prosecutors under certain circumstances.[14]

Romilly had one further object in mind. Several statutes removed the benefit of clergy from certain crimes against property when the value of goods stolen exceeded a specified amount. Over time, inflation had made greater and greater numbers of thefts capital. Romilly proposed to raise the values in the statutes to their modern equivalents. This would at least restore the value of men's lives to what they had been. But Romilly hoped for a second and equally important outcome: to bring an end 'to that shameful trifling with oaths, to those pious perjuries (as Blackstone somewhere calls them), by which juries are humanely induced to find things not to be a tenth part of what is notoriously their value'.[15] A 'pious perjury' occurred when a jury returned either an acquittal against the evidence, or a 'partial verdict' – as when a man accused of theft from a shop, of an amount above five shillings, was found guilty of stealing four shillings, eleven pence, despite all evidence of greater worth. This verdict brought the offense below the 'capital' threshold, and might be chosen for several reasons. Jurors might consider an offense too trivial to be worthy of death, but if they thought a person guilty, and believed the Crown might pardon him without significant penalty (as often happened in such cases), the partial verdict would guarantee some punishment. This 'trifling with oaths' was a much repeated complaint against the existing criminal laws, and Romilly would cite it as proof that the statutes did not have full public support. His objections were not merely that the violation of oaths indicated dissatisfaction with the existing law, but that morality, as well as law, required that oaths be taken seriously.

In late October 1807, Romilly had a plan to begin an effort to reform the criminal laws. By late January 1808 he had pulled back, in part because a petition from Horsham against his return was likely to be decided against him, and he would be out of Parliament anyway. But a conversation with his fellow barrister George Wilson raised another reason for hesitation. Wilson argued that any bill affecting the criminal law, to have a real chance of success in both Houses of Parliament, required consultation with the judges. Otherwise, it would not only be likely to fail, but would prejudice any future attempts to introduce measures for improvement. Romilly had encountered the notion that legal changes ought to be screened first by the judges when the Lord Chief Justice Ellenborough urged him to let the judges have time for comment on his bill regarding debts. Ellenborough had made judicial consultation into something of a sine qua non, and Romilly concluded that if any measure first had to be approved by the judges, it would never change the system, much less improve it. He even wondered about the constitutionality of such a doctrine, since it gave the judges an assured veto power. But Wilson's concerns caused him to hesitate. In any case, at the end of February he lost his seat for Horsham.

Romilly's Whig friends were not about to let him disappear back into his regular business in the Courts of Chancery. Within a month, Lord Henry Petty (the future the third Marquis of Lansdowne) told him of a seat available for the right price. The price requested was £3000, £1000 more than what Romilly would have paid for Horsham. Sir Arthur Piggott informed him that the difference could be made up from a fund hitherto unknown to Romilly 'which has been formed ... by the most distinguished persons in Opposition, to answer extraordinary occasions'.[16] Romilly's politics were clearly whiggish, but he objected to an apparently dependent position, especially as he could afford the additional cost; so he paid the full amount himself and reentered Parliament in mid April as representative for Wareham.

By this time his determination to try reforming the criminal laws had been buoyed by a conversation with another barrister, James Scarlett. Scarlett thought he should attempt to repeal at once all the statutes which made any non-violent theft punishable by death. While Romilly agreed with the goal, he thought he had no chance of carrying so comprehensive a bill. But Scarlett's comments encouraged him and he determined to try repealing the offensive statutes one by one, 'and to begin with the most odious of them, the Act of Queen Elizabeth which makes it a capital offense to steal privately from the person of another'. The choice of 8 Eliz. c. 4 was shrewd. It was seldom enforced. So far as he knew, only one person within living memory had ever been charged and executed under it, and that one because he was caught picking pockets during a court hearing on the Northern Circuit. Beyond being nearly a dead letter, the Act was one that even such a panegyrist for England's criminal laws as William Paley declared in need of amendment.[17]

On 18 May 1808, Romilly brought in two bills in the House of Commons, the first to repeal the statute of Queen Elizabeth, and the second for granting compensation to defendants in certain felony acquittals. He spoke briefly on the compensation bill, observing that while a man waited for trial (as much as eight months in most places, and up to a year in the four most northern counties) the poor rates often supported his family. But the bulk of his comments related his reasons for considering criminal law reforms. He recounted his original intention to increase the value of stolen goods that made thefts punishable by death, but told the House that he had abandoned this when he realized he would still be 'enacting capital punishments for offenses in which there are no circumstances of aggravation', a result he could not bring himself to accept.[18] Romilly instead proposed to bring capital statutes under review of the House one by one, beginning with the Elizabethan law on pick-pockets. No principle was clearer, Romilly asserted, than that certainty of punishment was a better deterrent to crime than severity, a principle widely acknowledged since the Marquis Beccaria's writings in the previous century. Many continental countries had reformed their laws to accord with this theory, diminishing the number of capital offenses while making more certain the application of lesser punishments. In England the exact opposite had happened: more capital statutes had been added, with the irony that these harsh laws were seldom enforced. His evidence showed that only about a sixth of those sentenced to death were in fact executed. The rest had their sentences commuted by the exercise of the Royal Prerogative of Mercy, either to transportation to Botany Bay or to some kind of imprisonment with hard labor. Because a pardon of some form was granted more often than not, it seemed to Romilly that the Crown, rather than reviewing cases for pardon, had to choose those who would suffer the full vigor of the law. Since the Crown depended on the recommendation of the judges, and the judges, having no set guidelines for recommendations, were notoriously inconsistent, the administration of justice took on an aspect of grim and random chance. Certainly this was an affront to the idea of majesty implied in the royal exercise of mercy.

The statistics prompted the question of whether laws should exist on paper that in practice were almost ignored, and whether such statutes could 'be deemed any longer essential to the well-being of the State'.[19] 'Pious perjury' and the uncertainty of punishment were but two of the problems that grew from the discrepancy between the letter and practice of the law. Romilly was as concerned for morality in this matter as for the skewing of justice: right laws should flow from and encourage right moral attitudes. Laws that failed this test had to be changed.

The basic outline of Romilly's later arguments could be seen in this speech. He had brought out the Beccarian argument for certainty over severity, and pointed to the evidence, gleaned from the Government's own records, that the English law promised severity, but produced uncertainty. He questioned whether the written law should be so much out of line with the practice of the courts. Finally, he used the frequency of partial verdicts and pious perjuries as proof of popular disapproval of the capital statutes.

In the debate that followed, little objection was raised directly against these points. Discussion focused on the second bill, regarding compensation. The first to speak after Romilly was Henry Arthur Herbert, an Irish member from Kerry, who claimed he approved of the laws in general and 'that very good grounds ought to be laid down before any innovation was made upon them'.[20] He disapproved of the bill for compensation, and suggested that many indolent people in Ireland would reckon confinement in prison no hardship. Sir John Newport questioned Herbert about whether Irish prisons were so comfortable as to prove an inducement to confinement, but Herbert stuck to his objections. The compensation bill also provoked protest on policy grounds, and at least one member questioned the cost of such a measure. Even the radical Sir Francis Burdett had difficulty with the wording, which seemed to place in the judges' hands the responsibility for deciding when an acquittal was justifiable, and the acquitted deserving of restitution, and when it was not, casting an even longer shadow over a person's reputation. The Solicitor General found similar difficulties, and Romilly later withdrew it.

The first to speak in favor of the general principle behind the bills was William Wilberforce, who told the House that he 'had experienced the most unmixed satisfaction' from Romilly's speech. He reminded the House that

> a great and lamented public character, at an early period of his life, had intended to have a digest made of the whole of our criminal code, with a view of lessening, in a great degree, the number of capital

punishments which it contained, and the objections to which it was impossible to confute.[21]

Wilberforce was referring to William Pitt, and his invocation of that late statesman was meant to forestall any charge that what Romilly intended was in any way radical, and to tie the measure to previous, impeccably respectable efforts. Still, the Solicitor General remarked on the novelty of the bills, and William Smith met the issue directly, only to dismiss it: 'As to the measure being a novelty,' Smith told the Commons, 'every improvement is a novelty.' Leave was then given to bring in the bills, and Romilly's campaign for criminal law reform was officially begun.

Aside from the conversations with Wilson and Scarlett, Romilly recorded no reference to discussions outside of Parliament in preparation for the bill. Neither does he appear to have approached the Whig leaders to gather support. Of the one group he actually avoided consulting, the judges, he finally did notify the Lord Chief Justice, but as a courtesy, and not for approval. He 'knew the severity of Lord Ellenborough's disposition', but since the Chief Justice had always shown 'great civility' toward him, Romilly felt he owed him some explanation before the bill came forward in the Commons.[22] Ellenborough responded politely, 'I shall be happy to find your plan such as I may fully approve. If I should not, I shall, with great respect for its author, do that which my own impressions of duty may require of me upon the occasion; as you will of course expect and wish that I should.'[23] Recording the letter in his diary, Romilly went on to reflect on the 'mischievous effects which have been produced in this country by the French Revolution', including not only 'a stupid dread of innovation', but also the infusion of 'a savage spirit ... into the minds of many of his countrymen'. Ellenborough's politics had been particularly affected by the dark turn of the Revolution in the 1790s, but it was not merely the change of opinion which Romilly observed; it was the intensity of the feeling behind the fear of change. He was appalled a few nights before his bill came up for further discussion, when he was approached while standing at the bar of the House of Commons by the brother of a peer, who declared, 'I am against your Bill; I am for hanging all.' Romilly, knowing that the man was drunk, tried to find some excuse for him, and suggested he 'meant that the certainty of punishment affording the only prospect of suppressing crimes, the laws, whatever they were, ought to be executed'. Of course, Romilly disagreed with such a argument, but had encountered it before. No, the man said, 'it is not that. There is no good done by mercy. They only get worse; I would hang them all up at once.'

Romilly was feeling the pressure of disapproval as he approached the second reading of the bill on 15 June.[24] This second debate centered not on the removal of the capital sentence from 'privately stealing from the person', which all appeared to agree ought to be done, but on the preamble to the bill and on what should be the maximum punishment attached to the crime of pick-pocketing. Francis Burton, a representative for the city of Oxford, who had over twenty years' experience in the criminal laws of England, contended that the bill's preamble was at variance with its actual enactments. While the intent of the bill was quite limited, the preamble was sweeping, declaring that 'the extreme severity of penal laws hath not been found effectual for the prevention of crimes' but actually rendered 'punishment extremely uncertain' by making conviction more difficult. This declaration condemned a great portion of the criminal laws, while nonetheless leaving them in full force, a situation to which Burton objected. Herbert and Plumer agreed with Burton's objection to the preamble, though none of them opposed the enacting part of the bill. Romilly had thought it necessary to lay a foundation upon which to bring in the bill, but he was not tied to the preamble and was willing to replace by the common formula, 'Whereas it is expedient', if this would render it acceptable to the House.

Another concern voiced by Burton was that Romilly's bill left too little discretion to the judges. The bill proposed simply to repeal the earlier statute, which would have reduced all cases of 'privately stealing' to simple larceny, for which the maximum punishment was seven years' transportation. For most capital sentences commuted to transportation, the term could be fourteen years to life. The final decision was usually left to the judge. Romilly had not set out to attack the discretion of the judges per se, but only to remove the possibility of the sentence of death for a particular crime. Yet the issue of judicial discretion was, both in this debate and in those to come, a matter of much discussion and concern. Burton and Plumer asserted that seven years' transportation might not be sufficient for some criminals. Citing his experience as a justice on the Chester circuit, Burton asserted his certainty that the longer sentence had more deterrent value. Plumer privately showed Romilly a letter from Lord Ellenborough which stated the Lord Chief Justice's concern to have the discretion to transport for life available. The Solicitor General said he had consulted other judges who felt the same.[25] Romilly pointed out that three times as many offenders were transported for seven years as were transported for any longer period, and that if this did not deter, a much greater portion of the penal laws needed amending than he was proposing, but rather than lose the bill, he accepted the 'altogether objectionable' amendment offered by Plumer, which made the *minimum* sentence seven years' transportation, but allowed discretion to give sentences up to life transportation or imprisonment for as long as three years.

Romilly had not intended to commit the House to a general review of the capital laws in 1808. He was nonetheless surprised by the amount of resistance to the bill, especially when so many claimed to support the actual proposal of removing the death penalty for pick-pocketing. He told the Commons near the end of the debate that 'he had not justly incurred the censure so liberally bestowed on him, of indulging in wild theories'. He had not proposed any fundamental change of system. He had offered observations on a problem in the enforcement of the law and suggested a small change as the beginning of a solution. That he believed the change humane is certain, just as he believed that it would remove difficulties which the consciences of jurors and prosecutors might have at imposing a death sentence on a pick-pocket, even if pardon were likely. The purpose of the criminal laws was, in the end, to prevent crimes, and Romilly believed that when criminals went unpunished, as they assuredly did when the severity of the statute discouraged prosecutions and convictions, crimes and criminals multiplied. In a sense, Romilly was arguing for more punishment: because so few received any punishment under the old law, a new and less harsh statute would catch many who had earlier escaped penal discipline.

With Plumer's amendments tacked on and the preamble removed, Romilly's bill passed the Commons and was sent on to the Lords, where 'it passed without opposition, and without a word being said upon it'.[26] It became 48 Geo. III. c. 129 when it received the royal assent in July. This small success was only a beginning. Before the Parliament was prorogued, Romilly moved for several sets of papers to be ordered for the Commons.[27] All dealt with statistics on prisoners and convicted felons in England and Wales. The first requested the number of those committed to gaols from 1800 through 1807, listing the charges against them, the numbers convicted, acquitted, or discharged for whatever reason, and specifying not only the number capitally convicted, but also the number who actually suffered the sentence. The second return dealt with convictions at quarter sessions, the third with the number of people sentenced to transportation in the specified years, including the length of their sentences. The fourth return was to report on the number actually transported, giving the date and place of each person's conviction and time of embarkation for New South Wales; the fifth return was to show the number of those who had died in the Hulks since 1780 while waiting to be transported. It was quite a list. The returns, which would serve as the basis for many future arguments, forced the Home Office to examine records which had never been regularly assessed and encouraged the movement toward statistical compilation.

Lines are drawn

While awaiting the outcome on his bill in 1808, Romilly heard of Sir James Mackintosh's efforts to improve the administration of justice in distant India. Mackintosh, who had shared Romilly's early enthusiasm for the French Revolution and had similarly found himself first disappointed and then horrified at the turn of events there, had obtained an appointment as the Recorder of Bombay. He began almost immediately to question the accepted way of doing business and law there. He resisted sentencing convicts to death (in seven years he condemned only one man to execution, an artilleryman who had wantonly murdered a native of Goa), and he had set about trying to improve other aspects of jurisprudence, both criminal and civil.[28] Romilly wrote to him that he 'felt great indignation at hearing how the attempts have been received', but that such 'endeavours at Reforms and Improvement should not be popular in India is not surprising when they are very far from being popular here'.[29] Romilly thought most people in Britain indifferent to his proposals, but others considered them 'with Jealousy and Alarm'. Those who approved them were unfortunately much less ardent than those opposed. His record was not very encouraging, but he was not yet discouraged, and he hoped that if he continued in Parliament, he would leave the laws less imperfect than he found them, 'which Ld. Coke somewhere says every lawyer owes to his profession'.

At the close of Parliament, Romilly retired to the country. His close friend Etienne Dumont accompanied him and brought along one of Bentham's manuscripts on penal theory, which Dumont was editing and translating into French. Romilly liked the work, though he did not record how it affected his pursuit of penal law reform.[30] Many encouraged him directly to continue his efforts, among them the radical cleric Dr Samuel Parr.[31] Parr had long had an interest in penal law reform, and he wrote to Romilly that his last conversation with Charles James Fox had turned upon the issue of the penal code and the disposition of English judges. In his biography of Fox, which contained a substantial discourse on the state of English law, Parr had few kind words for the English legal profession.[32] Of the criminal laws he told Romilly, 'I love them not, and I have not spared their principles, or the furred homicides who administer them.' He thought the law reformer's greatest challenge would be confronting the jealously guarded discretion of the judges, and it did not surprise him that he had to compromise precisely on this point. Nonetheless, Parr thought Romilly's achievement noble and told him to press on.

Romilly's request for the returns on trials, convictions and executions indicated that he very much intended to continue his efforts. In 1809, however, while he digested the information from the returns, he refrained from bringing in any bill dealing with the criminal laws. He was by no means idle that year, but he pursued careful and judicious changes in the laws of debt and bankruptcy instead of pressing penal reforms. His bills passed, though the bankruptcy bill encountered strong resistance and revision in the Upper House from Lords Eldon and Redesdale, 'two of the most strenuous enemies of innovation'.[33]

Most of Romilly's energy in 1809 was taken up with the debate concerning the Duke of York's allegedly improper disposal of commissions and promotions in the army because of the influence of his mistresses. The matter went beyond titillating scandal to become a matter of serious public inquiry. After all, Britain was at war, and the sale of military offices surely interfered with the successful prosecution of the conflict. Although the evidence was strongly against the Duke, neither the Government nor the Opposition wanted to press the matter severely for fear of alienating the royal family. Romilly, however, could not in good conscience remain quiet and spoke against the Duke on 13 March.[34] Those eager to see him one day in high office thought his speech impolitic, but his moderate and careful analysis convinced many in the House of his integrity and independence. It also raised his profile beyond the halls of Westminster. He received votes of thanks from several assemblies, including the Common Council of London. He did not wish to be seen as a 'popular' or radical politician, but acclaim for his apparent disinterestedness was a useful basis upon which to build his later appeals to public opinion on the criminal laws. Admittedly, Romilly may not have seen it that way in 1809, when all he had to console him was a clear conscience and the company of a few other independently minded MPs.

Romilly spent the late summer recess preparing papers on the criminal law, which he thought he could publish if he did not have the opportunity to bring in bills on the topic. Others were also busy in 1809 publishing material to aid reform of the criminal laws. Basil Montagu, a barrister at Lincoln's Inn and an expert on the bankruptcy laws, published the first of what grew to three volumes of opinions of famous authors on the punishment of death.[35] The book was sponsored by the Society for

Diffusing Information on the Subject of the Punishment of Death, founded in 1808 by Montagu and the Evangelical Quaker philanthropist William Allen.[36] The Capital Punishment Society (CPS), as Allen called it for short, was conceived independently before Romilly's parliamentary efforts began, but moved quickly to support them. This first publication contained excerpts from writers as diverse as Samuel Johnson and Beccaria, as ancient as Sir Thomas More and Erasmus, and as recent as William Paley, Patrick Colquhoun, and Jeremy Bentham.[37] Not all the quotations were against the capital statutes, but the bulk of the material supported mitigation. Although Montagu's book did not at first sell well, the members of the Society became the core advocates for mitigation of the death penalty, and eventually their 'diffusing information' did much to form and enhance public opinion on the issue of capital punishment.

Romilly had carefully studied the returns on capital sentences and transportation by the time he gave notice at the start of the 1810 parliamentary session of his intention of bringing in further measures for reforming the criminal laws. He rose on 9 February to ask the House for leave to bring in three very specific bills, each repealing a particular capital statute. The first addressed an act from the reign of William III, which had made shoplifting punishable by death when the amount stolen exceeded five shillings; the second would repeal a law from the reign of Queen Anne, which made stealing 40 shillings or more from a dwelling-house capital, and the third, a statute of George II, which removed the benefit of clergy for theft from boats and ships on navigable rivers.[38] The details of the returns suggested to him which statutes to attack, for he chose three laws that were among the least enforced.

Romilly's opening speech went far beyond justifying the repeal of these three bills and expanded the basic points he had made in 1808 to present a comprehensive argument for a thorough overhaul of the criminal laws.[39] To justify the introduction of amendments in the existing penal laws, he believed it necessary to lay a firm foundation, with arguments drawn from recent experience, from the statistics of the returns, and from reflection on the reasons for imposing the death penalty or any punishment. Romilly began his polemic by an appeal to necessity and expediency. If the multiplication of capital statutes was necessary, though so often the cause of complaint against England's laws, then everyone should be convinced of the need. He believed the reasoning against the widespread and indiscriminate use of capital punishments rested on solid ground, but did not expect that the practice of ages could be or indeed should be easily overturned.[40]

The returns on criminal prosecutions and convictions prepared by the Home Office had been laid upon the table for the reference and information of the House. Romilly pointed to them as providing evidence that pardons were granted far more frequently than executions were carried out. Many now expected this and believed that the criminal law was administered as it had always been intended, with only a few suffering the full rigor of the law. Romilly had become convinced that this view was wrong. Instead, the present operation of the law was the result of a slow change 'in the manners and character of the nation, which are now so repugnant to the spirit of these laws, that it has become impossible to carry them into execution'.[41] In earlier periods, he doubted any law was made which the legislature did not intend should be strictly enforced. While he expressed some skepticism as to their absolute accuracy, Romilly had gathered quotations and estimates from as far back as Sir John Fortesque in the reign of Henry VI, through the Tudor kings and queens and to the Stuarts; all clearly indicated a great many more executions in England than were now carried out, despite the increased number of hanging offenses.[42] The first relatively dependable numbers for convictions and punishments came from the middle of the eighteenth century and had been published by John Howard. Using these tables, Romilly illustrated that in the middle of the previous century, half or more of those convicted at the Old Bailey of capital offenses were executed. He compared this with the most recent tables from the Home Office for 1802–8. These numbers showed that no more than 20 per cent of those convicted in any year were executed, and that the average for all seven was slightly higher than one in eight.[43] To impress upon his listeners the incongruity between the written code and the law as it was actually practiced, Romilly isolated the statistics for two offenses he proposed to alter, shoplifting and stealing from a dwelling-house. For the whole period 1749 to 1771, those convicted of these crimes to the capital amount were 240; of these, 109 were hanged. The tables published by the Home Office did not distinguish how many had been convicted of these offenses for the previous seven years, but they did report that 1,872 had been committed to Newgate on a charge of one or other of the crimes. Of this total, only *one* had actually been convicted and executed. The numbers showed a clear decrease in the infliction of death over the previous fifty years.[44] They also gave substance to the assertion that the threat of death seldom acted as a deterrent to theft. If only one was hanged of almost two thousand accused, the chances of escaping death were almost certain; to these chances could be added the cases for which no statistics existed, those where a tender-hearted victim failed to bring prosecution, or those where prosecutions were stopped before they reached a point to be entered into the record.

Romilly went on to explain his reasons for objections to the scope of judicial discretion over life and death. A person condemned for one crime was often allowed to suffer for crimes he was only suspected of committing. Thus, a man found guilty of larceny, who had in addition a generally bad reputation, would be allowed to hang; another, suspected of murder, for which there was insufficient evidence to convict, but for whom strong evidence of a minor theft did exist, would also be left to die.[45] The inconsistency between judges was exacerbated by the failure to publicize the basis for their decisions. When some at an Assize Session were reprieved, and others found guilty of the same offense were left to hang, the judges gave no explanation of the mitigating or aggravating circumstances which made one more worthy of receiving death than another. All these factors contributed to the criminals' belief in 'the lottery of justice', which eliminated the deterrent value of capital punishment.

Though absolute certainty was unattainable, Romilly proposed four steps that would at least increase the probability of effective punishment. First, he called for vigilant policing. Second, he suggested more rational rules of evidence. Third, the laws had to be made clearer to the general public. Finally, punishments ought to be made as much as possible proportional to the guilt of the offender, based upon the seriousness of the crime.[46] Focusing on the last two of these points, he noted that one mode of making the capital statutes better understood would be to require judges to write down their reasons for letting a capital conviction stand. These could then be collected and published, as were the judges' decisions on the common law. Better still, however, was to specify sentences and degrees of aggravation in written statutes.

At this point the argument in favor of reforming the criminal laws was substantially complete. Romilly, however, turned to confront the ideas of William Paley, because Paley had presented the most reasoned and respected defense of the existing system. This move transformed his attack into a more theoretical exercise than the pragmatic and statistically based arguments would have supported alone. The shift haunted him in the debates that followed. Yet Romilly had to deal with Paley at some point. Paley's *Principles of Moral and Political Philosophy* had become one of the most widely read works in England. Originally published in 1785, it had shortly afterward become an examination text for Bachelor of Arts candidates at the University of Cambridge. By 1810, eighteen

British and six American editions had been published. Paley was arguably the most widely read contemporary theologian in the English-speaking world in 1810, and his reasoning in favor of the existing administration of penal justice was at least as well known as those of its critics.

Paley saw only two ways to administer penal law. The first was to have very few capital statutes and to apply them vigorously; the second assigned capital punishment to a wide range of crimes, but inflicted the penalty only in a few exemplary cases. The latter was the English way, which Paley considered far superior to the other. The public gained protection by the salutary effect of the threat of death. Paley wrote,

> by the number of statutes creating capital offenses, [the English law] sweeps into the net every crime, which, under any possible circumstances, may merit the punishment of death; but, when the execution of this sentence comes to be deliberated upon, a small proportion of each class are singled out, the general character, or the peculiar aggravations of whose crimes render them fit examples of publick justice.[47]

Paley's way insured a maximum amount of authority for the judges, who relaxed or maintained the rigor of the law, which in Paley's view raised the majesty of the Crown as the dispenser of mercy to the convicted.

Romilly's arguments against Paley built upon his earlier comments regarding the effect of discretion in the practice of the criminal law. He objected to Paley's dichotomy, finding it too exclusive of other alternatives. Further, rather than upholding the majesty of the Crown, Romilly thought the selection of those 'fit examples of publick justice' made the Crown and its officers appear cruel and arbitrary. His closing comments stressed two points. First, even if Paley were correct about the preventative efficiency of the terror produced by the threat of death, the system was indefensible because its net was not cast wide enough; the laws singled out for the punishment of death crimes of the poor against property, while the 'heinous' and 'enormous crimes' of the wealthy often went unpunished, even unnoticed. He gave as examples the guardian who defrauds his ward and the lawyer who steals a man's estate by legal conniving. These were not punished with anything, yet they destroyed a person's dignity and prosperity. Second, Romilly wanted to be clear that he was not disputing the Crown's power to pardon, which he saw as an essential part of the English constitution. He did, however, question the policy of a practice that was in effect 'an almost continual suspension and interruption of the law'.

Although Romilly's comments on Paley were not as developed in his Commons speech as in later published editions, they were enough to stir the waters. William Windham objected to the attack on Paley, though he claimed not to be completely adverse to reform.[48] Other opposition was more pronounced. Most followed the lead of Thomas Plumer, who declared with pride that he was 'an enemy to the opposition of theoretical speculation to practical good', whether this came from Adam Smith (to whom Romilly had referred in his opening comments) or Paley, or any other source. Far from showing the bloodiness of the English laws, the Prime Minister Spencer Perceval argued that Romilly's evidence proved that the present practice of the laws was quite humane. Like Plumer, Perceval suspected 'speculations to practical good', by which he meant any criticism of existing institutions that included even a minute trace of philosophy. He reiterated the need to support the authority of the judges and maintain a deference toward their opinions in matters of penal law.[49]

Romilly felt it necessary to respond to this implied accusation of disrespect for the judiciary, reminding the House that his whole livelihood as a barrister depended on the good opinion of the judges. William Smith vehemently defended Romilly against the charge of 'speculation', emphasizing that he had 'not advanced a step without facts to warrant all his conclusions'.[50] Smith also pointed out that Plumer's arguments tended to deny the possibility of any alteration that was not fully proved to be beneficial before it was made. Here Smith cut to the core of the difficulty faced by all reforms proposed in the era of the Napoleonic Wars: every effort of improvement was labeled a 'dangerous innovation', which would only lead to the destruction of existing institutions. Smith was careful not to invoke the specter of the French Revolution by name, but it nonetheless always floated in the background. Despite the constant suspicion of proposed changes, Romilly obtained leave to bring in the bills.

Not all who favored amelioration had attended the introduction of the bills. Wilberforce, who would prove a constant and indispensable ally, had been engaged in a series of conflicts with Perceval's government, the most recent of which was the inquiry into the expedition to the Scheldt. On the advice of James Stephen, he remained away from the Commons for a few days, though he wrote to Stephen on 9 February that he 'particularly wished to attend to-day to hear Sir Samuel Romilly on capital punishments'. He thought he agreed with him, and liked 'the spirit of his law better than that of his opponents'. He asked Stephen to explain his reason for being absent.[51] Wilberforce's practical and wholehearted assistance would be needed later.

Little immediate public notice was taken of the bills. Some private enthusiasm was voiced, however, and others saw the introduction as an opportunity to raise more widespread concern about the administration of the criminal law. Francis Horner wrote to Romilly, the day after the introduction of the bills, that he believed the opening speech should be published.[52] Horner was 'quite persuaded' that the public was 'ready for instruction' regarding reform of the criminal law, if it came with Romilly's authority and well-reasoned arguments and illustrations. The weighty opposition of Plumer, Horner continued, would only be overcome by the weight of the public opinion, which could be enlightened through the press. Horner thought himself better able to gauge the potential influence of Romilly's speech on a popular audience than Romilly was, and he was probably accurate in perceiving the reserved Chancery lawyer as less than eager to court the wider world in print. But Horner's advice did not fall on deaf ears, as Romilly had already contemplated publishing the material. Romilly's *Observations on the Criminal Law of England* appeared in mid March 1810, enlarged from the speech by more extensive criticism of Paley and some explanatory notes. Romilly rushed to complete the pamphlet while the bills were still under discussion; and it enjoyed immediate success. His speech received further circulation when Basil Montagu and the Capital Punishment Society published a full account of the debates on the 1810 bills.[53]

These works struck a cord with many outside Parliament and did much to enliven public interest in the issue. *The Times* printed letters of support from 'Anti-Draco' and 'Publico', who enthusiastically encouraged Romilly's effort, quoting from Blackstone, Samuel Johnson and Beccaria, and emphasizing the need for milder punishments to obtain more consistent prosecution.[54] Romilly had plainly succeeded in making the criminal laws an object of discussion in England, but not all were sanguine of the quick success of Romilly's proposals. Parr cautioned, 'Nearly all your brethren will be against you; and this spirit of the fraternity is an additional reason with me for leaving as little as possible in their power.'[55] The 'spirit of fraternity' was most manifest in the judges, however, and in fact many barristers sympathized with Romilly, though they moved only slowly toward public support of amelioration. Beyond England the Scottish philosopher Dugald Stewart, whom Romilly had known for several years, took special notice of the *Observations*. He wrote to encourage Romilly in late June. Stewart's optimism was greater than Parr's for a reason; he knew several of his former students would actively promote penal law reform, including Horner, Henry Brougham, and Lord Henry Petty.

Romilly had indication that the Ministry would oppose at least two of his bills, those dealing with theft from dwelling-houses and on rivers. When the report came up for consideration on 1 May, attendance in the Commons was very thin indeed, which made it more likely that the Government could crush all three bills at once. Romilly knew that even without organized opposition, the measures would cause a great deal of discussion, so he decided to bring out one certain to be opposed, let the heavy fire rain down on it immediately, and stall discussion on the others until a more propitious time. When he moved for consideration of the dwelling-house bill, the first to speak was Herbert of Kerry, who had opposed Romilly's 1808 measures. Herbert recited the standard litany of those who resisted any 'innovation' in the laws. Windham seconded his arguments and treated the three measures as part of a plan 'to overturn the criminal law of the country'. William Frankland, the Attorney General Sir Vicary Gibbs, Plumer, and Perceval all concurred, and only Davies Giddy restricted his opposition to the particular bill under discussion; Giddy even hinted that he would support the bill on shoplifting.[56]

The defenders of the law repeatedly expressed the belief that even if juries or prosecutors did not take the law as far as it could go, the terror of the threat of death still operated on the minds of potential criminals to prevent theft. Their certainty was challenged by all who spoke in favor of the bill, who were equally convinced that the terror of the punishment did more to deter prosecutors and juries than criminals. John Newport told the story of a gentlemen he knew in Ireland who had rejoiced when a law had been passed which made cutting down a tree a capital felony, since he kept orchards that had many times been pilfered and harmed. Eventually an occasion came when an offender was found in the very act of destroying trees and was committed for trial. Resolved to enforce the law, the gentleman began his journey to the assize session, but, Newport related, 'there his fortitude at last failed ... he declared that, after the most agonizing deliberation, he could not reconcile to his notions of justice the propriety of being the cause of the untimely death of a fellow-creature for having cut down a tree'. Edward Morris added his own observations of criminal trial juries: 'I have daily witnessed these pious perjuries, these amiable weaknesses, as they are called, by which the prosecution of offenders is prevented.' Wilberforce concluded that if only one was executed when 1,872 were found guilty, either the law or the practice was faulty; he was inclined to believe it was the law. Such examples confirmed William Grant's depiction of a 'universal confederacy amongst the middling classes of society not to punish these offenses by death'.[57] They found it hard to believe that anyone involved in the administration of the law could plead ignorance of these conditions.

Opponents of Romilly's bills treated them as a broad challenge to the existing laws, while supporters focused on their narrow impact. They repeatedly reminded their fellow MPs that Romilly had not introduced legislation to change the whole system, but only specific acts, and that the focus should be on whether the public would be better served by the proposed changes. Both Wilberforce and Newport had also called attention to the conflict between the letter of English law and the spirit of the Christian religion. But when the House divided, Romilly lost by two votes, 33–35. Perceval and the Home Secretary Richard Ryder pressed for the consideration of the remaining two bills, but Romilly urged that they be put off because of the thinness of the House. Davies Giddy, who had voted against the first measure, joined in this request. Giddy's switch on either of the bills would mean a tie, and possibly a defeat for the Government, so they relented and allowed a few days' postponement. The evening was discouraging to the reformers. Wilberforce wrote in his diary, 'Shameful house; they divided against Romilly', noting that Frankland and Windham were in the majority.[58] Romilly thought Windham's opposition the most effective, but that Windham did not dislike the bill itself, so much as the doctrines he had put forward and his attack on Paley.[59] Romilly was most vexed at the absence of members of the Opposition, who 'in general ... wished well to the Bill, but not well enough to give themselves the trouble of attending upon it'. Of those voting against him, Romilly counted 22 who held some form of office from the government, including the law officers, three lords and one secretary of the Admiralty, three lords and two secretaries of the treasury, the Secretaries of the Home Office, of War and of Ireland, and a few undersecretaries in various departments.[60] Romilly had not presented the measure in a partisan manner, and many who spoke for it would not have counted themselves Whigs, but it would have been a good opportunity for the Opposition to trounce the Government.

Only three days later Romilly won a small victory: the shoplifting bill passed the House without a division. The Government did not oppose this measure, but gave no reason why it differed in their eyes from the bill regarding theft from dwelling houses, and Romilly was hard-pressed to find any defining distinction. The statute against shoplifting was almost universally ignored, but that was also true of the dwelling house bill. Giddy had explained his probable support of the shoplifting bill in terms of prevention and aggravation – shoplifting could be better guarded against than theft from an empty home, and so required a less severe threat to deter it. Or the Government may simply have counted heads on 4 May and discovered they would lose if they opposed the bill openly. After all, it still had to pass through the Lords. And the Government had more certain allies in the Lords.

After the shoplifting bill passed, Romilly moved for further convict returns, with the stated intention of obtaining as comprehensive a review of the actual administration of the criminal law as possible. He also promised to renew the measure which had been lost in the next session.[61] He lamented the Ministry's opposition to a question so completely unconnected with party, but he also expressed his regret that so few had attended the actual debate. 'I do think it strange', he told his fellow MPs, 'that the Highgate archway, or the Holloway water Bills, should obtain a fuller attendance than a measure of such vital importance.'

Lord Holland had agreed to move the shoplifting bill in the Lords. Knowing that Ellenborough and Eldon were both ready to oppose the bill, Romilly encouraged Holland not to rush consideration, but to choose an auspicious time before the end of the session; as he wrote to Holland, 'I am only desirous that it should not die a silent death in the House of Lords.'[62] He supplied Holland with as much information as he could, including 'an account of the numerous innovations in criminal law' which Parliament had passed in recent years. They were all on the side of severity, and 'passed without objection from any quarter'. Romilly added that it was 'only when an attempt to innovate on the side of Humanity' was made 'that the Judges take the Alarm'. Among the recent capital statutes was 43 Geo. III c. 58, known as 'Lord Ellenborough's Act', the only penal statute the Lord Chief Justice ever framed and passed. The 1803 Act created nine new capital Felonies and, except for Ellenborough's introductory remarks, had passed 'without a word being said upon it in either House'.[63]

Romilly's information warned Holland of the kind of consideration the bill was likely to receive from the judges in the Lords, but the intensity of the opposition exceeded Holland's expectations. When the order of the day was moved on 30 May, Ellenborough rose before anyone could speak in favor of the bill. He set the tone when he told the House, 'I trust your Lordships will pause before you assent to an experiment pregnant with danger to the security of property.'[64] Like Windham and Plumer, Ellenborough spoke not against the bill itself, but against the system he believed the bill must represent. After all, he pointed out, the arguments in favor of repealing the capital statute on shoplifting could be used against dozens of other laws. Ellenborough claimed to represent the 'unanimous' opinion of the judges. Liverpool and Eldon also spoke against the measure. Only Eldon accepted that the bill's friends did not seek a general change of laws, but there was cause for concern specifically about the bill before them – he did not believe it expedient in and of itself. He pointed to the results of the repeal of the Elizabethan act which had made pick-pocketing capital; he held that the alarmingly increase in prosecutions was evidence against any further alteration.

The bulk of the bill's defense was left to Holland. While he again tried to concentrate the debate on the bill at hand, his comments often went beyond it. He used the details Romilly had given him on the number of committals and executions and added reference to the capital punishment attached to some of the new revenue laws; these provisions, he noted, had remained mostly unenforced. Besides the statistics, he quoted at length from Johnson, Blackstone, and the Westminster magistrate Patrick Colquhoun. He held that the original act had been passed in an 'unenlightened time' when 'legislators observed no degree of relative proportion between the crime and the punishment', but that since then the people of England had become more humane and justice more merciful – an argument that conveniently ignored the recent passage of new capital statutes.

As in the Commons, the measure's supporters emphasized its particulars, but their arguments often raised general questions about the system. Since the judges had appealed to their experience, so too did the bill's defenders. Erskine spoke as a former Lord Chancellor, who could conceive of no circumstances which would have induced him to advise the King to let a shoplifter suffer the full punishment of the law. Suffolk pointed to himself as one who had in fact refrained from prosecuting because of the severity of the code. As he told the peers, 'The prosecutors are those who fear death, and not the persons offending.' Lauderdale drew from the recent investigation on the consolidation of the revenue laws, where the testimony often supported the notion that many, revenue officers included, were reluctant to prosecute when the punishment might be death. He recalled that even one of the judges had 'emphatically' confirmed the 'difficulty of obtaining any conviction of this class of offenders, in consequence of the excessive severity of the law'. Only Lansdowne presented 'speculative' arguments, accusing the criminal laws of being 'so absurd, so injudicious, so inconsistent with the purposes and end of justice, that the judges of the land will not allow them to be executed'. He defended the change in the pick-pocketing law, pointing out that the argument for the removal of the punishment of death was that its severity deterred people from prosecuting. The increase in prosecutions – and that was all the judges could have observed – was not proof of the failure of the alteration, but of its efficacy.

All the efforts of Romilly's aristocratic friends proved inadequate to persuade the Lords to consider the bill more fully. Ellenborough's closing arguments against the 'dangerous spirit of innovation' and his remarks about not knowing where to stand should this bill be passed, because it would surely be followed by another and another, left little doubt of the bill's fate. Further consideration was postponed by a vote of 31 to 11, so that the bill was lost when Parliament was prorogued. Romilly had attended the Lords' debate, not so much to find out the fate of his bill, as to observe the nature of the arguments against it. Given the lateness of the year, he was most impressed by the number of peers which the Ministry had turned out against the bill, among them seven bishops, whose servility towards government evidently outweighed the mild doctrines of their religion. Romilly was again struck by the importance the threat of innovation seemed to have for the opponents of his bill, and feared that Ellenborough's suggestions that judges could have encouraged the attempts to change the law by too much lenience might lead to more regular enforcement of the capital statutes.[65]

The meaning of the debates in 1808 and 1810

By 9 June, when he acknowledged his navigable rivers bill would not get a reading that session, Romilly had a clear understanding of the nature of the resistance to his proposed reforms. He denied, even in his own diary, that his goal was a complete revision of the laws of England; since his personal prosperity depended on the legal system, he found it hard to believe that anyone could seriously think him eager to destroy it.[66] He fully expected that judges would and should exercise a great latitude of discretion, as the range of alternative punishments listed in the bills proved; Romilly simply removed hanging from the list. He had addressed the issue of discretion with regard to Paley's praise of it, but while he might have preferred a written code of laws, Romilly did not think it practical in the short run, and perhaps impossible in the long. Still, neither good policy nor good morals could support laws that allowed the penalty of death for trivial offenses. Furthermore, such laws formed 'a cruel standard', which allowed those in power 'to justify every harsh and excessive exercise of authority'.[67] New laws stipulating the punishment of death could be justified by appeal to precedent; existing practices such as corporal punishment in the army and navy could be defended on the basis that they were not as harsh as hanging.

George Canning's comments in favor of Romilly's bills contained the best synopsis of the reformers' views with regard to discretion. As to the power given the justices,

> ... it must be remembered that it is a most awful discretion; a discretion by one man to give or take away the life of another.... The trust of discretionary power in judicial proceedings is, indeed, from the difficulty of describing the gradation of crime, not always to be avoided; but, when this necessity does not exist, the legislature ought not to grant what every upright magistrate must reluctantly receive. Whether such necessity exists in the present case is the immediate subject of this part of our present inquiry.[68]

For the defenders of the laws the question turned upon an either/or: either give the judges a maximum amount of discretion, even allowing the penalty of death for apparently trivial property offenses, or come up with a system which codified every possible offense and every possible aggravating circumstance. It was an impossible standard, and the reformers simply did not believe the dichotomy necessary.

What the debates of 1808 and 1810 demonstrated was that the vision held by Romilly, Wilberforce, Holland and Lansdowne, of how written laws should be as much as possible consistent with practice, was a view which clashed with the expectations of those who still held the balance of power in England. The reformers proposed very specific restrictions, based on their desire for more proportional, regimented punishment, the result of which should be not only the prevention of crime, but, as will become clear in subsequent chapters, a reformation of the convict as well. This was not only a different image of justice, but a different model of government, which they believed would lead to fewer offenses and greater public safety. The Ministry response to Romilly's proposals also meant that the battle would not be won in Parliament until it had been fought outside in the public arena. Romilly had originally been reluctant to go directly to the public, but the debate convinced him to do so. The defeats of 1810 marked the start of the public battle, and outside Westminster Romilly would be aided by many able and eager hands.

3
Romilly, Bentham and Utility

Romilly had not exaggerated when he told the House of Commons that he had spent several years contemplating the criminal law of England. Although by 1808 his legal practice was exclusively in Chancery, he had got a start in the profession in more general practice in the Quarter Sessions and Assize Circuits. His interest in penal matters predated his call to the Bar, and his concerns for reform went far beyond criminal law. A study of Romilly's background demonstrates clearly that while he was a friend of Jeremy Bentham, his commitment and approach to penal law reform developed independently.

Romilly's background and early writings

Romilly's Huguenot grandfather had come to England in the first decade of the eighteenth century to escape the pressures of religious intolerance in France after the Revocation of the Edict of Nantes.[1] Although well-off in France, the family had little wealth in England and Sir Samuel's father was apprenticed to a jeweller when still young. In time he became well known for his workmanship, and he settled in Soho where Samuel was born on 1 March 1757. His father kept the house in Soho for business purposes when he later moved the family 'out' to Marylebone, then a little village far enough from the main centers of London activity to qualify as being 'in the country'.[2] Samuel had an older brother and sister, and their father provided the children with more than basic education; Samuel especially thrived on the Classics.

Finding a trade for Samuel was difficult. For a while he kept the books for the jewelry business, but had no love for it. His father eventually allowed him to pursue legal training, and at age sixteen Samuel was articled to William Michael Lally, a clerk of the Court of Chancery and an invaluable teacher. Although Lally also worked as a solicitor, he encouraged Samuel to continue his self-education, which turned more and more to literature. Through the Huguenot community in London the Romillys met the Genevan clergyman Jean Roget, who became a favored guest and eventually married Samuel's sister Catherine. Roget became a spiritual and intellectual mentor to Samuel, and introduced him to the writings of Rousseau, whose eloquence so captivated Romilly that he 'was blind to all his errors'.[3] In later years, Romilly considered Rousseau's writings as among the best to inspire young minds to a love of virtue and a hatred of oppression, even if they were wrong on many other topics.

Roget encouraged Romilly's ambition in the legal profession. Despite the economic risk, Romilly entered the Society of Gray's Inn when he was twenty-one.[4] He was there during the Gordon Riots in 1780, taking his turn as a sentinel with the barristers and other students at the gate in Holborn. The riots impressed him with 'how dangerous an engine religion is when employed upon the minds of the ignorant'.[5] The stress and turmoil of the time, added to his own strenuous study habits, weakened his fragile health, and he was advised to take an extended rest in late spring 1781. He traveled to Lausanne, where Roget and Romilly's sister had settled. The trip was fortuitous in many ways for the aspiring young lawyer. Having been impressed in his reading of John Howard's book on prisons, he was interested to learn about foreign penal systems and criminal laws and took advantage of an opportunity to participate as an assistant to a lawyer in Geneva in the trial of three accused burglars.[6] While in Geneva, Romilly met Etienne Dumont. Roget had known him for some time, and had described the one man to the other 'in such favourable terms', Romilly recalled, 'that we were desirous of becoming friends before we had met'.[7] The friendship would terminate only at Romilly's death, and few friendships have been more productive of lasting results. Through Romilly, Dumont became acquainted first with the Count de Mirabeau, for whom he wrote during the early stages of French Revolution, and later with Jeremy Bentham, for whom he edited and published philosophical works in French.[8] Romilly noted Dumont's 'vigorous understanding', 'extensive knowledge', and 'splendid eloquence', but was most impressed with 'his strict integrity, his zeal to serve those whom he is attached to, and his most affectionate disposition'.[9]

After exploring Savoy, Romilly headed back toward London via Paris. There he saw 'all that common travelers see', but also took advantage of family connections to gain an introduction to d'Alembert and Diderot.

The former was in precarious health, and Romilly found conversation with him difficult. Diderot was quite different, 'all warmth and eagerness', and talked to him of politics, Rousseau and religion. On politics, Diderot told him he had once intended a work on Charles I of England, and having studied the trial, he had planned to try him again, and again to send him to the scaffold if he had found him guilty. In England, Diderot said, he would have written it, 'but he had not the courage to do so in France'.[10] Toward Romilly's favorite Rousseau he was bitter, and clearly not looking forward to the publication of the *Confessions*.

On religion, Romilly recorded that Diderot was 'ostentatious of a total disbelief in the existence of God.' Romilly's impressions of these conversations reveal something of his own religious convictions, a subject he did not often speak of later in life. He wrote to Roget several months after meeting Diderot,

> With respect to the atheists of Paris, among honest men there can hardly be two opinions. A man must be grossly stupid who can entertain such pernicious notions on subjects of the highest importance without strictly examining them; and much is he to be pitied if, after examination, he still retains them: but if, without examination of them, and uncertain of their truth, though certain of their fatal consequences, he industriously propagates them among mankind, one loses all compassion for him in abhorrence of his guilt....I am not vain enough to pronounce what is the extent of Diderot's and D'Alembert's learning and capacity; but...I may judge of the subordinate atheists,...and in these I have generally found the grossest ignorance.[11]

A few months later he reemphasized his view:

> The more I reflect on the reasoning of the atheists of France, the more I wonder at their absurdity. I cannot forgive them that, not content with starting doubts, they are for utterly destroying every thing that falls not under the notice of their senses, which they preposterously regard as unerring, nay, as the only guides to truth. Wholly absorbed themselves in matter, they will allow nothing else to have existence.[12]

Despite his respect for the French Enlightenment writers, Romilly found the *philosophes'* reasoning on religion shallow, based more in scorn than calm reflection. Their flippant skepticism or outright atheism angered him and contrasted markedly with his own approach to religion.

Although Romilly's family remained in contact with its Huguenot heritage, Samuel was raised a member of the Church of England. His father's religious convictions inspired his charity and generosity, and in this the son would be much like the father.[13] With regard to doctrine, the situation is less clear, though some of his letters indicate a strong belief in the afterlife.[14] The Gordon riots gave him a suspicion of 'enthusiasm' and too ardent religious belief. His irregular church attendance as an adult has led some to suspect he was a Deist.[15] While not a model churchman, Romilly defended his commitment to the Established Church when questioned on his religious affiliations. During a debate on the removal of Catholic disabilities in 1812, he told the Commons that he could not remember ever being in a Dissenting chapel or service.[16] Thomas Belsham, a leading Unitarian minister and a friend of the MP William Smith, noted after Romilly's death in 1818 that while 'not himself a nonconformist, he was earnest to repeal the unjust and oppressive laws against the Unitarians', Dissenters, and Catholics, and indeed 'to extend to every peaceable subject the blessings of the British Constitution'.[17]

Perhaps the most instructive passage in Romilly's writings appears at the end of his political diary for 1812, included in his *Memoirs*.[18] Here he addresses 'Almighty God! Creator of all things!' and calls this Being the source of all wisdom, goodness, virtue and happiness. 'I bow down before thee,' he continues, but not to offer prayers, for he dare not think the unerring and supreme will 'can be in any degree influenced by any supplications of mine'. Neither does he pour forth praises, 'for I feel that I am unworthy to offer them'. Instead, his address is one brought forth in humility and with a great sense of insignificance 'to express the thanks of a contented and happy being, for the innumerable benefits which he enjoys'. It is essentially a prayer of thanksgiving, to express gratitude to God, 'from whom all this good has flowed'. The final paragraph is telling:

> I prostrate myself, O Almighty and Omniscient God, before thee. In endeavouring to contemplate thy divine attributes, I seek to elevate my soul towards thee; I seek to improve and ennoble my faculties, and to strengthen and quicken my ardour for the public good; and I appear to myself to rise above my earthly existence, while I am indulging the hope that I may at some time prove an humble instrument in the divine work of enlarging the sphere of human happiness.

While the prayer is reminiscent of reflections by Evangelicals advocating abolition of the slave trade or penal reforms, it lacks, or avoids, the language of the Evangelical revival. It has humility, but no dwelling on confession of sin. It expresses the sense of needing to carry out good works, and of God's providing one with opportunity to do so, but does not invoke Jesus or the Holy Spirit, or call upon God's special providence as a determining factor. An early twentieth-century biographer called this paragraph an illustration of Romilly's complete 'worship of humanitarianism',[19] but Romilly's 'humanitarianism' is informed by his religious upbringing, as much as by his Enlightenment education. It is focused on a humanity created by God and set in a universe that operates benevolently toward those who seek the wisdom and virtue of which God is the source. His God is a Being active in the lives of men, even if that Being is beyond the influence of human supplications or adoration. It is a view of a God who does not need humanity, but of a humanity that does need God. Romilly would not have denied supernatural intervention altogether, but like David Hume, whom he admired, he would emphasize the difficulties of evaluating evidence given by a zealot and demand very strong corroboration to establish the fact.[20] Romilly fits the definition of a 'rational' Christian laid down by Randall McGowen.[21] McGowen uses the term to indicate both rational Dissent (as in the case of the Unitarians) and those in the Church of England who, when turning to nature and reason to find evidence of God's purpose, 'claimed to discover a being who acted in history to encourage human improvement' and to increase the happiness of His creatures. Romilly's prayer and other theological statements certainly correspond with such an understanding of God.

Romilly's support of mitigation of the criminal law also fits McGowen's thesis that those who argued for penal reform tended to emphasize the reformative nature of God's justice on Earth, and to deemphasize or deny the doctrine of eternal damnation of unbelievers. Romilly himself does not, however, directly link his penal theory to his religious beliefs, so the connection is tentative. Still, he preferred the rational theologian over the traditional or the Evangelical. When he criticized William Paley in 1810, it was not because Romilly felt Paley to be a bad theologian; on the contrary, what frustrated him was that, with so much good in his writing, Paley still held onto the use of exemplary capital punishments for trivial offenses: 'Everything that is excellent in the works of so distinguished a writer, renders his errors, where he falls into error, only the more pernicious.'[22] Generally, he approved of Paley's writings, in marked contrast to Bentham's dislike of them.[23] To whatever extent one might characterize Romilly as a 'disciple' of Bentham, it is not with regard to religion or religious belief. Romilly had settled his basic ideas in this regard well before his friendship with Bentham developed, and he did not follow Bentham down the road of skepticism and rejection.

Religion aside, Romilly was sympathetic to Diderot's and d'Alembert's criticisms of the Bourbon Monarchy, and he returned to his legal studies much gladder for having been born in England. He was called to the bar in spring 1783. Soon afterwards, his friend and mentor Roget died unexpectedly. Significantly, one of the final letters Romilly sent Roget before his death dealt with the issues of public opinion and the criminal laws, and specifically with the question of capital punishment.[24] Romilly related the story of a duel between two English officers. Both were shot; one died immediately. At the coroner's inquest the jury refused to bring in a verdict of murder, though the law clearly defined death from dueling as such. Since the jury represented a cross-section of the middle ranks of society, Romilly thought it a fair barometer of popular opinion. Their refusal to return the obvious verdict pointed up a weakness in a system of laws dependent on a communal decision. The behavior of juries become a cornerstone in his later arguments for amelioration of the criminal code. On the issue of capital punishments, Romilly was responding to an earlier letter from Roget. He was much struck by Roget's argument against the punishment of death 'founded on the errors of human tribunals, and the impossibility of having absolute demonstration of the guilt of a criminal'.[25] This was the most forcible argument he had heard on that side of the question. But Romilly did not think that the death penalty could be excluded from the 'catalogue of human punishments'. He held that if a criminal resisted lesser punishments and continued to commit crimes, 'he must, at last, be punished with death'. Another reason why he thought that death should not be removed from human punishments, was that he did not think 'death the greatest of evils'. Even Beccaria admitted this: some punishments that could be inflicted, even some which were not torturous, were more terrifying than death, or more painful in the long run. Romilly found a logical flaw in Beccaria's reasoning. He seemed to forget 'that if human tribunals have a right to inflict a severer punishment than death, they must have a right to inflict death itself'. He was quick to tell Roget that this did not mean he approved of the existing penal codes of Europe; his own country's especially 'must be said to be written in blood'.

Romilly spent the remainder of 1783 getting set up in legal practice, and in 1784 he went on circuit for the first time. For a little-known lawyer with a reputation of being shy, he had a knack for making useful contacts, though he did not always think them so at first. One of these was his introduction in 1784 to the Count Honoré Gabriel de Mirabeau through an acquaintance from Geneva. Mirabeau was then in England on a self-imposed, though prudent, exile. The personal morality of the two men could not have differed more, but Mirabeau took a liking to Romilly and became convinced of his potential as Romilly helped him translate a pamphlet into English.[26] Mirabeau spoke of Romilly to the Marquis of Lansdowne, who had made his family home of Bowood a kind of English Salon, bringing together stimulating minds of divergent backgrounds, sometimes with remarkable results. Visitors to Bowood included Jeremy Bentham, William Wilberforce, the playwright David Garrick, the scientist and theologian Joseph Priestley, the Reverend Richard Price, and the political economist Benjamin Vaughan. Vaughan facilitated a meeting between Lansdowne and Romilly after the Marquis expressed interest in an anonymous tract on the power of juries published in 1784, which Vaughan knew Romilly had written.[27] Lansdowne cultivated the friendship and took an interest in Romilly's success. Although any actions taken to promote his legal practice went unrecorded, he did, somewhat inadvertently, further Romilly's interests in penal law reform.

Lansdowne asked Romilly to respond to a short work which appeared in 1785 entitled *Thoughts on Executive Justice, with respect to our Criminal Laws*. The book had received a relatively wide readership, with a second edition published before year's end, and Romilly thought Lansdowne himself was almost persuaded by it. The title page said it was written by 'a sincere well-wisher to the public', who was soon revealed to be the Rev. Martin Madan, a Methodist preacher and writer who felt that the overuse of discretionary pardon by the judges and partial verdicts of juries had helped provoke an increase in crime in England by rendering the punishment of crime uncertain.[28] Romilly had not taken much notice of Madan's book prior to Lansdowne's request that he consider it. A closer look prompted him to write a thorough refutation. Less than a hundred copies of his response would be sold, which might suggest, given Madan's success, the general receptivity of the reading public to arguments for mitigation in the 1780s. For historians the interest is not in how it shaped public opinion, then, but as an expression of what Romilly believed. He had no difficulty accepting the argument that only the certainty of punishment would deter crime; his main target was Madan's proposition that the existing laws were 'excellent'. Romilly contended instead that the laws were 'unreasonably severe', so that 'the punishment bears no proportion to the crime', and that it followed 'that strict execution of them is neither expedient, nor even possible'. Even a cursory glance would show a

> mass of jarring and inconsistent laws, which are severe where they should be mild, mild where they should be severe, and which have been, for the most part, the fruit of no regular design, but of sudden and angry fits of capricious legislation.[29]

Like Madan, Romilly emphasized the responsibility of legislators, but he also blamed them for enacting overly harsh laws, which, if enforced as written, would produce 'wanton cruelty and injustice'.[30] Passing new capital statutes was easy; even a novice MP could do it with little or no justification. Romilly doubted that the intention of Parliament was to create a hodge-podge of cruel statutes, but he considered the result of its short-sightedness almost criminal in its outcome. Far from castigating the magistrates and justices who mitigated the criminal code, Romilly praised them for acting humanely. Without their intervention, the administration of English justice would have been gruesome indeed.

Romilly based his criticism of the existing statutes on the idea that all punishment was evil and justifiable only when necessary to prevent a greater evil. He believed that real progress had been made in penal philosophy and that the 'absurd and barbarous notions of justice, which prevailed for ages', had been exploded and replaced by 'humane and rational principles', of which he posited four.[31] First, criminal prosecutions should serve the public good, rather than settle private scores or gratify the passions of individuals. Second, the primary goal of legislation should be the prevention of crime, rather than chastisement of the criminal. Third, the terror of a punishment alone was insufficient to prevent crime. And finally, unless some just proportion existed between a crime and its appointed punishment, the law would serve only to excite rather than repress crime. Romilly suggested that these points were so widely known as to be almost axioms of criminal law, thereby rhetorically throwing Madan into the category of barbaric, backward and reactionary. To support this position, he called not only on Beccaria, but even more heavily on William Blackstone, who argued, 'It is a kind of quackery in government, and argues a want of solid skill, to apply the same universal remedy, the *ultimatum supplicium*, to every case of difficulty.'[32] At the root of the problem was proportionality. Romilly could find no way of rationalizing the application of the death penalty to the multitude of crimes for which it was assigned. He could not agree with

Beccaria that it ought never to be inflicted, but it was abundantly clear 'that death cannot be inflicted for a mere invasion of property, consistently with reason and justice, nor without a gross violation of the laws of nature, and the precepts of our religion'.[33] 'Between a sum of money and the life of an individual', he continued, 'there is no proportion,' and without proportion, the administration of justice ran aground on popular sentiments. If statutes were 'repugnant to the character of a nation, they must remain unexecuted'.[34] For consistent enforcement laws had to be such that the best and brightest in society would agree with their execution, rather than being such as 'nature tells one it is a virtue to disappoint and to prevent their execution'. Undue severity led juries to judge the policy of the law, and they found it easy to 'quiet their consciences upon a perjury which was the means of preventing murder'.[35]

Besides these central arguments, Romilly presented several other comments on the laws and their administration. A speedy trial was almost impossible in Britain because of the infrequency of jail deliveries. The crimes of the wealthy often went unpunished. England needed a better system of policing, but Romilly rejected the idea of a centralized police force; at the time he could only imagine the French model, with its networks of spies and informers, which was an affront to English liberties. Romilly also proposed the propriety of addressing the root of profligacy by providing employment for the poor and suppressing the temptations to vice early, and he argued in favor of trying to reform criminals, which Madan had rejected as unfeasible. Not all systems had to operate like the Hulks on the Thames, Romilly contended, or like the prisons and 'houses of correction' that too often were simply schools of vice. Well-designed plans for reform were not invalidated because existing plans were 'ill imagined and ill executed'. At the heart of Romilly's hope for reform, of both law and convict, was his belief in the rational calculation of human beings, a belief shared by many in the eighteenth century, and a notion central to Beccaria's arguments as well as a foundation of Bentham's philosophy. Because 'every rational being does, unquestionably, in every action of his life, propose to himself some advantages, immediate or remote', certainty of punishment, made possible by proportionality and better detection, would deter potential offenders, since to commit a crime would be certain to bring down an evil on the offender's head.[36]

Romilly's penal philosophy was almost complete in this 1786 publication, and one can see much of his later parliamentary presentations. Romilly might not have convinced the reading public at large, but he did convince Lansdowne, who wrote that he was now inclined to think 'that a revision of our penal law is not only desirable, but necessary, for the purpose of making it agreeable to the spirit of the times, and such as can be executed'.[37] Besides Vaughan, a few others knew Romilly had written the book, including Sir Gilbert Elliot (later Lord Minto), Wilberforce and John Baynes, a barrister and friend of Wilberforce through whom Romilly first met James Scarlett.[38] Despite the publication's commercial failure, Romilly's acquaintances encouraged him, and he began to keep a record of observations on the criminal laws and their operation from his readings and experiences on the circuit. He examined not only the question of punishments, but also the rules of evidence and forms of proceedings, and pondered the effects that these might have on the 'manners of the people, and on the administration of justice'.[39] His conviction grew that the existing laws created unnecessary contradictions, brutalized the onlookers, and ridiculed justice.

Most of Romilly's unpublished notes and observations on English law have been lost. Scarlett recorded that he had read through a two-volume work on the criminal law, but had advised Romilly against publishing it, on the grounds that the style would not make him known as a writer and the part he took was still unpopular.[40] Romilly's *Memoirs* referred to many notes and essays which, the editors declared, Romilly himself considered unfit for publication.[41] They did, however, list 43 different essays, with titles ranging from 'On a Written Code of Laws' and 'On Bankrupts' to essays about the death penalty, punishments for children, and procedural issues, such as 'On allowing Counsel to Persons accused'.[42] The last essay listed was entitled 'Observations on Bentham on Punishment', suggesting a critical, if friendly, view of the philosopher's approach. Another list, now in the library at Lincoln's Inn, provides evidence of Romilly's breadth of interest, referring to topics from the laws concerning suicide and blasphemy, to cruelty to animals, to divorce among the poor and even to forensic medicine.[43]

Thoughts on England's laws were not Romilly's only concern through the late 1780s and 1790s. During further trips to Paris he became very interested in France's revolution. His friend Dumont had become Mirabeau's editor and ghost-writer, and Romilly helped both men, writing a tract on the debating procedures followed in the British Parliament, which Mirabeau translated and published.[44] Dumont's letters inspired Romilly with optimism, and in the summer of 1789 he set down his hopes in a short anonymous work called *Thoughts on the Probable Influence of the French Revolution on Great Britain*.[45] Romilly desired the pamphlet to inspire the hesitant among his countrymen to take heart and find encouragement from the developments in France. The

Revolution could only have positive results for Britain, chief among them greater security of their liberties and peace. France, whose many wars with England had been pressed by princely pride and dynastic ambition, would now be constrained by the need for popular consent, and Romilly trusted that where 'such consent must be obtained, no wars will be undertaken, but what are just and necessary'.[46] Their rivalry would now be over 'who shall soonest and most effectually promote the happiness of mankind, and extend the empire of reason, humanity and true philosophy'.[47] Ironically, Romilly early believed that the spectacle of great change across the Channel might 'diminish some of that horror at innovation, which seems so generally to prevail amongst us'.[48] Should this happy circumstance come to pass, he had a few questions prepared to set an agenda for discussion of change at home. His list covered issues of religious conformity, education, the structure and practice of English law, issues of military service, questions of trade and parliamentary reform. He put it all very tentatively, but he went beyond traditional Whig causes in his speculation. The pamphlet did not sell well compared with others of the time, but it revealed much about Romilly's thought in 1789.

His aspirations for France and England were soon tempered by a visit to Paris during the late summer court recess. Everyone Romilly met seemed to be convinced he had to play a great part, certain that he individually was of great consequence to the Revolution. It was a tumult he could hardly respect, even if he had great sympathy for Mirabeau and others who really seemed to strive to do what was in the interest of the French people.[49] He still wished the French *bon chance*, however, and he became convinced that Dumont's letters and eye-witness reports should form the basis of a history of the Revolution. The idea went through several forms before Romilly settled on producing a book which would contain the supposed letters of a fictitious German traveller, Henry Frederic Groenvelt, about his observations in France and England.[50]

With Dumont's permission he set to work on the book with Scarlett, who helped translate Dumont's letters. They added several short essays, almost all written by Romilly, describing institutions and manners in England.[51] Scarlett's later evaluation that these essays were written by Romilly as 'mere sketches for his own amusement – experiments upon style – and are not to be taken as the true representation of his sentiments' was overprotective of his old friend's reputation (as well as his own), for he had to admit that Romilly was among the many thinking men in England inclined to favor the French Revolution in its early stages.[52] Dumont's letters were true historical testimony so far as they came from a source close to the events described, though they contained much commentary, irony and sarcasm. A reader would certainly be inclined to take the remainder in a similar way. Romilly might have exaggerated his case sometimes, as a foreigner might be supposed to do, but he certainly was not writing anything he absolutely disagreed with. The 'letters' by Romilly presented observations on many aspects of English society, law and politics.[53] Written with a satirical turn reminiscent of Swift, they were full of real criticism. Unlike his speculations in the *Probable Influence*, *Groenvelt's Letters* do not contain suggestions for change so much as ridicule of the system in place. Romilly emphasized the incongruities and contradictions of English institutions and customs. Though by far the best written of Romilly's publications to that date, *Groenvelt's Letters* had a short shelf-life. Soon after the book's appearance, the atrocities of the Revolution increased. Romilly soon thereafter took every unsold copy of the work he could find and burned it.[54]

The remaining copies of *Groenvelt's Letters* were either in safe hands like Scarlett's, or in libraries of deposit like the British Museum. It therefore had no 'influence' on the culture that one can trace. The essays have historical interest, both in the scenes which Dumont records, and also in displaying further the ideas Romilly was playing with by 1792. The fictitious 'letters', along with his early reflections on the Revolution in France, reveal that Romilly's views on the criminal law were part of a larger perspective and program for reform. With regard to English laws and legal administration, the *Letters* show the strongest touch of Benthamic language of any of Romilly's published works. Indeed, prior to *Groenvelt's Letters* nothing Romilly wrote would have suggested familiarity with Bentham's writings, much less friendship with their author. Because of the supposed importance of Bentham in English criminal law reform, we need to clarify the relationship between him and Romilly, both personally and theoretically.

Romilly and Bentham: independent minds in a common cause

Romilly's place in law reform is certain. His friendship with Bentham is also certain from the testimony of both men. What is not at all certain is that Romilly's efforts were a result of this friendship. Indeed, analysis of Romilly's arguments and examination of his criticisms of Bentham suggest a significant distance between them when it came down to the actual practice of law and how to reform it. I do not intend an exhaustive discussion of the contrasts between them, but even a simple exploration shows that Romilly's approach to law differed from Bentham's enough to treat them as practically independent, if philosophically sympathetic. Noticeably absent from the list of those who knew about Romilly's response to Madan was Bentham. They first met in 1784 at a dinner given by a mutual friend, George Wilson.[55] Bentham remembered dining with Romilly in Chancery Lane sometime later in 1784, but recorded that their acquaintance had not yet become an intimate friendship.[56] Between 1785 and 1788 Bentham was not in the country, having gone to Russia to visit his brother Samuel, then working on the Czar's navy. He was, therefore, absent at the time of Romilly's publication of the *Observations* on Madan's book, and that work shows no sign of being influenced by any of Bentham's writings, published or private. With its positive use of 'natural rights' language and its relatively uncritical acceptance of Blackstone's views on law and the British constitution, Romilly's *Observations on a Late Publication* contained much that was in conflict with Bentham's early writings. Compare, for instance, the language in Romilly's book with that in Bentham's *A Fragment on Government*, published in 1776; it is not merely the subject matter which differs, but the use of phrases such as 'natural rights' or 'Law of Nature', which Bentham considered fictions, while Romilly in the mid 1780s would still quote Grotius and admire Rousseau.

Bentham had turned his thoughts toward issues of penal law in the late 1770s, but his attempts to write a complete work on the issue had been side-tracked in some of the thornier questions of translating the principle of utility (defined by Bentham, after Beccaria, as the 'greatest happiness to the greatest number') into an applicable legal system.[57] He had printed his *Introduction to the Principles of Morals and Legislation* in 1780, but for various reasons did not release it until 1789. Even then, it received little notice. Certainly he had not spoken with Romilly at any great length about the penal law before Romilly had set himself to examining and gathering information for criticism of the criminal statutes and their administration. Moreover, their approaches to criticism were crucially different. Bentham, though called to the bar in 1769, practiced law only a few years and never argued a case in court. His attack upon the English system was theoretical: in the language of the day, 'speculative'. Romilly was a practicing barrister, whose material came not only from his reading but also from his observations on the Circuit. His criticisms would always have the flavor of actual experience. Thus, Romilly's particular suggestions in the *Observations* were oriented toward specific abuses in the administration of justice. To the extent that it raised a challenge to the system, it was to the lack of coherence and the blanket application of the punishment of death. Bentham's *Introduction*, on the other hand, sought to shift the whole basis of penal law and offered a foundation upon which to build a new code. Although politically conservative in the 1780s, Bentham's approach to law was radical from the start. He said that what was, ought not to be, in contrast with Romilly's style which suggested that what was could be amended to better serve the community. Romilly's was an approach of reform; Bentham's was essentially one of replacement.

Only after Bentham's return from Russia and his reacquaintance with Romilly in 1788 in the comfortable atmosphere of Bowood did their friendship really begin to grow. They dined together frequently, and after Romilly's marriage in 1798, he and his wife were 'among the few who could ever induce Bentham to quit his Hermitage and mingle with the world'.[58] The friendship proved useful to Bentham especially. Through Romilly, his writings became known to Dumont, who became his translator, editor and publisher on the Continent. Indeed, it has been argued that the *Traités de législation* (1802) and the *Théories des peines et des récompenses* (1811) made Bentham an international reputation as a legal theorist before he had one in Britain.[59]

Romilly served as an intermediary for Bentham in other ways as well. In 1791 Bentham published a plan for a new kind of prison, the *Panopticon*, and he had made a model to help illustrate it. Although the Panopticon has been attacked by Michel Foucault and by Michael Ignatieff as part of a new technology of repression, many contemporaries thought it a striking improvement over the existing system, even if they could not accept some of the more extreme elements.[60] In the early 1790s the plan received much attention from members of Parliament and some cabinet ministers, including William Pitt. In 1794 an act was passed to provide for the construction of a prison along Bentham's lines, and preparations started. Bentham spent a good deal of his own money trying to find a suitable location and, when he found it, trying to obtain permission to build. He encountered resistance at every turn, eventually giving up the project in 1803. Between 1794 and 1803 Romilly continually sought to assist Bentham in getting the prison built, and much of their correspondence from this period deals with attempts by Romilly to get explanation or action from the officers of the Crown, particularly through the Solicitor General and Attorney General, whom he dealt with regularly. Romilly was frustrated for Bentham, for whom he could get no satisfactory answers, much less commitments. Bentham eventually came to believe in an almost conspiratorial opposition to his plan. When Romilly, with the help of Wilberforce and others, managed in 1812 to get Parliament to vote Bentham a sum of money to reimburse him for his costs in trying to put together the plan, he wrote to Romilly that while the current members of the Government were very kind and just toward him, he was well aware of the 'secret' history of the Panopticon plans.[61] The full history of these frustrations has remained mostly secret, but it is generally agreed that the frustrations over this project fueled Bentham's later radical attitudes about political reform.

Although they were friends, the evidence suggests that Romilly always maintained a distance from Bentham's ideas, and could at times be almost cruelly ironic about Bentham's eccentricities. In 1791, when he was preparing the *Groenvelt Letters*, which contains the most Benthamic language of any of Romilly's publications, he wrote to Dumont, 'Bentham leads the same kind of life as usual at Hendon; seeing nobody, reading nothing, and writing books which nobody reads.'[62] In truth, he and Dumont read much of what Bentham wrote, but critically. Dumont, when publishing Bentham's writings in French, found it necessary to edit them severely. When the *Traité de législation civile et pénale* was due out in 1802, Romilly told him Bentham was very 'impatient to see the book, because he has a great curiosity to know what his opinions are upon the subject'.[63] In part Romilly thought this was a curiosity to see these opinions in print, but Dumont's skill at smoothing out the rough edges of Bentham's prose was immense.[64] Romilly wrote both privately and publicly of the difficulties of Bentham's style. Commenting on Bentham's tract on judicial oaths, *Swear not at all*, he noted, 'It is like most of that extraordinary man's late publications, written in so involved & obscure a style that it will meet with few readers, if indeed there should be found any who will have the patience and perseverance to read it through.'[65] He was equally critical of the other's language in his 1817 *Edinburgh Review* article on the publication of some of Bentham's letters on the codification of the law.[66] In this very public forum, Romilly praised Bentham, but also observed the philosopher's distance from everyday realities and his stylistic shortcomings, and he told the readers that Dumont deserved great credit for making Bentham understandable to a continental audience.[67]

Romilly was annoyed not only by Bentham's new language of law and philosophy, but by his tendency to exaggerate a case and his want of tact when proposing reforms. On more than one occasion he had to warn the prophet of utility about the libel laws.[68] During the very period when Romilly was pursuing penal law reforms in the Parliament, Bentham obtained an interview with Lord Sidmouth, who had become Home Secretary in 1812.[69] Encouraged by the conversation, certainly more than Sidmouth had intended, Bentham offered to draw up, not suggestions for specific reforms in the English criminal law, but an entire penal code for Britain, for Sidmouth's consideration.[70] He considered it too much to hope that the Home Secretary would actually approve such a code, but he asked only for encouragement to complete the project which he felt would surely 'be of advantage to the country, and thence to mankind at large'. Bentham had, with typical modesty, sent the US President James Madison a similar proposal, to which he referred in trying to persuade Sidmouth.[71] A greater contrast with Romilly's cautious proposals could hardly be imagined.

Bentham's description of English criminal law to Sidmouth demonstrated how confusing and confrontational he could be:

> As to the existing Penal Code – but there *is* no existing Penal Code – (those fragments, those deplorably scanty, as well as frequently exuberant and throughout inadequately expressed – those perpetually incommensurable, never-confronted and ever-inconsistent fragments which are in the state of *statute law* excepted) existence cannot be predicated of it. Be it *law*, be it what else it may, that *discourse* which has no determinate set of *words* belonging to it, has no existence.[72] [Bentham's emphasis]

This was written to the Secretary of State for Home Affairs, the minister who oversaw a good portion of the administration of justice, and an individual not known for his friendly attitude toward moderate change, much less real innovation; one could easily see why Romilly grew frustrated with Bentham's manner. On an earlier occasion, when Romilly was Solicitor General and looking into reforms in the Scottish courts, Bentham decided to write a pamphlet on the topic, for which Romilly himself provided much of the information.[73] Bentham wrote him a 26-page letter of proposals and arguments, telling his plan and asking Romilly to lay his offer to write up a reform 'gratuitously' on the table in the Commons. Romilly reassured Bentham that he had no fear of his reputation being tarnished by association with Bentham, but told the would-be law reformer that he was wrong in his understanding of how to move such reforms through the Parliament. One could not simply lay them, or an offer to work on them, on the table and expect acceptance. Such action would only 'afford a pretext for that ridicule with which many persons would be glad to cover us both'.[74]

Bentham's good intentions did not matter, Romilly continued, and in fact would probably 'afford a strong objection to it'. He felt the legal philosopher's time would be better spent in working on his book on the laws of evidence. He thought if anyone could present a whole code of alteration from scratch (Bentham was largely ignorant of Scots law), Bentham could; but he did not think such a thing could be done at all.

The proposal to Sidmouth presented one of Bentham's major complaints about English common law, the *lex non scripta* as it was sometimes called. According to Bentham, for a law to be a law, for it to have positive and real existence, it had to be posited by a legislator, whether a king or queen, or a collective body like the Parliament, and it had to be written down.[75] All else was fiction. Thus, to the extent that the common law was unwritten, it did not exist. In the common law tradition, according to Bentham, all one could talk about intelligibly was 'judge-made law', since the decisions and reports of the judges provided the precedents and guidelines for its practice. Unfortunately, precedents were often inconsistent, and when new situations and conflicts arose, judges in fact created legislation by their decisions, even if they claimed to base them upon the common law precedents.

Romilly largely agreed with Bentham's analysis of the indefinite nature of the common law. But their perspectives were rooted in different concerns and led to different applications. Bentham said unwritten law was non-existent law, and therefore no law at all. Romilly did not attack the common law as such, but expressed concern for the uncertainty inherent in it. In his observations on Madan's book, he had discussed the problem of people not knowing the written statutes, which could be found if one really tried; how much more frustrating were unwritten laws! A section of *Groenvelt's Letters* also addressed the problem of judge-made law. 'Letters' on civil and criminal law in England and on the British constitution criticized the practices of English law and Blackstone as its chief proponent, but the essay on 'Judicial Legislation' showed the strongest marks of Bentham's influence.[76] The practice of common law, according to 'Groenvelt', was 'more a science of memory than of reason', was concerned more with precedents than legal principles, and was treated as if it had been in existence since time immemorial. The judges, the author declared, behaved as if they were as infallible as priests, who, rather than admitting the law did not cover a new situation, claimed instead to 'remember' it; 'the consequence is, that they are obliged to do what is usual with persons who are ignorant or forgetful, while they pretend to remember, they in fact invent'.

The language in these fictitious letters was more Benthamic than usual for Romilly, and they certainly support Scarlett's assertion that Romilly was experimenting with style. But if Romilly soon returned to the language of a practicing lawyer, he also carried his unease with the uncertainties of the common law. He favored a written code: 'It is vain to hope that clear, precise & certain laws can ever be obtained by any other means, than by the positive, & written enactment of a legislator.'[77] But he drew back from an outright condemnation of the common law tradition. When pondering in 1801 what he might do, were he ever to reach high office – especially that of Lord Chancellor – he took particular note of the responsibility of a judge:

> In England it derives peculiar importance from the circumstance of its being, in a great degree, an unwritten law that is administered, where every decision becomes in its turn a precedent; and where it is impossible, in many cases, to decide as a judge, without laying down a rule as a legislator.[78]

Though he considered many reforms which a person might pursue as Lord Chancellor, he did not include codification of English law among them. Instead, Romilly's reasoning flowed out of an acceptance of the basic structure of English government and law, with the presumption that careful and specific reforms could better the whole.

Romilly's concern about unwritten law can be seen as part of a growing anxiety in late eighteenth-century Britain, about the place of legislation in making and shaping law. David Lieberman has placed Bentham at the end of a series of thinkers who had moved British legal theory away from stressing the centrality of the judge and his decision and toward the realization of the sovereignty of the Parliament over all law in the United Kingdom. Against this background, Lieberman has portrayed criminal law reform as another manifestation of the general concern for the failures of the statute law. As he writes further,

> To place the legal criticism of a William Eden or a Samuel Romilly within this broader context of legal orthodoxy is also to explain the extent of the hostility to the penal law among England's legal establishment, and why, for example, penal reform should have provided common cause for such an unlikely partnership as William Blackstone and Jeremy Bentham.[79]

Lieberman's study grants Romilly's ideas and efforts for reform an independence minimized by historians who have tied him too closely to Bentham, but it also explains some of the underlying agreement. Lieberman also shows that criticism of the penal law was necessarily, though not always consciously, related to criticism of the entire system of laws and law-making in late eighteenth-century England. Bentham's philosophy may have imagined the greatest possible competence of statute law, but he shared the age with Romilly and others whose abilities and efforts had a lasting, if frequently forgotten, impact.

Romilly's political tactics also revealed his independence from Bentham. Even Elie Halévy noted that in Parliament Romilly appeared to have 'systematically... avoided naming Bentham, preferring to invoke the authority of Blackstone, 'the great commentator', or of Beccaria.'[80] This tactic would make considerable sense if, as Lieberman has argued, these eighteenth-century writers had been fairly well absorbed into the thought of England's legal professionals by the beginning of the nineteenth century, when Bentham was still considered an innovator and projector. Romilly did not need Bentham's rather idiosyncratic language and argument to present the case for penal reform when accepted authorities had already done so. And contrary to Halévy's view, Romilly's efforts at law reform did not become 'more consistent' after he became one of Bentham's intimate friends. In the very years that Romilly was most active in pursuing criminal law reform, Bentham was becoming more reclusive, and they were moving apart on what constituted practical measures. While he argued for a 'direct and profound' influence from Bentham, Halévy did note the differences:

> Romilly defined his own conception, which was opposed to the Benthamite conception, of a policy of reform: it was wrong to take a simple principle as starting point and draw from it certain consequences which would be true independently of consideration of times and place; it was enough constantly to adapt the laws to the changing conditions of customs and civilizations.[81]

Perhaps because they differed so much on the tactics of reform, Romilly did not record having spoken to Bentham about his plans to introduce bills in 1808. Even if they did discuss the measures, Romilly clearly did not feel dependent on Bentham's approval or suggestions.

Though Romilly rarely employed Benthamic language in his writing or speeches, two notable exceptions are worthy of comment. We have already observed the evident deployment of arguments from Bentham's writings which appeared in *Groenvelt's Letters*. In one of the letters based on Dumont's description of the 'Declaration of Rights' from August 1789, Groenvelt says,

> A little senseless jargon about the *law of nature*, and *natural rights*, is an excellent auxiliary to a professor, who would involve his ignorance in the cloud of a loud and elaborate harangue; but we who understand what they talk about, and are desirous to be understood by others, will readily agree to reject altogether these vague and unmeaning expressions. To speak correctly, rights have no existence but by virtue of the law; they do not precede society, but are produced by it; ... When the constitution and laws of a country are complete, then is the time to make a *declaration of the rights of a citizen*.[82]

One wonders whether this could have come from the hand of Dumont, Mirabeau's secretary, or from Romilly, the enthusiastic admirer of Rousseau, before they encountered Bentham's criticism of 'law of nature' language and his insistence upon legally defined rights. Later in the same letter, Groenvelt declared, 'I wish to reason in a language that is intelligible to all mankind, and would gladly annihilate some thousands of volumes on metaphysics, jurisprudence, and morals.'[83] Such a project was imagined by Bentham as early as the 1770s and was the goal of his unfinished *Comment on the Commentaries*.

The second example of Romilly's deployment of Benthamic language appeared in his arguments in 1810 against Paley's statements in favor of judicial discretion. These heavily reflected unpublished writings by Bentham on Paley's infamous 'net', into which any crime meriting death might be swept.[84] Bentham wrote the pieces between January 1809 and July 1810, and perhaps they were actually prepared for Romilly's public efforts.[85] In any event, Romilly criticized the latitude which Paley would allow the judges, arguing, like Bentham, that this discretion made the punishment of criminals unpredictable, and so removed the deterrent.[86] But once again, though he argued that if possible the guidelines for sentencing should be written down and incorporated into statute, he did not go as far as Bentham in condemning judicial discretion. Neither did the bulk of Romilly's arguments rest on his criticism of Paley; he simply filtered and mixed Bentham's ideas with his own. Certainly this added to the power of his 1810 address, and he would not have denied it, but this direct incorporation of Benthamic language into his public rhetoric was the exception to Romilly's preference for other sources.

In his study of the first generation of Bentham's followers, which rather debunks the image of the Philosophical Radicals as organized, effective political shakers and movers, William Thomas suggests that no 'one who has read Bentham and felt the fascination of the vast enterprise he set himself can doubt that he had considerable influence'.[87] The exaggeration of this influence is understandable, but regrettable for having distracted historians and legal theorists from other strands of thought in the efforts to alter England's penal laws. Bentham's contribution was unparalleled at the theoretical level, and he gave the arguments of utility with regard to criminal law their most comprehensive expression. In the melee of parliamentary politics, however, his language was too cumbersome and unwieldy, his theory too radical and too complete, to effect the alterations Romilly and his allies sought. Bentham proposed to annihilate too many volumes on jurisprudence and morals to become an active contributor to the debate.

Some, like Halévy, have tried to portray Romilly as simply an imperfect disciple of Bentham, who strove to put the master's thoughts into actual legal form. This study has shown that Romilly ought not to be called a disciple at all, but at most a friend and colleague, who took sympathetic interest in the trail Bentham was trying to carve in the English law, but who really cut his own path toward reform.[88] They agreed at many points, but Romilly had his own voice, and it was more in tune with the structures of English practice and tradition. The criminal statutes needed a more general overhaul than Romilly felt it politically possible to propose in the 1810s, but in the end the reforms looked more like his proposals than Bentham's. Those who have written of these reforms with disappointment, because they did not more fully reflect Bentham's theory, and those who have blamed them for reflecting too much, have both erred in seeing Bentham as the spirit behind the attempts at amelioration. We must not dismiss the Philosopher of Utility completely, but neither his rhetoric nor his personality was ever a driving force behind the campaign to mitigate the capital statutes. Romilly's utilitarianism was less theoretical than his friend's, but for that very reason it was more in keeping with English attitudes, and was therefore a much greater force in bringing on practical and gradual reform.

4
Evangelicalism and Penal Law Reform

William Wilberforce was among the first to endorse Romilly's campaign for criminal law reform. A group of between twenty and thirty Evangelical members of Parliament followed him.[1] These famous 'Saints' have been remembered best for their antislavery campaigns. They shared many political views, including a dislike of party and concern for voting according to one's conscience. They have sometimes been mislabeled 'Tories', but the Saints were far more interested in reform than such an appellation allows. Detailed study has revealed that the Saints were a minority of the Evangelical MPs in Parliament, but they were very active, exercising an influence out of proportion with their numbers. Other Evangelical MPs associated more openly with the Tory leadership, especially after Spencer Perceval became Prime Minister; a few others were strongly committed Whigs. Contemporaries often saw Wilberforce as a spokesmen for the Evangelical laity in the Church of England, but while Wilberforce certainly shared many convictions with his fellow Evangelicals, not all agreed with him on how to apply their faith to public life. Perceval was the most striking contrast. As Prime Minister, Perceval opposed criminal law reform. Though he agreed that the laws as written were harsh, he believed the practice of the courts sufficiently mitigated their rigor, and that changes ought not to be made in a time of war and social unrest. This was an opinion about timing more than penal theory, but while it did not really deny the arguments of the reformers, it did reveal a different approach to politics from that of Wilberforce or Romilly. Since the votes of the Saints often tipped the scales in favor of penal reform during and after Perceval's administration, an assessment of Evangelicalism and criminal law reform requires some clarification on the sources and direction of public attitudes of Evangelical politicians. For many, support for penal law reform resulted as much from practical experience in working with the poor and their efforts to improve the country's moral behavior, as from the conscientious application of a specifically 'Evangelical' penal theory. Their views of crime and the reformation of criminals did have a basis in theology, but this grounding was supplemented and sometimes suggested by the lessons learned in philanthropic involvement.

Evangelical theology and public life

1) Evangelicals in politics

While a mark of Evangelicalism was activism in some form, its specific manifestation in politics varied. Ian Bradley has identified 112 MPs between the years 1784 and 1832 who were either self-professed Evangelicals or whose associations and extra-parliamentary commitments strongly suggest Evangelical leanings.[2] Besides 30 'Saints', Bradley identified 15 Evangelicals who sat with the Whigs and 56 others among the Tories; in both these groups, political loyalties appeared to derive from traditional family ties and interests, as much as from personal conviction. The final 11 Bradley labeled 'Recordites' because of their adherence to theological and political views voiced in *The Record* newspaper, which Alexander Haldane first published in 1828. Because they came relatively late in the period, the Recordites played little part in criminal law reform, though Boyd Hilton has linked them to the emergence of a new Tory paternalism, whose most famous advocate was Anthony Ashley Cooper, 7th Earl of Shaftesbury.[3]

Aside from those who served in office, such as Perceval and Vansittart, Evangelicals outside the Saints were much less active in Parliament, speaking only infrequently. They generally agreed with the Saints on matters of probity in government and often voted with them on issues not closely associated with party, including antislavery measures. On more partisan issues, Evangelical Whigs adhered to the party's long advocacy of the rule of law and the rights of Dissenters, stressing the primacy of personal religious conscience and, increasingly, the utility of more representative government. Evangelical Tories held to the view that Government was to be obeyed unless clearly threatening the faith, and their religious beliefs do not seem to have created in them as great an anxiety to challenge socially accepted practices as did the Saints'. Their political activities have supported the view of Evangelicalism as socially conservative or at least passive, in keeping with doctrines which taught the transience of human life and institutions and raised skepticism that public action could bring lasting change. Such beliefs, however, did not keep these Tory politicians from occasionally aligning themselves with the Saints, as many did with regard to slavery and, though less overwhelmingly, to penal reform.

In contrast, Wilberforce, the Thorntons, Thomas Babington, the Grants and the other members of the Clapham Sect thought their religion called them to be involved in public life in an assertive manner. The Saints voted as a solid block on questions of antislavery, economy in government, and criminal law reform. On many other issues, the Saints took no group policy and voted independently, each according to his conscience. For Wilberforce, a close friend of William Pitt, this insistence upon obeying conscience meant foregoing any ambition of holding office. He recorded in his diary in August 1802 that his part was 'to give the example of an independent member of parliament, and a man of religion, discharging with activity and fidelity the duties of his trust, and not seeking to render his parliamentary station a ladder by which to rise to a higher eminence'.[4] Pitt would have agreed about Wilberforce's independence, to Pitt's frustration. Nor was Wilberforce alone in putting aside personal friendship when political conscience demanded it. James Stephen, who entered the Commons by Perceval's help and invitation, wrote the Prime Minister plainly that if confronted with the unpleasant event of 'not being able to concur in a course of proceeding proposed or recommended by *you* to the House ... I should of course not vote with you'.[5] Stephen did vote against Perceval on occasion, including the 1810 votes on Romilly's bills, and he eventually retired from Parliament because of differences with the Government over the handling of slavery matters.

During a particularly contentious election, when Henry Thornton received considerable criticism from Sir Francis Burdett, whose brother was running against him, Thornton overcame initial dislike of attending a dinner of a fellow candidate who was distinctly a government man, only because the man was such a 'sturdy friend to œconomical reform', of which Thornton was a leading proponent. 'As to Parliamentary politics, the path of duty is clear', Thornton wrote; 'it is not to bend an inch either way, I mean upon great public questions, to the humour of any of the parties'.[6] This commitment to independence encompassed some religiously influenced issues, such as Catholic emancipation and the Irish Church, where some might vote for, others against.[7] It also meant supporting the Opposition when they supported a cause of the Saints. In 1806, after Pitt's death, Wilberforce responded positively to

Henry Brougham's request that he support Lord Henry Petty's bid to fill Pitt's vacant seat for the University of Cambridge.[8] Wilberforce ruffled a lot of noble, and more than a few Evangelical, feathers with this support, but it demonstrated his distance from uncritical support for the King's Ministers.

The Saints were among the most conscientious attenders at parliamentary debates, and they served on select committees far more often than the average member. They allowed that many political issues could be religiously neutral, but they consistently favored fiscal and administrative reforms to curtail abuse of offices and were generally in favor of moderate political reforms. Henry Thornton took an active role on the Commons Select Committee on Finance during the first decade of the nineteenth century, writing an influential tract on the effects of paper credit, as well as advocating the elimination of many sinecures and other drains on the public purse.[9] On parliamentary and electoral reform, they showed varying degrees of enthusiasm. Thornton and Babington, and later Buxton, had the greatest openness to alterations in the electoral system, though they were never willing to go so far as the 'democracy' advocated by the Painites and later radicals. Wilberforce's attitude was not untypical. He feared the

> progress of that increasing luxury and dissipation in private life, together with that party spirit and political corruption under the name of the influence of the crown in public life, which was gra-dually... sapping the very vitals of our body politic.[10]

He felt that all well-disposed men could agree that the bribery and expense of elections ought to be lessened. Yet, the answer was not to be found principally in political reform. In 1815 he told the radical Major Cartwright that he could not cooperate with him in his particular scheme of electoral reform, because he and Cartwright differed 'so widely both as to the importance of the measure itself and as to the extent to which it ought to be carried... in my judgment the diseases of our country are of a moral still more than a political nature'.[11] The tree of British politics was bad at its moral root, and cutting off branches would not solve the fundamental problems. Pruning might be part of the cure, but one had to dig down deeper if lasting changes were to come. The most important practical implication of this focus on the moral source of public ills was to place political problems and solutions on a secondary tier of concern.

2) Salvation and doing good

All orthodox Christianity has been concerned with issues of sin and human redemption and of right belief and right behavior. One distinctive element of Evangelicalism has been the emphasis placed on individual experience and the self-conscious commitment to Jesus Christ as one's personal Savior and Lord.[12] Conversion proved to be one of the bothersome elements of Evangelicalism; it was an all or nothing personal commitment that affected not only the convert, but all of his or her friends and acquaintances. Moving away from earlier discussions regarding the marks of the true church, Evangelicalism focused instead on the characteristics of a true Christian. It brought the focus to the individual level, declaring that each person had to examine his convictions in a way that neither Church of England nor most Dissenting churches consistently demanded of their members. Evangelicalism said not only that Christianity was the right religion – that was of course the common belief in Britain – but that salvation required an uncompromising personal belief in Christ. As Wilberforce argued in his evangelistic treatise, *A Practical View of the Prevailing Religious Systems of Professed Christians, in the Higher and Middle Classes in this Country, Contrasted with Real Christianity* (1797), if one admitted to the doctrines of the church, one ought to allow that

> our dependence on our blessed Saviour, as alone the meritorious cause of our acceptance with God, and as the means of all its blessed fruits and glorious consequences, must be not merely formal and nominal, but real and substantial; not vague, qualified, and partial, but direct, cordial, and entire.[13]

Not only one's intellect, but all one's emotional and practical energies should be transformed as well.

To Evangelicals, conversion logically followed from consideration of mankind's spiritual situation. Sin, human rebellion against God and his precepts and the resultant inhumanity to one's fellow creatures, was a grievous condition to live in – only God's loving patience prevented the universe from coming undone. For the sinner, eternal damnation was the penalty, unless some other satisfaction for God's justice could be found. That satisfaction came through the sacrificial death of Jesus, understood as God Incarnate or God the Son. One's salvation was a gift from God and rested solely on one's belief in this atonement, but full awareness of one's natural sinfulness appeared at times to be the prerequisite to believing fully in Jesus. Wilberforce provided a clear summary:

> We must be deeply conscious of our guilt and misery, heartily repenting of our sins, and firmly resolving to forsake them. . . . we must found altogether on the merit of the crucified Redeemer our hopes of escape from their deserved punishment, and of deliverance from their enslaving power. This must be our first, our last, our only plea. We are to surrender ourselves up to be washed in his blood.[14]

This 'surrender' served as the basis of one's present and eternal condition before God. All else was of secondary or derivative concern.

The historian David Bebbington has argued that one important result of a conversion was a sense of assurance of God's forgiveness and a certainty of one's salvation.[15] This assurance inspired and sustained Evangelical missionary and reform efforts and marked the movement as something different from those grounded in the earlier Puritan tradition of conversion. The Puritans had exercised restraint in declaring individual certainty of being among God's elect. Careful self-scrutiny helped provoke this caution, which, the divines hoped, would lead to greater reliance upon God, and less upon human knowledge. Evangelicals showed a much greater confidence than their Puritan predecessors in the power and capacity of human knowledge. D. Bruce Hindmarsh has rightly pointed out 'that there was a spectrum of opinion on assurance among evangelicals as surely as there was among Puritans', but it is clear from the notes of the Eclectic Society, composed of leading Evangelical clergymen and laymen from both Established and Dissenting churches who met bi-weekly in London between 1798 and 1814, that assurance was a recurring topic and concern.[16] Indeed, it was the internal knowledge of one's dependence on Christ, of 'him affecting the heart', that gave one confidence that one's faith was true and thus that one's salvation was sure. The eighteenth-century Evangelical divine Henry Venn declared that this 'dependence is so easy to be known, that no one can possess it without being conscious of it'.[17] Bebbington has traced this confidence in human knowledge to the acceptance and promulgation of epistemological theories from the early Enlightenment.[18] John Locke's *Essay Concerning Human Understanding* was especially important to early Evangelicals such as John Wesley and Jonathan Edwards, though he was by no means the only contemporary philosopher to affect their understanding of the sources of human knowledge.[19] They used the language of empiricism to describe a spiritual sense, akin to the five physical senses, which accounted for the inward perception of grace and acceptance felt by a new convert. The connection to empiricist ideas is further seen in the frequent description of Evangelical piety as 'experiential religion'.

Conversion led to a changed life, in which practical behavior reflected the internal change of character. Besides the commands to avoid sin, there were many positive mandates for action – to promote justice and mercy and to cultivate attitudes of compassion and generosity. 'You are every where commanded' by Scripture, Wilberforce observed, 'to be tender and sympathetic, diligent and useful; and it is the character of the "wisdom from above", in which you are to be proficients, that it is "gentle and easy to be intreated, full of mercy and good fruits"'.[20] In working out their faith, Evangelicals exhibited what has been called a 'frenzied determination to use every precious minute and not to waste a single opportunity for doing good'.[21] 'Frenzied' might be an overstatement, since members of the Clapham Sect at least enjoyed their times of leisure and play, but they understood rest and recreation as the appropriate balance to an otherwise active, energetic life.

With their emphasis on personal salvation, one might have expected Evangelicals to propagate a pietistic and private religion. They were certainly influenced by continental pietism, which tended toward social and political quietism, and the concern that worldly activity should not lead one away from ultimate realities appeared as a recurrent theme in sermons and publications. John Wesley and other early leaders were at pains to contrast their revivals with the disruptive 'religious enthusiasm' of the previous century by emphasizing the socially conservative nature of their religion. Wilberforce's *Practical View* also stressed order. True Christianity, he thought, supported social order by teaching all classes how to behave in their proper station:

> Affluence she teaches to be liberal and beneficent; authority, to bear its faculties with meekness, and to consider the various cares and obligations belonging to its elevated station, as being conditions on which that station is conferred. Thus, softening the glare of wealth, and moderating the insolence of power, she renders the inequalities of the social state less galling to the lower orders, whom also she instructs, in their turn, to be diligent, humble, patient; reminding them that their more lowly path has been allotted to them by the hand of God.[22]

The result, Wilberforce declared, was a softening of class distinctions: a stress not on social mobility, but on a respectful flexibility which promoted merit and good morals while correcting the wastrel and the profligate.

For all their social conservatism, Evangelicals did place heavy emphasis on activity in this life. Hannah More, the eighteenth-century blue-stocking whose literary talents made her one of the most widely read Evangelical moralists, provided this succinct summary, 'Action is the life of virtue, and the world is the theatre of action.'[23] Evangelical activism was related to the notion of conversion, but even more to the experience of it. To be converted, emotionally and intellectually, resulted in a strong desire to share the experience and to see others converted as well. The call for a thoroughgoing application of scriptures led to concern for the poor and, as the eighteenth-century revival spread up the social ladder, to new efforts of philanthropy. The idea that the wealthy had a responsibility to the poor was not new, but Evangelicalism gave new impetus to the formation of innumerable charitable and moral reform societies in the late eighteenth and early nineteenth centuries.[24] The historian Michael Watts has called it a paradox that 'the men who had their eyes fixed most firmly on eternity did far more than their contemporaries to improve the temporal existence of their fellow men here on earth'.[25] Most of the participants, however, considered all these activities as the logical result of working out their salvation.

The knowledge of one's salvation bolstered confidence to take action, by giving hope to those who acted boldly to do the works of God. Further, 'experiential religion' caused the faithful to consider how God's salvation was to be made manifest in their lives. The striving to do good works has often been misinterpreted as a belief that salvation came from doing good, of earning one's redemption by making one's efforts and sufferings in this life an atonement for one's sins.[26] Such an interpretation stands in complete contradiction to the message of every Evangelical preacher, from Wesley and Whitefield, to Charles Simeon and Thomas Chalmers: all proclaimed that salvation comes only by faith in Jesus Christ as the Son of God, whose death atoned for human sin. Rather than good works leading to salvation, saving faith would manifest itself in the works one did. As Wilberforce wrote for his educated and nominally Christian readers:

> It is the description of real Christians, that 'they are gradually changed into the image of their Divine Master;' and they dare not allow themselves to believe their title sure, except so far as they can

discern in themselves the growing traces of this blessed resemblance.[27]

The demand for self-scrutiny lay in the hope of discovering and assessing the 'traces' of one's 'resemblance' to the character of Christ, and many Evangelicals followed the Puritan custom of keeping a journal to record these self-critical reflections.[28] Most could find personal habits and persistent vices ('besetting sins') which were less than Christ-like, and which called for repentance and self-discipline. But it was not merely the personal that concerned them. The cognitive dissonance created by the gap between the moral values drawn from Scripture and the observation of injustice and poverty in the world gave strong motivation to attack specific maladies in society. Taking action with a sense of mission provided another assurance that one was fulfilling 'the good works which God had prepared in advance' for those who were His own.[29] Quite often the private expression by an Evangelical writer of concern for the reality of their conversion could be found in a context suggesting not so much fear of having a false salvation, as wrestling with the gulf between what they could see in the practice of their lives and the life of virtue and love to which they believed themselves called.[30] They sometimes pondered how deeply they felt that belief.

Depth of feeling was to be cultivated, for it led to greater attention to the works of God. Cultivation implied some effort. Wilberforce provided an apt example in his 1803 New Year's Day reflection, when he expressed his desire to 'press forward and labour to know God better, and love Him more'.[31] To fulfil this desire required 'watchfulness, humiliation, and prayer', for, Wilberforce observed, 'Heaven is not to be won without labour.' Out of context, such expressions provided superficial support to the view that good works were a prerequisite to eternal life,[32] but the whole of the passage had a far different concern: deepening a devotion already begun and in some measure secured, a hungering after more, not a begging for admittance to the feast. The springs of human motivation are multiple, and fear and guilt certainly did play a role in Evangelical activism, but their theology gave them other reasons for acting. The Saints accepted the notion that one might believe, and yet still have room for greater faith, knowing that living in faith meant praying, 'Lord, I believe; help thou our unbelief.'[33] They desired their daily thoughts to be shaped by the impression of God's holy and omnipotent presence, which provided the psychological assurance that one was accepted by God and confidence that one's decisions and hopes were shaped by the divine hand.[34] That such devotional energies might lead to lives of 'frenzied' activity was hardly surprising.

3)   The principle of utility and Evangelical public action

Discussions of criminal law reform have overwhelmingly emphasized the impact of utilitarianism. Evangelicals very often appeared among the most vehement critics of the principle of utility in early nineteenth century Britain. Yet Wilberforce and other Evangelical leaders frequently supported measures suggested by utilitarians. Rather than Halévy's 'paradox' of cooperation, close analysis reveals that despite some root differences, utilitarianism and Evangelicalism shared many basic assumptions about the nature of human thought and action in society. The phrase 'principle of utility' had a history of its own, and Bentham was not the first to define it as the greatest happiness to the greatest number; as late as 1803, the Evangelical *Christian Observer*, attached the 'principle of utility', a phrase used interchangeably with 'general benevolence' or 'general expediency', to the writings of David Hume, William Godwin, and William Paley more readily than to those of Bentham.[35] Evangelicals objected to the utilitarian judgment of actions exclusively by their results as being a false foundation. Even the best-formed human mind was subject to the whims of temper and passion, a point which the Evangelicals connected to human sinfulness, but which even a skeptic like Hume had recognized.[36] Since the principle of utility inevitably rested on private judgment, it was easily open to abuse and self-deception and likely to be swayed by personal ambition and desire.

On a another level, the Evangelical writer and minister Thomas Gisborne attacked the principle of general expediency because a finite being could not possibly know, or adequately consider, what measures in fact might tend to produce greater happiness without recourse to other criteria. Gisborne was a regular advisor to Wilberforce and the Saints, but his influence reached well beyond that circle.[37] He entered the debate in response to the adoption of Paley's *Principles of Moral and Political Philosophy* as a preparation text for the Cambridge BA examination. He explored Paley's assertion that the way to understand the will of God 'by the light of nature' was to ask whether any specific action tended to promote or diminish general happiness. Gisborne thought this would make good sense, 'were the powers of the human intellect unlimited, and capable of deriving knowledge from *any* specified source, of drawing it forth from *every* secret repository in which it is stored'.[38] But, Gisborne argued, human powers were not unlimited, and were in fact subject to the immoral tendency of human desire. Furthermore,

Paley had not shown that man even had the faculties to discern what general happiness meant. The appeal to utility was, therefore, less than useful, and could be blasphemous, since, as Gisborne wrote, one might interpret it 'as authorising every man to disobey the most positive divine commands whenever, in his opinion, the observance of them would, on the whole, be inexpedient'.[39]

Gisborne's interpretation of Paley had critics of its own, and some defended Paley by arguing that he meant utility to apply primarily in those cases when God's revelation did not provide direction. Gisborne, however, believed that Paley had employed expediency even in cases when the scriptures gave explicit instruction, and most Evangelicals agreed.[40] But having displayed the weakness of appealing to utility as the *primary* guide to action, Gisborne admitted that its basic concern, the promotion of the greater happiness of mankind, had an important place in moral reasoning, so long as it was understood correctly. Gisborne put an Evangelical spin on the definitions:

> The first step of Mr. Paley's reasoning, that 'God wills and wishes the happiness of his creatures,' if understood in the full latitude of the terms, demands our unconditional assent. We know that the divine Author of the universe is a being of unbounded benevolence. We know that a desire of promoting happiness, or in other words general expediency, extending to *all* created beings, is an unchangeable motive of his conduct.
>
> The consequence deduced from the foregoing fact by Mr. Paley, that 'those actions which promote that happiness must be agreeable to him, and the contrary,' is also strictly true, if Mr. Paley be supposed to speak of actions in the abstract without any reference to the motives of the agent. The Almighty approves or disapproves of actions viewed in this light, accordingly as they further or impede his plan of universal good.[41]

The problem with expediency was the condition of man: first, his limitations – one just could not know enough to rightly judge the full impact of an action; second, his sinfulness – intentions and motives mattered to the moral state of human beings; God did not judge merely by externals. If one controlled for these factors, remembering that human happiness had both temporal and eternal components, then the standard of utility could be incorporated into Evangelical reasoning.

Like other moral thinkers, Evangelical ministers took notice of the difficulty of giving clear or universal definition to the content of 'happiness', and in this case some found guidance in Paley's own exploration. They were careful to denounce the idea that happiness could be got simply through material possessions, and instead focused on the importance of human spirituality. 'God can make us happy in the destitution of all outward good,' argued Josiah Pratt, who instead linked happiness to acquiescence in the will of God. 'Temperance; moral habits; gospel hope; reliance on God's overruling care – these give human happiness,' another minister held. The Rev. Henry Foster summed it up this way: 'Happiness is the application of God's remedies to man's miseries,' and this had as much to do with the present life as with the eternal.[42] The Evangelicals regularly reasoned in terms of utility, but always with the sense that while the temporal was important, it was not the only reality: a spiritual man had also to remember God's final judgment.

The appeal to general happiness and public utility appeared in numerous Evangelical publications. Wilberforce believed that 'true Christian benevolence is always occupied in producing happiness to the utmost of its power', and further asserted, 'Happiness is the end for which men unite in civil society.'[43] The editors of the *Christian Observer*, with all their stress on the inadequacy of expediency as a guide, nonetheless conceived that their purpose was to present subjects 'intimately connected with the real welfare and true happiness of mankind', while providing careful and critical analyses of literature which promoted 'tenets hostile to piety, order and general happiness'.[44] Another Evangelical periodical, the *Eclectic Review*, was even clearer in its objectives. 'To blend with impartial criticism an invariable regard to moral and religious principle' was 'its leading object', but with regard to the selection of materials for review, 'whether of science or amusement', the editors would choose writings, 'an account of which may be conducive to public utility'.[45] Concern for adapting the publication 'in every respect to public utility', also led the publishers 'to offer it at the lowest price that is likely to be consistent with respectability'. In their reviews and feature articles, both the *Eclectic* and the *Christian Observer* expressed interest in the general happiness of society, though the *Eclectic* was more likely to make direct reference to 'principles of utility' and to employ the language of utilitarianism. It showed more enthusiasm, for instance, for the publications of Jeremy Bentham.[46]

Another periodical which easily mixed Evangelical and utilitarian language was *The Philanthropist*, published and edited by the Quaker William Allen between 1811 and 1819. In the first edition, Allen wrote 'On the Duty and Pleasure of cultivating benevolent Dispositions'. He asserted that the Creator's purpose must be the happiness of his creatures, 'and that it is the duty as well as the interest of his rational beings, to co-operate with him, in producing this desirable end'.[47] The sole object of the *Philanthropist* was to stimulate 'to virtue and active benevolence ... and to shew that all, even the poorest, may render material assistance in meliorating the condition of man'. As the articles in the *Philanthropist* made clear, bettering the 'condition of man' included the abolition of slavery, reform of England's penal code, numerous acts of charity, and the spread of Christianity and civilization through missionary and commercial activity.

Evangelicals often linked the purposes of God to the happiness of man. The reason, as Wilberforce wrote to Lord Grenville, was that they esteemed 'Christianity not only as the foundation of our future hopes, but as the only source even of our present happiness'.[48] This conviction provided the basis for a strong Evangelical belief that in public matters, what was morally correct or biblically directed would also make good, expedient policy in law and government. Commenting on Lord Grenville's support of the slave trade abolition bill in 1804, Wilberforce wrote that he 'spoke like a man of high and honourable principles, who, like a truly great statesman, regarded right and politic as identical'.[49] Or, as Hannah More put it negatively, but succinctly, 'It should be held as an eternal truth, that what is morally wrong can never be politically right.'[50] As in the antislavery campaigns, the Evangelicals linked good morality to sound political policy when pursuing reform in the laws of criminal justice. Part of their definition of justice was the concurrence of the policies of government and Christian principle. For the state to act unjustly was always bad policy, which would end in social or political turmoil and disruption. General happiness could only be secured when the Crown and its officials followed the principles of Christ, and when the Parliament adhered to them in making or revising the laws. In the Evangelical view, not a few of the problems relating to the administration of the criminal laws stemmed from the failure to consider the principles of Christianity which applied to them.

By extending the interest in general happiness beyond the temporal, the Evangelicals converted the central concern of the principle of utility into a call for deeper spirituality and moral reform, the consequences of which included the amelioration of public institutions and laws that affected the welfare of people in the here and now. To separate Evangelical social thought sharply from the utilitarian ignores this central agreement on ends – the promotion of the greatest happiness. Once this concurrence is admitted, the consensus with regard to the reformation of criminals and the inefficacy of the capital statutes becomes plainer. True, Evangelical views on the penal law included elements beyond the reach of an appeal to general expediency. The stress on eternal well-being made a difference in their views on the content of prison discipline, but the connection Evangelicals made between the will of God revealed in scripture and its implications for how a Christian society should treat its criminals, provided an appealing rhetoric which more secular utilitarian arguments could not muster.

Evangelicals and penal theory: the demands of justice and mercy

Amelioration of the penal laws was an even greater challenge to established interests than abolition of the slave trade. It brought the Evangelicals into direct political conflict with the administrators of the law, both judges and Government ministers, whom they had spent much time and ink supporting during the French Revolution and Napoleonic Wars. The judges, so Lord Ellenborough claimed, saw the attack upon one part of the criminal law as an attack on the whole. While conservatives graciously acknowledged the good intentions of the reformers, and were always cordial to them outside the Houses of Parliament, their rhetoric tried to make amendment of the laws seem a radical, unnecessary innovation that might well have dangerous consequences. Despite this, Wilberforce and the Saints pressed on in their support of Romilly's efforts.

From one perspective, the interest of Evangelicals in criminal law reform was paradoxical. Few groups preached the depravity of man more consistently or believed more readily in the eternal punishment of Hell. Both these doctrines have been blamed for giving justification to capital punishment.[51] But neither led necessarily to support of the death penalty. Reforms on the continent, especially in countries with strong Calvinist histories, showed that belief in human depravity might well lead to an awareness of human frailty and an emphasis on the impossibility of absolute certainty of criminal guilt, which argued for reserving capital punishment for only the most desperate cases. As for the everlasting punishment of Hell, Evangelicals well knew that the most seductive sins were not within reach of legislation, capital or otherwise, and they considered Hell the great equalizer, where the scheming and the rich, whose sins lay beyond the purview of earthly tribunals, would suffer as they had made others suffer.[52]

One might well have expected Evangelicals to have developed some coherent view of penology, since their message concerned divine punishment and reward. In fact, though, Evangelical penal theory was never organized into one coherent statement, but rather found expression in diverse writings. Their 'good news' was that, while all human beings stand condemned before God because of their sin, the death of Jesus had provided atonement. Although believers were saved from the ultimate punishment, they did not escape suffering in this life. Indeed, the Evangelicals, like Christians through the centuries, acknowledged that pain in this life had a purpose – to bring one to God or to refine and discipline one's understanding of Him. Conversion did not take one out of this world of tears, but in fact called one to face more resolutely not only one's own hardships, but those of others also. To account for this aspect of the Christian life, they generated a theodicy to make sense of suffering, to give it purpose. At the high level of theology it was recognized that when man fell from grace, all of nature suffered a corruption.[53] This did not mean that nature was evil, but that it was subject to the consequences of human sinfulness. Disease, disasters and famines all had natural origins according to the mechanistic natural philosophy of the eighteenth century, but the Evangelical would have insisted that behind all these lay the consequence of sin – God had so ordered the universe that human actions contrary to his created order would bring pain, often to others even more than to the one who sinned initially. The first theological fact of suffering was that it had its origins in human sinfulness.

The second point was more a matter of dispute. All agreed that suffering in this life could help one to closer dependence on God, and so to a fuller experience of the eternal life He gave. But some groups interpreted suffering, personal or communal, as a sign that sin had been committed and believed that suffering would cease once the sin were truly repented.[54] For others, suffering was simply a fact of living in a fallen world, something to be endured, but which might, through endurance, bring about a closer understanding of Christ's own death and, through such an identification, of his resurrection as well. On the whole, the Evangelicals in the late eighteenth and early nineteenth centuries emphasized versions of the former explanation, that suffering, personal and national, resulted from unrepented sin.[55] In either case, however, suffering could and should serve to discipline one's heart and refine one's habits, so that in thought and deed one conformed to the image of Christ. This description defined the doctrine of *sanctification*, the lifelong process of Christian discipleship which led to deeper understanding of God and greater personal holiness.

The idea of suffering as sanctification had practical implications. It meant, paradoxically, that Christianity provided a means for making life better by helping people learn from suffering to change destructive habits and environments. Wilberforce thought that while religion in general was advantageous for civil society, Christianity in particular had proved good for the poor 'by changing the whole condition of the mass of society', turning the most populous districts from 'scenes of...wickedness and barbarism' into settings known for 'sobriety, decency, industry, and, in short, for whatever can render men useful members of civil society'.[56] The combination of conversion and spiritual discipline made suffering efficacious, temporally and eternally. To provide the possibility for both was one reason for the Evangelical commitment to religious instruction and to periods of solitude as necessary parts of the improvement of prison discipline.

While this overall Evangelical perspective on suffering supported the adoption of punishments oriented toward the reformation of offenders, the specific rejection of the death penalty for all but the most grievous crimes had bases in biblical commandments as well. From at least the time of the Interregnum writers reflecting on the morality of capital punishment had referred to the comparatively short list of crimes which the Mosaic law had made capital.[57] The Pentateuch imposed the death penalty for crimes of murder, blasphemy, rape, fornication and sexual deviation, but never proposed it for property offenses, and property offenses were the focus of the vast majority of England's capital statutes. Writers critical of the death penalty in the seventeenth century agreed that the New Testament brought greater mercy to human transgressors than the Old Testament law recognized, which meant that human laws based on Christian principles might be more lenient than the Mosaic law, but certainly not more severe.[58] Few eighteenth- or early nineteenth-century writers made direct reference to the seventeenth-century debate, but any who considered it agreed that while Scripture might uphold the penalty of death as permissible for some extreme offenses, it gave no support to most of England's statutes.[59] Even William Blackstone had used the biblical standard to judge England's laws 'protecting' property.[60]

Instead of the death penalty in cases of theft or unintentional injury, the biblical guidelines laid down restitution as the just and appropriate condition for the community to impose on the offender. The Bible ordered a thief to repay his victim at a rate of two, four or five to one, depending on the property taken and its condition when the thief was caught.[61] The English common law by itself did not provide for restitution, because an order for restitution had to come from the Crown. A statute from the reign of Henry VIII, however, did allow a judge to order restitution to be made to the plaintiff out of the offender's goods, which would have been forfeited to the Crown upon conviction.[62] Because English law treated larceny, and all felonies, as crimes against the Crown, as well as against the injured party, it required a further punishment beyond restoring the property.

Many religious writers disagreed with this procedure of administering punishment, few more than Gisborne, whose *Principles of Moral Philosophy* offered the most developed Evangelical statement on the limits of legitimate punishment. Part 1 of the *Principles* was devoted to the examination and refutation of Paley. Part 2 developed a theory of general rights and obligations, and Part 3, the final section, dealt explicitly with the application of these rights and obligations to the constitution of civil society. Gisborne concentrated on moral rather than legal principles, but he was quite certain that moral philosophy provided the only solid foundation for civil society. Deducing his conception of offenses and punishments from his general theory of human rights and obligations, Gisborne could not view the destruction or theft of property as a public offense separate from the injury to an individual. He first showed what rights could clearly be deduced from the concurrence of natural reason and the Holy Scriptures. His interpretation was expansive, asserting that every man originally has a right, by the gift of God, 'to unrestrained enjoyment of life and personal freedom; and to such a portion of the unappropriated productions of the earth as is necessary for his comfortable subsistence'. To deprive another of these rights without the sanction of 'divine authority' made one guilty not only of injustice to the individual, but of sin against God. Human beings in society could create laws to restrain or guide the exercise of these rights, but only when such restraint was directed by the command of God, necessary for the defense of other people's rights, or when such restraint or deprivation had 'the consent of the individual suffering it'.[63]

Just as the improper restraint of another's rights was a sin, so was the careless use of one's own freedom. Gisborne continued, 'Every man sins against God who does not act in such a manner with respect to the use, defence, and disposal, of his rights' as 'will on the whole, fulfil most effectually the purposes of his being'. The gifts of God had a purpose, and from the one to whom much was given, much was expected. Gisborne allowed a large measure of private judgment in fulfilling one's purposes, but he observed that the Scriptures

continually inculcate on every individual, that it is his duty to use these gifts in such a manner as may best enable him to fulfil the ends for which he was made: namely, to promote and secure his own final welfare, together with the final welfare of others, and their present happiness as well as his own.[64]

In describing rights and obligations, Gisborne defined justice as promoting the good of oneself and others, as much as defending oneself and others. With this definition, he deftly reconciled self-interest and charity; since the purpose of one's existence included securing the happiness of others, failure to act justly had negative consequences for the actor. Acts of injustice included any unauthorized restraint on a person's rights, such as theft of property or physical assault, but might also included neglecting another's welfare, such as withholding assistance from one in need.

With regard to issues of injury and punishment, Gisborne returned to the notion of restitution and greatly limited the scope of formal punishment. If one had obtained 'complete satisfaction for the injuries he has suffered' by restitution or indemnification, he had no further claim on the offender, 'except for security against future violence, when it is on good grounds supposed to be intended'.[65] By 'indemnification' he meant 'the receiving of an equivalent for an injury done', the most natural and equitable means of rectifying an injury. In all the cases where indemnification might apply, Gisborne specified that restitution could be made either through the offender's giving over his own property or by appropriating to the injured party 'such a portion of the other gifts which God has bestowed upon him, such a portion of his strength, or of his industry, or of his skill, as will answer the remaining claim. What he cannot pay with his property, he must pay with his service.' Even those cases in which pain or bodily injury had been sustained should be resolved through indemnification.

Unlike punishment, indemnification was not primarily concerned with the infliction of suffering on an offender. Instead, indemnification and restitution always implied a restoration, not only of goods, but of community tranquility and personal relationships. Indemnification recognized the offender as a human being who had rights and a need to work out his own salvation. Punishment was reserved for those cases when future violence might be expected, and Gisborne treated the right of punishment as 'a branch of the right of defence against an aggressor'.[66] The justice of punishment rested solely upon the basis of obtaining present and future security for an individual or society. All other reasons were insufficient. Punishment as a vengeance for crimes was a usurpation of the prerogative of God, a view repeated in later Evangelical discussions of penal reform.[67] Punishment in lieu of indemnification was 'too absurd to merit much attention', since then it would be 'nugatory, and would therefore be an unauthorized attack'.[68] Perhaps most striking, Gisborne objected to the idea that natural justice authorized the infliction of punishment on an offender to deter others from crime. He acknowledged that this was a prevalent belief, but argued it was false because it was 'directly repugnant' to the principles he had earlier established for the restraint or deprivation of any individual's rights; specifically, punishment simply as deterrence was neither authorized by God, nor necessary for the defense and protection of others, nor would it be a restraint authorized by the consent of the individual suffering it. However, if deterrence was not a primary reason for punishment, Gisborne did allow that if punishment were already justified by his principles, and one had a choice of punishments, then one was bound 'in the sight of God' to choose the one which appeared 'most likely to deter others from engaging in criminal undertakings'.

Gisborne clearly limited the space for the exercise of punishment. If some cases might be so extreme as to require a punishment that absolutely deprived an aggressor of committing further outrages, in many others the end would 'be sufficiently answered by measures less violent, which, in all probability', would 'deter the criminal from his purpose', though they did not altogether disable him.[69] By stressing the role of indemnification, he had already limited the possible scenarios for punishment. He contended further that if a lesser punishment would achieve the security desired, it should be chosen over a harsher one. Gisborne never, therefore, directly advocated the death penalty; indeed, he was loath even to admit it could be justified. The danger was in the infliction of unjust punishment, since any excessive penalty was a violation of the God-given rights of the one experiencing it and benefited neither the offender nor the injured party. Indeed, the choice to punish an offender had to be made consciously, for, Gisborne declared, every man had duty to exert the right of punishment or to refrain from inflicting it, as he was persuaded that 'such exertion or forbearance will most effectually promote the great purposes of his being'. In deciding upon this, one had to consider the 'ends for which the aggressor was created', along with all the other issues to be weighed.[70] Ideally, therefore, punishment should not only serve the needs of the injured, but of the offender also, because the criminal was a creature of God as much as was the victim of crime.

Gisborne's views on rights and punishments were liberal and likely more extreme than those of many who looked to him as an advisor.

But the insistence that criminal offenders be treated as human beings with rights given by God was indisputably connected to the Evangelical support of penal law reform, as was the view that punishment was primarily for protection against an aggressor. Many involved in the debate on the penal laws echoed Gisborne's arguments. In an article in 1819 the *Eclectic Review* considered that the effective authority of laws rested on a combination of conscience and self-interest, and that 'punishment, when conformable to our ideas of what the laws justly require as the sanction of that authority, is viewed with unmixed approbation'. The *Eclectic* reviewer, like Gisborne, argued that the law was a 'salutary restraint' upon a man's natural freedom, 'the price of his enjoying the benefits of civil society', and that its simple purpose was 'the protection of life and property'.[71] Thomas Fowell Buxton built on the argument for the God-given rights of offenders in his 1818 study of English prisons and showed that its grounds were not merely religious speculation, but that the laws of England themselves supported it. After reviewing the opinions of legal writers from Bracton to Coke to Blackstone, Buxton listed the statutes concerning the treatment of felons and concluded unequivocally, 'The convicted delinquent then has his rights.'[72] After entering parliament, Buxton expanded this point to mark out the limits of government authority with regard to punishment. In 1821 he declared,

> Necessity alone can justify the infliction of death. But if any minor penalty is equally effectual, there is no necessity; then there is no right – and then, the infliction of death can be considered in no other light, and called by no other name, than that of legal murder.[73]

This rhetoric went further than Gisborne, but it did represent the logical extension of his argument.

These later writers reasoned in the same way as Gisborne about the nature of the criminal and appropriate punishment. As the *Eclectic Review* article argued, punishment ought not to be the mere infliction of pain, but a positive control or restraint, and the best way to restrain a criminal was 'by taking away the disposition to offend, that is to say, by the reformation of the offender'. This of course was not a new argument. Wilberforce had long been considering the uses and limits of punishment in civil society, and when he spoke in favor of the reformative possibilities of prison discipline in 1810 he went beyond a simple concern for moral reformation. He advocated not only corrective training that would include religious and moral education, but also instruction in how to read and write. Prisoners should be taught a trade and have a portion of their earnings while in prison set aside for when they were released.[74] By advocating a reformatory program, Wilberforce, and writers like Buxton and the *Eclectic* reviewer, in essence endorsed Gisborne's view that punishment should help the offender fulfil 'the ends for which he was created', though their rhetoric was seldom as philosophical as the clergyman's.

Certainly this view that reformation was preferable to execution was not restricted to Evangelicals. Law reformers could draw upon the prayers of the Church of England itself for support of it. Both the morning and evening services contained a prayer of absolution, which invoked 'Almighty God, the father of our Lord Jesus Christ, who desireth not the death of a sinner, but rather that he may turn from his wickedness, and live'.[75] The Anglican prayer was based on Ezekiel 33:11, a call to repentance in the Old Testament. This particular text would be employed with increasing frequency in the second decade of the nineteenth century as a support to the argument that the death penalty was contrary to the mild spirit of the Christianity, even if religion allowed for it in extreme cases. In 1818 Buxton combined this prayer with endorsement of the reformative view of the purpose of punishment, succinctly laying out the Evangelical justification of penal law reform:

> A merciful and enlightened jurisprudence, like the Author of all that is merciful and wise, does not rejoice in the death of a sinner; but rather, that he should turn from his wickedness, and live. Punishments are inflicted, that crime may be prevented, and crime is prevented by the reformation of the criminal.[76]

God's mercy, rather than his wrath, was to serve as a model for human jurisprudence. The duty of finite men and women who had come to Christ was to help those in error to repent, to show to others the grace that God had shown to them. The *Eclectic Review* article in 1819 made explicit that all needed forgiveness for their transgressions, and urged the reader not to 'forget the claims which the vilest participants of our nature have upon us, who, not less than they, derive all our hope of salvation from pure, unmingled, Infinite Mercy'.[77] Both the criminal and the saint depended on God for mercy in the end. The difference between the offender and the respectable member of society was not that one was sinful and the other was not, but that one's sins were evident and disruptive to civil society, while the other's were secret and less obviously detrimental. The criminal was a human being and therefore a potential brother or sister in the family of God. To seek the reformation of the criminal was to acknowledge that God could change lives.

Although the Thorntons and Grants, Wilberforces and Buxtons might not have come from backgrounds conducive to criminal activity, they had the imagination to recognize the temptations which might lead one astray. They leaned toward an environmental view of the origins of crime, while at the same time taking for granted that offenders could learn to reason as well as law-abiding citizens when given the opportunity. The Saints assumed that it was often a combination of poverty and the influence of seasoned criminals that led the young and inexperienced into criminal activity. Describing the potential of a well-designed penitentiary, Wilberforce called it an 'asylum' and considered among its virtues that it kept the prisoner 'apart from the contamination of a society worse than himself'.[78] In his *Inquiry*, Buxton observed the 'system's' tendency to encourage and refine criminal activity by associating the novice and the unconvicted indiscriminately with hardened felons and accomplished thieves. Buxton believed that if a prison separated an offender from his previous associates, he would cease to think as they did.[79] He went so far as to quote John Locke, that nine-tenths of what a man was, he was because of his experience and education.[80] Buxton illustrated his point about English prisons with numerous examples. One particularly poignant tale described a young man referred to as GM, the son of a journeyman butcher. GM had been arrested and tried for selling religious tracts without a hawker's license and sent to the Bridewell for thirty days. There he encountered youths whose experiences and crimes were of an entirely different order from his own, and who encouraged GM to join them. The father told Buxton that his son was now a wretch, rebellious and surly, and he did not know what to do. Reflecting on this boy, Buxton wrote, 'let us turn from his crimes to his misfortunes, and perhaps we shall find that depraved as he is, "he is more sinned against then sinning"'.[81] Buxton believed not only that the environment in which the boy was placed was largely to blame for his becoming incorrigible, but that the larger public was guilty of harming both the boy and itself, since it suffered jails and prisons to be houses of corruption, rather than correction. Buxton certainly did not mean that a criminal bore no personal responsibility for his actions, but the *Inquiry*'s stress on moral education and improved environs indicated his conviction that human choices were heavily influenced by one's background and friends. Indeed, one purpose of the regime Buxton advocated was to make a prisoner fully aware of his choices and their impact. Like Romilly and Wilberforce before him, Buxton held that a primary reason for penal law reform was to make clear the consequences of crime, since the lottery of justice encouraged criminals to think they would avoid all punishment.

Evangelical theology called upon Christians to recognize themselves as sinners saved by grace and to see other men and women in the same predicament. The world was full of temptations, and one might easily slip from the narrow way and tumble down the slope toward criminal behavior. Yet God's grace could pull one back and restore one to righteousness. While Wilberforce and his colleagues would have acknowledged this even in the first bloom of their faith, it did not lead them automatically to pursue penal law reform. Even as some became convinced of defects in the laws, the practical politics of the issue often prevented immediate action. This chapter has examined how penal reform was connected to other Evangelical ideas, and has suggested how religious conviction and concern for personal salvation were easily wed to arguments for the better protection of the public. Evangelicals were just as convinced as Romilly that the laws as they stood were one of the grand impediments to bringing thieves to trial. After a visit from Elizabeth Fry in 1818, Wilberforce reflected, 'Our murderous laws prevent prosecutions, and often harden convicts' hearts.'[82] The next chapter follows the paths that led Wilberforce and Buxton to take an active role in criminal law reform.

5
The Evangelical Approach to Criminal Law Reform

Evangelicals certainly were not the first ones to have been led by their religious convictions to call for restrictions of the death penalty. Sir Thomas More's doubts on the efficacy of capital punishment, voiced in 1513 in *Utopia*, became a standard reference in reformist literature. During the seventeenth century, Puritan reformers questioned harsh punishments, as did the Quaker followers of William Penn.[1] The influence of both these groups could be seen in the American colonies under their control: Puritan New England saw no proliferation of capital statutes in the eighteenth century, and Pennsylvania resisted applying the death penalty to property offenses until taken over by the Crown. After the Restoration in England, however, during the period of reaction against religious 'enthusiasm' in Parliament, the number of England's capital statutes grew steadily, and the Bloody Code has rightly been called the creation of the aristocratic government of the late seventeenth and eighteenth centuries.[2]

Public criticisms of the penal laws had been voiced in the 1750s, but all attempts to mitigate existing legislation failed, and the creation of new capital statutes did not appreciably slow until the advent of Romilly's reforming campaign. Evangelicals had become interested in penal issues by the end of the third quarter of the eighteenth century, though their focus was primarily on jails and prisons. The initiative came not from members of the Established Church, but from Dissenters such as John Howard and Jonas Hanway. Howard, whose name became synonymous with humanitarian prison discipline, was from an Independent background, with strong ties to the Baptists and a definite bent toward 'serious religion'. Although his personal asceticism, reflected in his approach to prison reform, has produced a few modern critics, his motivations were humane and religious at base.[3] Compassion for people in miserable conditions and belief that the reformation of the criminal ought to be the main concern of jails and prisons prompted Howard to advocate hygienic and dietary improvements as well as religious and vocational instruction for prisoners. He was willing to learn from his errors as well, evidenced by revision of his opinion on solitary confinement when too long a period of isolation was shown to bring on madness and hysteria in prisoners.[4] To his concern for penal reform Howard added criticism of the death penalty, since he could find little evidence that it really deterred crime, and even less that most capital statutes could be reconciled with the Christian religion. Howard's statistics and arguments concerning penal reform became one of the primary sources in the discourse on criminal law reform, in part through the excerpts in Basil Montagu's *Opinions of Different Authors upon the Punishment of Death*.[5] Perhaps more important than Howard's direct criticism of the death penalty was the potential he envisioned for the use of prisons as places of reform rather than punishment. Although Bentham's schemes for the Panopticon were widely discussed in government circles in the 1790s and first two decades of the nineteenth century, the philosophy guiding prison reform owed as much or more to Howard.

When Wilberforce entered Parliament in 1780, one could not have found a general constituency for amelioration of the criminal laws. William Eden and William Blackstone had both offered critical remarks on the frequent application of hanging, but they had stirred very little interest.[6] That a growing number of people felt uncomfortable with the broad application of capital punishment has been shown, but those who expressed doubt did not constitute themselves into an active movement. The lack of public interest in Romilly's response to Madan's *Thoughts on Executive Justice* illustrated the prevailing mood toward criminal law reform in the mid 1780s. Although recurring alarm over increased crime in London and Middlesex provoked public interest in the criminal trials and led to publication of the Old Bailey Sessions Paper,[7] expressions of disapproval for hanging were in fact relatively rare compared to other matters, and those who made them did not strike a responsive chord, at least not with the policy-influencing public.

Wilberforce: moral reform to criminal law reform

Precisely when William Wilberforce first entertained thoughts about criminal law reform is unclear. In his early years in Parliament he associated with many reforming elements, and his friendship with Pitt during that period certainly encouraged some optimism about the possibility of change. Pitt's early views on political change were revealed during a visit with Wilberforce to France in 1783. Pitt told the Abbe De Lageard that the first part of the existing English constitution which would perish 'is the prerogative of the King, and the authority of the House of Peers'.[8] He would back away from such positions as time went by, but Pitt was much interested in measures to improve government. Though Wilberforce's views were less clear than Pitt's at the time, he showed no hesitation in supporting his friend in motions for such measures as electoral reform.

Sometime during 1785 Wilberforce first met Samuel Romilly through the Comte de Mirabeau, who was then in England following his escape from prison in France.[9] Wilberforce was among the few who knew of Romilly's authorship of the tract against Madan.[10] He approved of the arguments, and they may have been among the factors prompting him to attempt a minor reform in the criminal law in 1786. The bill, which was also one of Wilberforce's first legislative attempts after his conversion, was limited in scope. It had two provisions, the first substituting hanging in place of burning to death a woman convicted of petty treason (either the murder of her husband or a servant's murder of her master); the second would allow judges to deliver up for dissection the bodies of felons executed for rape, arson, robbery or burglary, a power already granted them for the bodies of murderers. The mitigation here was small indeed. In the first proposal, Wilberforce was simply making the penalty for murdering one's spouse neutral with regard to gender, since no special punishment was meted out to murderous husbands. The second proposal might better come under the heading of a 'scientific' improvement, since its purpose was to provide bodies for medical instruction and research; but it was entirely insensitive to the popular controversy surrounding such treatment of the dead.[11] It had been suggested by William Hey, a political correspondent and eminent physician in Leeds, who was also a friend of John Wesley's.[12] In any case, the bill, which passed the House of Commons, was stopped in the Lords by the opposition of Lord Chancellor Loughborough. His opposition had as much to do with his dislike of Pitt's law officers, who had drawn up the bill, as with Wilberforce's intentions.[13] Loughborough made much of the fact that the judges had not been consulted prior to the bill's introduction. He also defended the existing statute's deterrent value. The Lord Chancellor was most strident, however, in expressing his disapproval of 'men not conversant with the law, turning projectors to it,' by introducing 'raw, jejune, ill-advised, and impracticable schemes' for amending its execution. Loughborough told the House 'that the judges were the persons with whom alteration of the conduct of criminal justice ought to originate'. The Lord Chancellor distrusted any alteration in the law suggested by the first part of the bill and suspected the second would reduce the deterrent value dissection was believed to have. Wilberforce may have found it hard to understand the effective deterrence which Loughborough declared the existing punishments provided, but the message was clear that his meddling in matters of law was unwelcome. He had made definite political mistakes in this attempt. Besides the failure to consult the judges, linking the bill's dissimilar provisions was a tactical error, because as a result neither proposal received adequate consideration. The heavy-handed opposition to the bill, though, bore witness to the prevailing attitudes of the day.

Since Pitt's attempt at parliamentary reform the year before had been similarly rebuffed in the Lords, as had his proposal for police reform, Wilberforce doubted he could push any law reform through the Parliament.[14] His concerns for penal matters, however, contained an element that suggested that direct legislative action might be less advantageous than other approaches. Following his conversion to 'vital religion' in 1785, Wilberforce began to see the condition of England in a different way, one which emphasized the prevalent mood of moral laxity and religious indifference. British support of the slave trade was part of the evidence of the country's ungodliness. So too were its harsh penal laws. If the problems of society were at base spiritual and moral, with bad laws, a corrupt commerce and corrupt politics the proof of the country's condition, then perhaps one should focus on changing the public's view of morality and religion. In the apt words of one biographer, 'If he could reform the morals (or 'manners') of England, he would help empty the prisons and cheat the gallows.'[15]

With this possibility in mind, Wilberforce approached Bishop Porteus in early 1787 with a plan for promoting the reformation of manners. Porteus found the idea laudable. The goal was 'to check as much as possible that deluge of vice and immorality which was overflowing this country', by enforcing existing 'laws against drunkenness, lewdness and indecent prints and indecent publications, disorderly public houses, and the various profanities of the Lord's Day'.[16] Wilberforce's plan was inspired by the Society for the Reformation of Manners that had operated during the reign of William and Mary almost a century earlier. That society had based its mission on a proclamation made by the King and Queen in 1692, 'for the Encouragement of Piety and Virtue; and for the preventing of Vice, Profaneness and Immorality'. This proclamation was regularly issued by each monarch upon ascending the throne, and

George III was no exception. Wilberforce proposed that the King reissue the proclamation, while his subjects organized themselves to carry it out, primarily by encouraging local magistrates to enforce the laws referred to in the proclamation, and in some cases by actually undertaking prosecutions. Bishop Porteus strongly supported the effort, but he cautioned Wilberforce that such a project would encounter difficulties, and advised that the organizers be circumspect from the outset. The high goal of reducing crime might be praiseworthy, but not all would be eager to see the laws strictly enforced, and others of elevated social station would be openly contemptuous of the idea. Knowing this, Wilberforce prepared cautiously.

When George III gave the Proclamation for the Encouragement of Piety and Virtue, etc., on 1 June 1787, much of the ground-work had been laid, but Wilberforce continued to build support through the summer to form the association to ensure the proclamation not be quickly forgotten. On 25 July, he wrote to the political organizer Rev. Christopher Wyvill, and after assuring him of the strong arguments in favor of the measure, penned his most famous words on penal reform:

> The barbarous mode of hanging has been tried too long and with the success which might have been expected from it; the most effectual way of preventing the greater crimes is punishing the smaller and endeavoring to repress that general spirit of licentiousness which is the parent of every species of vice. I know that by regulating the external conduct we do not at first change the hearts of men, but even they are ultimately to be brought on by these means, and we should at least so far remove the obtrusiveness of the temptation that it may not provoke and call forth the appetite which might otherwise be dormant and inactive.[17]

He attached a copy of his measure, with a list of those who had agreed to support it, and others whom he hoped soon would. The Society for Carrying into Effect His Majesty's Proclamation Against Vice and Immorality (dubbed the Proclamation Society for short) got underway quietly in autumn 1787.

The story of the Proclamation Society and other associations for moral reform has been told at length elsewhere.[18] For the purpose of this study the connection Wilberforce made between moral reform and the reduction of crime is central. He clearly disliked England's sanguinary laws. At least one aristocratic observer understood Wilberforce's object to include a more direct assault on the hanging statutes. The Duke of

Manchester wrote that it gave him 'great pleasure to find you join the ideas of many humane and thinking men, in reprobating the frequency of our executions and the sanguinary severity of our laws', and expressing hope that Wilberforce and other young members of Parliament might take up the hard task of revising the laws.[19] While Wilberforce was doubtful that a direct attack upon them was feasible in the late 1780s, he did some quiet canvassing of opinion. On a journey back from Bath in August 1789 he met Lord Kenyon, then Chief Justice, while the judge was on circuit. At dinner Wilberforce spoke to him about the criminal law and recorded that he was 'glad to find him favourable to penitentiary houses and a less sanguinary system of penal law'.[20]

Such conversations might have helped Wilberforce form his views more fully, but they did not lead him to make criminal law reform his focus. He had been called in a different direction. As he recorded in his journal on 28 October 1787, he believed he had been given a sacred charge: 'God Almighty has set before me two great objects, the Suppression of the Slave Trade and the Reformation of Manners.'[21] Of these two, the more overarching was the abolition of the slave trade, but he put much thought and effort into moral reform, and Wilberforce's connection of moral reform to diminishing crime pointed to a fairly complex perspective. He considered the custom of hanging 'barbarous', because it was a holdover from a ruder and less civilized period in history, when the principles of true Christianity had not penetrated so far and so deep among the English people. That the spread of Christianity resulted in the refinement of manners generally and in the raising of moral standards particularly, Wilberforce stated repeatedly in his *Practical View*, first published in 1797.[22] He made the connection between the spread of Christian morality and the alteration in criminal jurisprudence explicit when he told the House of Commons in 1810 that after 'the reformation introduced a purer religion and more humane conduct' in the reign of Elizabeth, the number of executions in England had declined steadily.[23] Like many others educated in the 'enlightened' eighteenth century, he believed the refinement in manners which had taken place over the previous two hundred years had rendered hanging less acceptable to the general public. The evidence of that was to be found in the infrequency of execution for petty offenses, which he was quick to appropriate from Romilly's illustrations in 1810. For Wilberforce, hanging was a 'barbarous mode' also because of the spectacle of it all. Like Romilly, Wilberforce believed that those witnessing an execution were less affected by the example of the punishment, than by its brutality, which blunted people's sensitivity to violence and accustomed them to bloody entertainments.[24] For an evangelically-minded individual, this dulling of impression was doubly perverse, as it tended to harden the hearts of the condemned to any appeal to repent before God, an argument which was strongly voiced during the debates in Parliament after 1810.

The barbarousness of the Bloody Code having been declared, it remained for Wilberforce to find a means to secure the 'most effectual way of preventing the greater crimes' by 'punishing the smaller'. The Proclamation Society strove to suppress the spirit of licentiousness in general, but what might be done for those who had already committed and been convicted of crimes? As early as 1786 Wilberforce had raised the issue of penitentiary houses with the Prime Minister. But then, and again in 1788, Pitt turned the matter aside by agreeing that action must eventually be taken on the question, but at some unspecified future date.[25] The pressure for improvement of the prison system dated back at least to the 1770s and the investigations by Howard and Hanway. Both men acted from strong Christian convictions, and both went beyond demanding merely healthier conditions to planning for the reformation of prisoners.[26] Their arguments inspired a bill for the construction of houses of labor in each county, which was drawn up by Sir William Eden with the help of Blackstone and Howard. The bill eventually passed in modified form as the Penitentiary Act of 1779.[27] The act was never put into effect, however, as the committee in charge of finding suitable locations for the penitentiary houses could not come to an agreement.

Pitt's first real opportunity to put the penitentiary ideas into action followed the publication of Jeremy Bentham's *Panopticon* in 1791. Bentham's proposals renewed the debate on building new prisons and infused vigorous new ideas into it. His plan was based on a revolutionary prison design, which placed inmates under perpetual observation, and on the employment of the prisoners in profitable production. Indeed, Bentham believed his Panopticon should not only pay for itself, but bring a profit to its share-holders. Never shy about the correctness of his ideas, Bentham sent a letter to William Pitt in January 1791 with an outline of his project.[28] Pitt did not at first respond, and Bentham sent his plans to Wilberforce and other MPs, including Sir Charles Bunbury, who had been part of the commission charged with finding a site for the penitentiary authorized in the act of 1779. Slowly, support grew for taking some action, and in 1794 Henry Dundas, Pitt's Home Secretary, framed a bill for the purchase of property on which Bentham's prison might be erected. As in 1779, difficulties quickly appeared. The Penitentiary Act of 1794 called for the government to purchase a piece of Lord Spencer's Wimbledon Park estate, but Spencer managed to have inserted the clause, 'or any other as convenient and proper Spot of ground'.[29] Spencer, who was First Lord of the Admiralty, fought the original choice and forced Bentham to look elsewhere. The Treasury hesitantly looked into the possibility of purchasing Tothill Fields, a marshy area south of Westminster Abbey owned by the Dean and Chapter. The Dean resisted, negotiations dragged on, and Bentham grew increasingly frustrated, having invested a good portion of his own money in the project by this point. Wilberforce, like Romilly, was sympathetic throughout, meeting with any who would listen to him on Bentham's behalf. Wilberforce thought Bentham was badly used in the whole matter and believed that the actions of the Dean and the overall intransigence of the Treasury helped to alienate Bentham from the Established Church and the Government.[30] But Bentham could be belligerent himself, at one time writing to Wilberforce that the next time he met the Attorney General in the House of Commons, he should 'take a spike, the longer and sharper the better, and applying it to the seat of honour, tell him it is by way of *memento*, that the Penitentiary Contract Bill has, for I know not what length of time, been sticking in his hands'.[31]

By the end of the decade, neither Bentham nor Wilberforce were hopeful that the Panopticon would be built, though Wilberforce continued to make periodic inquiries about it. Not until Romilly, with Wilberforce's support, again raised the issue of penitentiary houses in 1810 would substantive action take place. By then Bentham was disillusioned with the project, complaining to Wilberforce that he was 'so far from solicitous' that he gave Romilly 'no expression but that of *reluctance*: having no such ambition as that of passing the short remainder of my life among the Treasury Porters'.[32] Wilberforce encouraged him to have hope and not to separate himself from this new effort, since his friends would not wish him to 'lose the just praise of originating or at least devising the means of carrying into effect, the true principles of jurisprudence'.[33]

The Millbank penitentiary would be built as a result of Romilly's 1810 motion, but the committee appointed to look into the plans, chaired by the conservative Evangelical George Holford, rejected some of Bentham's basic assumptions about the purpose of the prison. Essentially, the Holford Committee became a forum for discussion and decision 'between the principles of Blackstone, Howard, and the 1779 Penitentiary Act and of Jeremy Bentham, the panopticon, and the 1794 Act...Holford came down firmly on the side of Blackstone and

Howard'.[34] For the future of English prisons the decision was definitive: they were to remain government-run institutions, with an emphasis on religious reformation, and not to become private ventures using convict labor. Wilberforce was not entirely satisfied with the final plan, but accepted it when the vote came up to provide funding for the penitentiary's construction in 1812. The act also included, by Wilberforce's advice and Romilly's agitation, a clause stipulating compensation for Bentham's long years of effort and expense.[35]

In addition to his support for prison reform, Wilberforce periodically tried to intervene in the administration of punishments for worthy cases. The interventions in capital cases were not always successful, especially when the charge was forgery, which made the laws appear to him all the more sanguinary and barbaric.[36] By the time the Holford Committee began to meet to consider plans for a new prison facility, Wilberforce had become Romilly's firm ally in restricting the death penalty. Romilly met at least part of the criteria Lord Loughborough had laid down in 1786: he was a lawyer, and though most conversant in the laws of equity, he had experience in criminal cases. Although Romilly had never been a judge, he made sound objections to the notion that only judges should bring forward amendments in the laws, and he did have the personal respect of every judge who knew him. The Saints had no difficulty in supporting Romilly's campaign, and they knew him well because of his active parliamentary support for abolition of the slave trade. Moreover, it was clear to the Saints that Romilly was as committed to penal law reform as they were to antislavery, showing a willingness to introduce and argue for measures he believed in, even though they were defeated time and again in the House of Lords. He had the kind of certainty, moral strength and perseverance that brought him admiration among the Saints, even if his rationalistic religious views placed him outside their number.

Wilberforce's political commitment to criminal law reform was somewhat dependent on finding an appropriate leader, but the timing probably had much to do with the success of the abolition of the slave trade in 1807. The success of abolition not only freed time for attention to other issues, but gave the Saints and their allies a confidence in the possibility of carrying measures for social and government improvement through Parliament. Others became committed to ameliorating the criminal law because of personal experiences outside Westminster. They too gained assurance from the success of the antislavery campaign, but they treated penal issues as a separate concern, and it was personal experience leading to an internal conviction which turned them toward efforts to alter the existing laws. The story of Thomas Fowell Buxton's gradual commitment to political action in behalf of criminal offenders illustrates this process well.

Buxton: the growth of commitment

Thomas Fowell Buxton first came to wide public notice through a speech given in behalf of the distressed in Spitalfields in November 1816.[37] He had not begun his life in London with the intention of becoming a philanthropist and law reformer, although his family background encouraged a positive view of charity. Beginning with a few moral commitments and practical opportunities for service, Buxton's analytical mind and leadership ability brought him into ever greater involvement in the social issues of his day. He was not primarily interested in politics, but he believed political action was necessary to achieve practical changes, both in penal matters and, later, in colonial slavery. He was, therefore, an unusual political figure. His progressive stages of involvement demonstrated one Evangelical approach to political activism as well as criminal law reform.

Buxton came from a moderately wealthy family in Essex.[38] His father, Fowell Buxton (Fowell was the family name of Thomas's grandmother, and son followed after father in preferring to be called Fowell), was of sufficient social standing to have been appointed high sheriff. Both privately and in his official capacity he was said to have been interested in improving the living conditions of prisoners. Any direct influence on his son's career is doubtful, however, as the father died in 1792, when Thomas was only six. Although Buxton's father was a member of the Church of England, his mother was a Hanbury, a Quaker family involved in the brewing trade. This Quaker connection was important. Buxton reflected later in life that he had been raised 'in some sort a Quaker – or half a one',[39] though more socially than religiously. He considered that he had learned little of the Bible or doctrines of the Christian religion while a boy. Indeed, he was a strong-willed youth, not much interested in the serious side of life at all. This was reflected in his schooling, where his early performance left much to be desired.

A marked change in Buxton's attitude came after his first visit with the family of John Gurney of Earlham Hall, near Norwich. The Gurneys were distant relatives of Buxton's mother, they were Quakers, and all eleven children were keen on self-education. This put a fire under Buxton, and at the age of sixteen he finally started to take learning seriously. Perhaps the motivation was to prove himself to the Gurneys, for he married one of the sisters, Hannah, in 1807. Her brother, Joseph John Gurney, became Buxton's role model. Hannah's older sister was Elizabeth Fry, who also played a large role in prison reform.

In 1803, not long after his introduction to the Gurneys, Buxton began attending Trinity College, Dublin. When he graduated in 1807 he was asked by several of his teachers and peers to consider representing the University in Parliament. The twenty-one year old Buxton was greatly flattered, but he passed by this opportunity to enter politics because of his approaching marriage, which also meant having to find employment. He toyed with entering the law, and read Blackstone and other legal treatises, but was pleased when he was able to join Truman's Brewery on the invitation of his uncles, Sampson and Osgood Hanbury. He was industrious and did well at the Spitalfields brewery, living with his wife in Brick Lane for the first few years. He became a partner in 1811, and the business continued to thrive.

When Buxton married Hannah Gurney, she did not leave the Quakers; instead, Fowell joined. They were both received into the Devonshire House Meeting in London in 1807, the same meeting attended by William Allen and several leading Quaker families in the metropolis.[40] His formal attachment to the Friends was short. In 1811 he began attending Wheler Chapel (Church of England) in Spitalfields to learn from the ministry of the Rev. Josiah Pratt.[41] Pratt was solidly Evangelical, having been part of the Eclectic Society since 1798 and the founding editor of the *Christian Observer*, which was closely related to the concerns of the Clapham Sect. Pratt also served as the secretary of the Church Missionary Society for twenty-one years, beginning in late 1802.[42] One could hardly have found a minister more thoroughly committed to 'vital religion'. From Pratt, Buxton gained his first solid understanding of Christian doctrine, but it would be wrong to say that his earlier thoughts and actions were uninfluenced by religion. In October 1809 he wrote to his wife about reading the Sermon on the Mount, having been especially struck by the verse which begins, 'If your righteousness exceeds not the righteousness of the scribes and Pharisees...'. Pondering this verse, he turned to 'thinking of what I can do for the poor this winter'.[43] Certainly, though, Pratt's ministry affected Buxton, and he went less and less to Quaker worship. In 1817, he was officially disowned by the Devonshire House Quakers 'for not attending meeting and worshipping elsewhere', though he maintained relationships with several members of the Friends and periodically joined them in worship.[44] His wife Hannah and his close friend Samuel Hoare, Jr., part of a Quaker banking family, also joined Wheler Chapel and were similarly 'disowned' by the Friends.

The income from the brewery allowed Buxton to turn more and more to other endeavors. William Allen led him into many projects in greater London to relieve the poor, promote education, and promote the Bible Society. When Allen, Basil Montagu and others set up the Society for the Diffusion of Knowledge upon the Punishment of Death in 1808, Buxton delayed a holiday visit to be part of it.[45] Buxton studied Montagu's collection of *Opinions of Different Authors upon the Punishment of Death* in preparation for his own speeches on criminal law reform years later.[46] While he did not serve on the governing committee of the society, Samuel Hoare, Jr., did, and Buxton was keenly interested in the Society's efforts.

Buxton's more direct encounters with the administration of the hanging statutes began in 1815, when he was part of a committee who called on Lord Sidmouth to provide a stay of execution for a boy found guilty of attempted robbery.[47] Although the entourage included Dr Stephen Lushington, and Thomas and Edward Foster, men better established and more widely known, Buxton was the spokesman, describing the details of the case which had convinced them that the boy was not guilty. Sidmouth was unpersuaded and unwilling to overturn the jury's verdict, and the youth was hanged the following Wednesday. According to one of the participants, this incident precipitated the founding of another society, 'for Investigating the Causes of the Alarming Increase of Juvenile Delinquency in the Metropolis'. Besides Buxton, the new society's members included Montagu, Allen, David Ricardo and many others. The investigations by the society led to several efforts to provide alternatives for boys and girls in London who, whether from poverty or bad associations, had turned to crime for a living. Buxton was an active and prominent participant in these projects.

Since the Truman Brewery was located in Spitalfields, Buxton became familiar with the difficulties of those who lived there. Among these were a large number of silk weavers whose trade had been ill-affected by the peace following the Napoleonic wars. When wintery weather set in early in 1816, the weavers' situation turned desperate. Buxton joined the Spitalfields Benevolent Society, an organization connected to Pratt's ministry, instituted to provide soup and basic necessities to the impoverished in the district. He was willing to act, he wrote at the time, 'rather because my judgment is convinced, than because my feelings are moved'.[48] This comment reflected much of his philanthropic activity: it began by an intellectual conviction, which later might find emotional expression, but the sympathy for the suffering was often a phenomenon separate from Buxton's decision to take action for their sake. Indeed, he often prayed that he might feel more strongly what he knew to be right in his mind. The distress in Spitalfields was greater than the soup society's means to relieve it, and the society determined to hold a public meeting at the Mansion House to appeal for assistance. Buxton was chosen to deliver the address on 26 November.

Buxton perceived the weavers' distress as a temporary phenomenon in the wake of peace. His speech described not only the need of the poor, but a compelling social and religious responsibility of his listeners for them. Buxton told the audience of London alderman, magistrates and commercial leaders that

> this district [Spitalfields] has claims, not only on your compassion, but something like claims, even on your justice; not only those claims which distress always has on the benevolence of the affluent, but on those intimate and almost legalized claims which the labourer possesses on his own employer, the mechanic on his own master, the pauper on his own parish.[49]

Most of those in need worked in the City of London, but lived in Spitalfields, which was technically in a different county, and so got no poor relief assistance from the Corporation. Buxton told his listeners, '...you have the man, and the labours of the man when he can work, and we have him & his family when he cannot.' Upon this basis, he built a case for his audience's compassionate and willing assistance, while taking subtle notice of the flaws in the existing poor laws.

Initially, Buxton felt he had failed to do much good and told his wife that he 'felt very flat', leaving out many topics he had hoped to cover; he only hoped he had spoken 'well enough not to injure our cause'.[50] Others took a different view and soon the praise began to come from all corners. The speech's arguments were claimed by the Benevolent Society as the best way to raise concern, by some radicals as giving evidence of the deficiencies of the existing system, and by the friends of government 'because it forms so beautiful a contrast to the language of those wretched demagogues'.[51] A couple of days after the speech, Buxton wrote to his wife that one person said the speech had produced a cask of tears, another that he had seen 'the whole Bench of turtle fed Aldermen wimpering,' and another 'that it produced three miscarriages amongst the ladies', but Buxton discounted the last account as being that of a mere flatterer.[52] The speech certainly helped the cause, bringing in over £43,000, including a £5000 donation from the Prince Regent. It also elicited a note from William Wilberforce, expressing hopeful anticipation for the

> success of the efforts which I trust you will one day make in other instances, in an assembly in which I trust we shall be fellow-labourers, both in the motives by which we are actuated, and in the objects to which our exertions will be directed.[53]

Buxton was not ready to enter Parliament in 1816, but his public career essentially began with the speech in the Egyptian Hall of the Mansion House.

Earlier in 1816, impressed by the visits of Elizabeth Fry and the efforts of the Ladies Committee for the women in Newgate Prison, Buxton and Samuel Hoare decided to extend the efforts of the society which had investigated juvenile delinquency, to work on behalf of men and boys confined in the prison.[54] The reorganized society was officially dubbed the Society for the Improvement of Prison Discipline and the Reformation of Juvenile Offenders, or the Prison Discipline Society for short. In January 1817, Buxton found himself visiting the condemned in Newgate. There he observed four youths sitting apart from the others and looking especially miserable; of the convicts most recently sentenced to death, all but these had been pardoned. 'It has made me long much that my life may not pass quite uselessly,' he wrote his wife the following day, 'but that in some shape or other I may assist in checking & diminishing crime & its consequent misery.'[55] All have the power, Buxton reasoned, to do something in the service of their Master. Since he had the capacity, and no mean talent, he had also the responsibility. He intended to pray that he might

> be enabled to feel somewhat the real Spirit of a Missionary – & that I may devote myself, my influence and my time and above all my affections to the honor of God & the happiness of Man – my mission is evidently not abroad, but is not less a mission on that account.

Buxton saw himself at a fork in a road, and he must choose one way or the other; the one, a continued life of business and gaining of wealth, where he might do some good, but as least as much evil; the other, a more arduous road, to become 'a real soldier of Christ', with 'no business on earth but to do his will & to walk in his ways'. Buxton made no commitments in this letter, but acknowledged that while the spirit was willing, the flesh was weak: 'In short the cares and the pleasures, & the business of this world check the good seed – & we are perpetually deceived, we would sow to the Spirit, & we sow to the flesh – we desire heaven, & we are chained to the earth.'

If Buxton expressed no certain plans in early 1817, he clearly gave more thought to entering Parliament after this. Buxton went down to Weymouth (to which he had a family connection through his grand-mother) to observe an election later in 1817. He refrained from offering himself as a candidate when invited because he could not obtain a seat independent of party connection that year. He shared the Saints' com-mitment to independence, and he hoped that his abstaining from run-ning in 1817 would pave the way for his independent entry at the next general election.[56]

In the meantime, he was not idle. Aside from carrying on business and various charitable activities, Buxton became increasingly interested in the condition of England's jails and prisons. This came to the fore late in 1817 when he visited the Maison de Force, a house of correction at Ghent in Flanders. The contrast with his experience of British jails was startling. Whereas dirt, noise, idleness, and a high rate of recidivism marked most British prisons (not all, as Buxton was careful to explain), the Maison de Force was clean, quiet, and the prisoners busy with employment under the supervision of an outside contractor. Even more astounding to Buxton, only 5–10 out of 100 prisoners ever returned after release.[57] Upon consultation with others in the Prison Discipline Society, Buxton embarked on a project of research and writing to show the varying conditions in prisons both in Britain and abroad, illustrating what might be done through a careful plan of prison discip-line. The result was *An Inquiry Whether Crime and Misery are Produced or Prevented, By our Present System of Prison Discipline*, published in February 1818. The work was an immediate and unexpected success, running through six editions in 1818 alone. It attracted attention from all quar-ters, and Mackintosh referred to it in parliamentary debate later that spring. Perhaps most satisfactory to Buxton's political interests, Wilber-force wrote him a more direct plea to run for Parliament as soon as possible, so that God might use his 'benevolent zeal', and 'direct it to worthy objects'.[58]

The pamphlet brought Buxton a step further into the criminal law debate, for while his focus was on the operation of jails and houses of correction, he was quick to point to the benefits brought by restricting the death penalty to willful murder in the Netherlands and parts of America. The *Inquiry* immediately made Buxton a national voice for penal reform, and the general election in 1818 allowed him to obtain the political position from which to use it more effectively. He was elected an independent member for Weymouth, without debt to any party, but clear as to his own agenda. Buxton's friends had high hopes for him and were firmly persuaded he had entered Parliament with only the most noble of intentions; J. J. Gurney recorded that Buxton 'was rather a singular instance of a person going into parliament for the *sole and single* purpose of doing as much good as he can'.[59] Buxton immediately joined the reform effort, working closely with Sir James Mackintosh after Romilly's death late in 1818.

Buxton had not rushed to enter Parliament. It had been eleven years since he had been invited to represent Trinity College, Dublin. He was distrustful of making a name simply for the sake of reputation. Like Wilberforce, Buxton struggled with how to react to temporal accolades, and asked his wife to pray that he serve others in the spirit of Christ, that he might 'have the high privilege of being his servant – and that the performance of his will & not the applause of men may be the wages I seek'.[60] He had done much by private philanthropy, and he would not turn away from these efforts as a public figure. He had come to a point where he knew that further progress required legislative action, though he carefully reviewed his reasons for being in Parliament before each election over the next nineteen years.

As he began his parliamentary career, Buxton's theory of punishment was still being worked out. He certainly had an opinion about what was just and what would work, but these were not part of a system such as Bentham would have insisted upon. Buxton's commitment to penal reform had grown slowly and was a result of exposure to the real conditions in the prisons and investigations into the backgrounds of the convicts. His interest in penal matters, therefore, was personal rather than abstract, experiential as well as theoretical. His religion and friends had led him to investigate the problems of the poor and to visit those in prison; his encounters in these situations made him reflect on causes and effects. When he went to Westminster, Buxton had concluded that to improve prisons and pave the way for a system of reformation of offenders, the criminal laws had to be changed.

Criminal law reform and the middle class reform complex

As Wilberforce's linking of penal issues and moral reform demonstrates, Evangelical interest in criminal law reform could be viewed as part of a larger concern for the values of civil society. David Turley has included the amelioration of prison conditions and amendment of the capital statutes in what he calls the 'middle-class reform complex'.[61] Turley uses 'complex' to refer both to the multiplicity of social institutions of middle-class origin and to suggest a mentality of reform peculiarly strong in the British middle-class. The complex encompassed the causes of educating and improving the condition of the poor, assisting the sick, widows and orphans, ameliorating prison conditions, restricting capital punishments, and antislavery. In all these cases, Turley writes, 'a necessary step to improvement was the recognition of the essential humanity of these victims rather than their animality, an animality which required the equation of control with physical restraint or brutalisation'.[62] Turley goes on to observe,

> The performance of the humane as a product of recognition of the human was thus in part the effect of the development of evangelical themes in theology. Even sinners in their sinfulness declared their humanity since sin itself was universally present. The impulse to reform had one source, in other words, in the urge to encourage self-order in individuals who appeared to lack it, either because they seemed evil or were ignorant of what was required.

Evangelicalism, therefore, played a special role in providing an impetus to the middle-class reform complex.

Many have raised questions concerning how far the humanitarian sensibility of reformers should be linked to middle-class attitudes about order and the proper regulation of civil society in an age of commercial expansion. Turley himself argues that, despite some strong voices critical of the emerging commercial and industrial society, reformers' arguments and activities tended to favor 'the hegemony of capitalist values'.[63] Indeed, Evangelicals held a more positive view of commerce than has been generally acknowledged.[64] One need not demonstrate again that these capitalist values were held dear by the middle-class in Britain, and it is also clear that those sponsoring criminal law reform, whether of utilitarian, Evangelical or 'rational' Christian orientation, often came from the commercial middle-classes. One may, therefore, ask how far the Evangelical sponsorship of penal reforms should be construed as an extension of middle-class efforts to control the lower orders.

The observation is common that middle-class activists, while pressing their own claims for political reform, were leery of extending political power too far down the social ladder. Evangelicals especially have been subject to the accusation, from William Cobbett, Karl Marx, and

E. P. Thompson, to name a few, that their rhetoric about obeying God by obeying the government was no more than an attempt to keep the working class docile and in check. Penal law reform at first seems an odd component of this social control thesis. But since one element of reform was to provide laws which, by being more agreeable to general opinion, might also be more enforceable, the contention that humanitarian penologists in the early nineteenth century were bent on social control has been widely argued.[65] One need not disagree with this thesis to observe that it has become less than interesting; yet it might never have sounded original or revisionist at all, had it not been for the exaggerated praise by historians of the reform movements, who depicted these movements as proof of the onward and upward march of humanity. The reformers themselves never denied their interest in social order, nor did they think this unusual or contradictory to their appeals to humanitarian values. Criminal law by definition was, and always has been, about social control. It has always concerned the protection of persons and property from those who, willfully or out of necessity, choose to attack these objects for personal gain, survival, or political protest. Reform of the criminal laws and the restriction of the death penalty meant the expansion of secondary punishments, and the search for effective secondary punishments led to the position that it would be better to reform an offender than to keep him locked up forever or turn him lose on society unchanged. That prison discipline aimed at providing a regime which fostered religious repentance and the internalization of norms held by the middle-class should not therefore be a surprise. These norms included Christian morality and respect for private property, upon which the activists believed civil society rested.

That middle-class reformers should desire criminal offenders, whom the reformers knew came predominantly from the lower classes, to accept these values is not astonishing, yet neither need it have been sinister or duplicitous. The assumptions that reformers made about the lower orders in this period were largely assumptions they made about themselves, and this was especially true among Evangelicals. If they thought that the lower classes had a propensity for evil, it was because they believed all people had a propensity for evil, themselves included. If they thought that material want and lack of moral education increased the temptation for ill-gotten gain, it was because they thought they themselves would be so tempted under such circumstances. In a like manner, they believed that criminals were capable of rational calculation because they assumed they were like anyone else in this way, when given proper instruction and opportunity to exercise judgment. Moreover, the values of self-control, disciplined labor and moral probity which they hoped prisoners would internalize were values the middle-class reformers hoped they and their families had internalized already.

The question is moot, therefore, whether Evangelical penal reformers advocated change in the criminal statutes to enhance social order – that was their claim from the start. But they also believed their reforms gave more dignity to offenders than the punishments of the existing system. They supported these views by personal observation, which had proved that the laws as they stood provided the criminal with no way out of his or her dilemma. In the case of hanging, this was more than obvious. In the reform of prison discipline, the goal was to provide a prisoner with the means to reenter society with the ability to achieve some level of self-support, perhaps even respectability. This was the reformer's understanding of humanitarian punishment, and as it became apparent that specific technologies of reform proved ineffective or were applied in such a manner as again to affront their sense of human dignity, they, or their successors in the next generation, pushed again for changes.

The accusation, vulgar or scholarly, that early nineteenth-century humanitarianism was only a mask for social control would have been incomprehensible to Wilberforce, Romilly or Buxton. That fetters of love and humane prison discipline were somehow just as constraining as fetters of iron and hours of idleness in an ill-lit, musty jail would have sounded ridiculous. They believed in social order, and they believed that laws existed to protect that order; they also believed that some laws were better than others.

6
The Conservative Resistance

Modern ideas about law and punishment have been so completely infused with the arguments of penal reformers that the appeal of the conservative view of criminal law and its administration has been largely lost. Spencer Perceval, Lord Eldon, and the other defenders of the existing system certainly did not consider themselves less humane or less concerned with effectiveness than the reformers. Indeed, in their own view at least, they were advocates of a system which was as humane as any in the world, and better than most. Their arguments and actions, however, revealed a quite different vision from that of the reformers, both of how criminal justice should operate and of the just and necessary powers of its enforcers.

Those against criminal law reform in 1810 included all the ministers of the Government as well as their Tory supporters. As we have seen, Romilly counted 22 office-holders in the Commons on the night his dwelling-house bill was defeated; when the shoplifting bill came up in the Lords, Government supporters were again out in force. The opponents of amelioration were not simply unthinking reactionaries. That the law officers and leading judges were chary of any innovative measure cannot be doubted, but their position was not entirely without theoretical support. Simply stated, the defense of the existing capital laws rested on the doctrine of maximum deterrence, the steadfast belief that the humane administration of justice required that judges have the greatest possible discretion in recommending punishment, and the presumption that changes in criminal law should originate with the judges themselves. In addition to these basic foundations were general fears of innovation, made plausible and to some degree popular by implicit and explicit reference to the course of the French Revolution.

William Paley and the conservative defense of the law

In the debates in 1810, Romilly attempted to outmaneuver the defenders of the criminal law by an attack upon one of its most distinguished apologists, the theologian and moral philosopher William Paley. Even when they were not drawing directly from them, the advocates of the existing statutes often echoed the arguments found in Paley's *Principles of Moral and Political Philosophy*.[1] As the work was dedicated to the Bishop of Carlisle Edmund Law, whose son Edward became Lord Chief Justice Ellenborough, Paley's popularity with Ellenborough and his close associates was not surprising. The conservative acceptance of the reverend philosopher's version of utilitarianism was doubtless not lessened by his glowing praise for the British constitution, which anticipated, and perhaps shaped, the arguments of Edmund Burke's *Reflections on the Revolution in France*.[2] The conservative acceptance of Paley meant that they held to the principle of general expediency as firmly as any group in the early nineteenth century; what was really under contention was the precise meaning of 'general' and the best measure of expedience.

Paley proposed that the 'proper end of human punishment is, not the satisfaction of justice, but the prevention of crimes'.[3] Like Gisborne, Paley declared that only God could award justice in the sense of truly appropriate retribution of 'so much pain for so much guilt'. The sole reason for demanding punishment of any sort was to preserve social order, for, Paley asked, 'What would it be to the magistrate, that offences went altogether unpunished, if the impunity of the offenders were followed by no danger or prejudice to the commonwealth?' He did not altogether reject the notion of proportionality, but thought that the cause of human punishment was founded not on the degree of guilt of the offender but 'in the necessity of preventing the repetition of the offence'. Paley believed that no government punished, or ought always to punish, criminals according simply to the atrociousness of their crimes; rather they punished 'in proportion to the difficulty and necessity of preventing them'. Though one offense may appear no worse than another, if it were more difficult to detect or prevent, a government would be justified in applying a more severe punishment to it.

Paley used the specific example of privately stealing from a shop, which did not differ in its moral quality from stealing from a house. Since the former was more difficult to detect and prevent than the latter, the law had wisely attended it with more severe punishment.[4] When Ellenborough refuted Romilly's shop-lifting bill, he referred to this argument. The great mass of property was subject to depredation, but in particular it was an 'unavoidable hazard to which retail dealers are exposed, arising from the facility with which the theft is committed, amidst the bustle and confusion of a number of customers'.[5] Davies Giddy borrowed a similar example from Paley with reference to sheep stealing, urging that because sheep must be raised on extensive downs, they were exposed to extreme depredation, while sheep poachers were exceedingly difficult to apprehend; hence, sheep stealing ought to remain a capital crime.[6] While proportionality in punishment might be ideal, Giddy asserted that 'the punishment should increase with the difficulty of detection'.

Paley also supported the notion that whatever means prevented crimes might be justifiable, regardless of proportionality. He did not jump to the conclusion that any and all means were justifiable, however; rather, his argument took a slight twist. Paley believed, like many Enlightenment theorists, that human punishment was always the lesser of two evils, and the magistrate could justifiably inflict punishment only to prevent some greater evil to individuals or society. Paley could agree, therefore, that no necessity of punishment existed, if the prevention of crime could be obtained by any other means. But given the vagaries of detection and prevention in so many cases, a maximum amount of deterrence had to be built into the laws. He was not unmindful that what he suggested appeared to fly in the face of what the 'the justice of God' taught one about looking for gradation in punishment. His warrant for going beyond the laws of God in severity was the fact of human imperfection and limitation. God was omniscient and could perfectly inflict punishment, but man could not. Whereas the Evangelical Gisborne, Wilberforce, or Buxton considered human ignorance a reason for mitigating even the harsher aspects of the biblical law, and others used it to question the certainty of guilt and the justness of capital punishment altogether, Paley maintained that the limits of human knowledge gave full vindication to harsher penalties. Because of the difficulty of discovering crimes and catching offenders, 'the uncertainty of punishment must be compensated by the severity' and by 'additional penalties and increased terrors'.[7] The paramount terror was to be found in the threat of death. This was the doctrine of maximum deterrence.

Paley reduced the ways of applying this deterrence to two: either a society had few capital statutes and inflicted them invariably, or else it had many but applied them infrequently and with deliberate discretion. The English law followed the latter pattern. Its application of the death penalty to a broad range of offenses allowed, in Paley's mind, for the widest efficacy of its terror to deter crime, sweeping into its net any and every possible crime and circumstance which might merit the punishment of death. The appeal to this need for terror was made at every turn by those who would preserve the criminal law against Romilly's assaults. From Herbert of Kerry, to Windham, to Lord Ellenborough, all declared their conviction of the power of this terror to prevent crimes and their belief in the likely dangerous effects were this constraint to be removed. Lord Eldon amplified the psychological angle in explaining his opposition to Romilly's bills. It was not, he explained, the 'circumstances of the severity of the law being put into execution to the fullest extent, so much as the imaginary terrors of it on the mind', that produced the 'abhorrence of crime'.[8]

Eldon's words revealed another facet of this reasoning. If the terror of the potential consequences of the law operated on people's minds as its defenders believed, then executions and the rigor of the law need only be exercised infrequently, even sporadically, allowing for mild practice despite apparent brutality in theory. As Paley put it, 'By this expedient, few actually suffer death, whilst the dread and danger of it hang over the crimes of many.' The total sum of pain might well be less than in a system which advocated that each crime be punished proportionally. The advocates of the established laws charged that this humane aspect was either overlooked or willfully ignored by the detractors of the law. The problem for the conservatives, as Sir Vicary Gibbs pointed out, was that the efficiency of terror was 'impossible to adduce', 'because acts that are prevented are never seen'.[9] This unfortunate flaw put the best defense of the capital statutes (that it in fact prevented crimes) into the category of the unprovable.

The certainty and the flexibility of the established law

The champions of the established system had another reason for objecting to the measures for reform. They maintained that while many who were found guilty were not executed, all suffered some form of punishment, so that none escaped 'with impunity' as Romilly and his associates claimed. The Attorney General pointed out that while few hanged when found guilty of stealing from a dwelling house, 'there is a certainty of the same punishment which is intended to be introduced by the Bill', which was transportation for not less than seven years or imprisonment with hard labor. Eldon went so far as to claim that 'as the law is at present, you have in effect what is sought by this Bill'. Their confidence in the certainty of some punishment for the guilty derived from their denial that the harshness of the statutes discouraged prosecutions. The law officers and leading judges one by one denied this charge; they had not seen any reluctance to prosecute in their experience in the courts. If some victims of crime did fail to prosecute, the conservatives were convinced that it was because of the cost of legal action and not out of humanity. As Eldon put it, the 'true cause of that tardiness to prosecute, proceeds from a principle of parsimony. Sore already with the loss of their property, they are unwilling to risk the expense of a prosecution, which may in the end fail, from the difficulty of proving the crime'. This was not a reason to amend the punishment, the Lord Chancellor explained, but an argument for supporting prosecutions at public expense.[10]

Neither the judges nor the law officers entertained the consideration that since their daily experience was with those who had already chosen to prosecute, they were not really in a position to discern how many might have chosen not to.[11] They were satisfied that most people did bring cases to trial if they had sufficient knowledge of the culprits. That juries often devalued stolen merchandise to avoid the capital punishment was not directly contradicted. Instead, this 'flexibility' in the law was praised as one of the strengths of the existing system. It meant that guilty parties were punished, but not capitally, so that the certainty which Romilly asserted was lacking, was in fact present. Some of the law's defenders, like Solicitor General Thomas Plumer, went so far as to advise the use of lesser statutes for the purpose of ensuring prosecution, while protecting tender consciences. Lord Eldon took a similar line. In response to Lord Suffolk's testimony that he had chosen not to prosecute a servant for theft because of the severity of the potential punishment, the Lord Chancellor declared that the noble lord 'had nothing to do but indict her for stealing in his dwelling house to the value of thirty-nine shillings'. Such equivocation with regard to the law had not evidently occurred to the 'noble' lord.[12]

Flexibility went along with the assumption that the justices who administered the criminal law should be allowed the widest discretion possible to determine actual sentences. As has been observed, the practice of the courts required that anyone convicted under a capital statute must receive the capital sentence from the judge before the court adjourned. In the great majority of cases, however, the judge would temporarily reprieve the felon, while an evaluation was filed which usually recommended mercy and meant that a pardon or commutation of sentence would be delivered from the Home Office within a few weeks. The basis for a relaxation of the letter of the law was the judge's evaluation of the particular circumstances of each case. The judges did not have to recommend mercy, and in situations where a crime was complicated by 'aggravating circumstances', a judge might well refuse to take any further action and simply 'suffer the law to take its course'. The opponents of reform attempted to portray the attack on the capital statutes as an all-out offensive against this judicial discretion. By directing their rebuttal at the implied limitation on magisterial discretion, instead of at the proposed changes to limit punishment, the conservatives shifted the argument from the question of punishments as such, to the issues of privilege and prerogative which were part of the Crown's administration of justice.

The discretion of those in authority was thought to be an absolute necessity, because true and complete certainty embodied in legislation was an impossibility.[13] The appeal to judicial discretion appears at every turn of the 1810 debates, but the most complete exposition of the virtues of the existing system of statutes and the dangers of alteration came after Romilly's bills were reintroduced in 1811. Colonel Frankland, who had confined his remarks in 1810 to a few short observations, mounted an all-out counter-offensive in defense of the status quo. Frankland's remarks surprised some, because he was considered among the 'thick and thin' supporters of the Whig Opposition.[14] He was a friend of Windham's, however, and he took up his ardent defense of the criminal laws in Windham's place, after that politician's death in 1810. But his presentation could not be dismissed as blind support of the governing party. Frankland argued that not only was a criminal code of perfect proportionality impossible, but that the attempt to form one would remove the human spirit from the law and was immoral:

> The system which attempts to affix prospectively an exact punishment to an exact offence, antecedently endeavouring to define every shade of distinction which a case may receive from its circumstances, trusting nothing to the discretion of the wise and the good, and thus presumptuously making the human code all in all, hardens men's hearts, and destroys all moral sentiments.[15]

Frankland objected to proportionality not only because it limited the judges' powers of discretion, but, in a twist on the reformers' arguments, because it would teach criminals to become shrewd calculators of costs and benefits, which he believed would result in encouraging 'the breed of these senior wranglers in crime'. Better to maintain a measure of uncertainty of the exact nature of a punishment, than bet on a thief's choosing to avoid a crime because of a certain, though proportional, punishment if caught. Thus, the opponents of reform did not deny the instructive capabilities of the law, nor did they refute the belief in criminal calculation. Instead, they felt it was an argument in their favor, which demanded the retention of a maximum discretion so that those individuals who had the greatest abilities to calculate the relative success or failure of a criminal undertaking might be dealt with most severely.

Frankland also asserted that the combination of the threat of severity with the discreet exercise of mercy was peculiarly suited to the manners and customs of the English nation. Frankland observed that 'without a strict penal law, there must be a strict police'.[16] The very love of liberty which so marked the English as a people, the argument went, precluded a more intrusive and effective policing of crime, which conformity to the certainty of punishment seemed to demand. Paley also had raised English liberty as a reason for the 'frequency of capital executions'.[17] As the reformers had not yet moved for greater powers for the discovery of crimes (though most did favor improved policing), their proposal to amend the punishment would be removing the one check to a wanton rampage of criminal elements. Although the English system might preserve the maximum penalty for many varieties of offense, it also allowed for the maximum liberty of the subject to pursue his legitimate business. That the system especially preserved the liberty of the judiciary went without saying, and required no further defense from the conservatives than their appeal to the need for discretion in determining degrees of guilt.

To the conservatives, then, the operation of the criminal law appeared to be as humane as the proposed amelioration would have made it. The terror of the threat of death was necessary to keep in check those sources of evil and disorder which a free society could not entirely eliminate without also sacrificing liberty. Of course, this was a liberty exercised under aristocratic rule, which implied a personal and paternalistic government. In his reevaluation of the debates on criminal law reform, Randall McGowen agreed with the conservatives in seeing Romilly's objectives as an attempt to replace the personal decision-making process of the judges with an impersonal, but predictable, rule of law.[18] While McGowen's insight has served to remind us that the defense of the old system was based on an entrenched view of how society did and ought to work, the suggestion that at base the issue between reformers and conservatives was not really about humanity or even 'how to secure the greater efficiency of the criminal justice system, but how to present a more pleasing image of justice', has obscured very real disagreements.

There was a real difference of opinion about what crimes one should hang for. Paley had said it was necessary to place a boundary on one side of the criminal law, which punishment could not legitimately exceed.[19] Romilly intended to set that boundary at a distance far short of the penalty of death, which seemed nature's limit of punishment, and which one could hardly conceive of exceeding. The conservative claims about discretion and its propitious flexibility, which was indeed part of the aristocratic order, were only part of the picture. Their repeated demands for the preservation of judicial discretion could be seen as a rhetorical move to shift the focus of the debate. Not all the conservatives were aware of what they were doing. Plumer revealed his confusion over how to react to the proposed amendments when he first attacked Romilly for wishing to minimize the judges' power of discretion, and then accused him of inconsistency because Romilly desired 'that the judges may be impowered to inflict a discretionary punishment when the punishment of death is abolished'.[20] The reality was that Romilly did not attack discretion as such at all – his comments regarding it had been restricted to its application in capital cases. He simply wanted to remove the penalty of death from the list of possible punishments administered at the judges' discretion.

If Plumer was genuinely confused, others were more disingenuous in their pontifications. Ellenborough's obfuscations about the absurdities of implementing proportional punishments, his hyperbolic statements as to the danger that 'depredations to an unlimited extent would be immediately committed' were the death penalty removed from privately stealing in a shop, and his claim that were the bill to pass, it would lead to another and another, until 'we shall not know where to stand, – we shall not know whether we are upon our heads or our feet',[21] all rang of deliberate exaggeration to draw attention away from the fact that he differed fundamentally with the reformers on the appropriate use of the death penalty. He was not afraid to illustrate his reasoning on discretion with examples of when simple crimes appeared to him to warrant hanging, but his method of polemic drew attention away from this primary distinction. Soon after Romilly's *Observations on the Criminal Laws* appeared, Ellenborough told Lord Lauderdale of an episode when he tried a man in Worcester for shop-lifting.[22] The man 'lolled his tongue and acted the part of an idiot'. When the jury decided he was not weak-minded, and was guilty of the crime, Ellenborough thought it right to leave him for execution, reasoning that the feigning of idiocy or lunacy ought not to be rewarded with mercy. Lauderdale thereupon asked the Chief Justice what law there was which punished 'counterfeiting idiocy' with death. To Lauderdale, Ellenborough's example provided better support for the amendment of the law than anything Romilly had argued. But the story also indicated the essential conflict over the appropriate reach of legal punishment: Ellenborough thought some people should hang for crimes of fraud and property.

Eldon and Gibbs were more straightforward about their positions. Eldon simply did not think a statutory mitigation of the punishment would achieve what its proponents thought it would. He too cited the necessity of providing room for the harsher punishment of crimes committed with aggravating circumstances.[23] He agreed with Gibbs that some cases of apparently simple crime merited the harshness of the existing statute. Gibbs illustrated his belief with reference to a practice he had known of in his younger days, when groups of burglars had broken into the homes of those who were out in the fields at harvest time, plundering them of all their belongings. 'Ought not the punishment [of death] to be inflicted for such atrocity?' he asked, maintaining that the salutary effects of the existing law had caused this offence to diminish.[24] Gibbs also held that the 'effects of this law are apprehended rather than felt; it acts by prevention and not by punishment'. Like Eldon and Ellenborough, he believed in the beneficial results of terror, on the assumption that the threat of death was humane because it prevented crimes without a great amount of blood being spilt. Conversely, these defenders of justice supposed that crime would not and could not be prevented without some blood being shed. This was a substantive disagreement with Romilly and Wilberforce and not merely a matter of the image of justice.

The fear of innovation

Those who might wish to believe that a less sanguinary system could work might be given doubts by another pervasive argument. This was expressed succinctly by Frankland in 1810:

> By altering part of our criminal code, we shall produce no certain good; but the alteration will be attended with the certain evil of destroying the lofty spirit...upon which our liberties so much depend. I must therefore oppose this Bill, which I consider as the first step towards an important, and, as I conceive, a dangerous innovation.[25]

For many, to question the criminal laws was to declare one's lack of trust in them, which would in turn lessen their effectiveness among the population at large. Some, therefore, objected to any public discussion of the possibility of amendment. But even for those conservatives who did not go so far, the discussion was viewed as a sneaky way to introduce the spirit of innovation into the public mind. Innovation, the threat to all established order, the risk of the destroying all that was good in the name of correcting anything that was wrong, was as much a part of the debate on mitigating the criminal laws as it was in the case of parliamentary reform.

The charge that any change in the criminal laws of England would be an unwarranted and dangerous innovation was intoned again and again, like a mantra of destruction against the reformers and their proposals. Plumer's response to Romilly's bills included his confession: 'I am ready to admit, that I long have, that I now do, and that I ever shall, view all innovations on established systems with a jealous eye.'[26] He insisted that this did not mean that he was 'averse from all improvement', but he wanted to have proof that a thing was an improvement, without attendant evil consequences, before he would feel comfortable endorsing it. The accusation against the proposed alterations was not merely that they were innovations, but innovations stemming from 'theoretical speculation to practical good', what Ellenborough called 'speculative legislation'. The repeated plea that amendments in existing institutions should proceed from experience alone seemed to place an immoveable barrier in the way of reform. One might have seen it as another rhetorical move employed merely to block discussion, but it reflected a serious aspect of the conservative viewpoint.

Opponents of reform did not claim that changes in the law had not occurred. When Canning charged that the original act making theft from dwelling houses capital was itself an innovation on the law, no one refuted him.[27] Conservatives did not deny historical change; but they did look upon the steady process of modification differently. First, the alterations were slow; they denied that abrupt reforms ever lasted. Second, modifications were made in response to specific needs. Since Romilly was not responding to any social crisis or addressing the demands of any particular constituency when he introduced his legislation, it was quite easy to characterize as 'speculative'. Finally, in the case of the expanding capital statutes, changes were merely seen as extensions of existing practices, so that the innovation was inconsiderable. This last reason gave credence to Romilly's claim that the criminal law formed a cruel precedent, and well illustrated the disparity of vision between the two sides with regard to the appropriate powers of government in the infliction of punishment.

Although the fear of innovation was present in British political debate prior to the French Revolution, the extreme events across the channel, and the subsequent wars it brought upon England, provided an ample supply of pretexts to resist 'speculative innovations'. Windham specifically raised the specter of the French Revolution by reminding the House that one of the voluntary associations spawned by that failed experiment also favored the elimination of capital punishment: '[G]lorious society it was,' Windham declared; 'they began by putting their king to death'.[28] France was also the implied reference in Frankland's remarks to the Commons about not being surprised that nations which sought, 'by taking off restraints, or by other unskillful means, to improve their liberty and happiness, should suddenly revert to a degraded state, and find they had only taken so many fearful strides in the high road to despotism and misery'.[29] The general influence of the French Revolution on projects of improvement had been observed by Romilly, and it was considered a contributing factor in Ellenborough's movement away from his whiggish heritage and into the Tory camp in the 1790s.[30] The link made by the Tories between innovation, speculation and the French Revolution, forced members in both Houses of Parliament to deny their interest in speculative reasoning about practical matters and made it necessary for participants in the early debates to disclaim any desire to pursue an extended program of legal reform.

The alternative to 'speculative legislation' in the conservative mind was the introduction of specific measures by those who were most able to evaluate the needs and limitations of the existing law: the judges ought to introduce changes. In cases when they did not themselves provide the initiative, they ought always to be consulted before any measure reached the floor of either House of Parliament. Romilly's failure to confer with the judges was observed by the Attorney General and the Prime Minister, and Ellenborough's pronouncements on the importance of this practice sounded like an accusation of heresy against those who failed to follow it.[31] To reformers, the shortcomings of this doctrine were obvious – if one waited for the introduction of substantive alteration to the system by those whose way of thinking had been molded by the system, whose livelihood was intimately bound up in the existing operation of that system, one was unlikely ever to see change, or at least not of the kind that Romilly, Wilberforce or Lord Holland desired. For the defenders of the law, any amendment had to have the approval of those who would be required carry it out, whose experience gave them the greatest knowledge of crime and the practice of criminal law. Without that experience to give credence to proposed reforms, they were only speculation.

A closer look at Eldon and Ellenborough

The claim to what amounted to a judicial veto on legal changes revealed something about the character of the most adamant defenders of the existing laws, Lords Ellenborough and Eldon. Neither man has received kind treatment from later historians. John, Lord Campbell, author of *The Lives of the Lord Chancellors* and *Lives of the Chief Justices of England*, recorded that he had many a personal conflict with Ellenborough, but that he nonetheless had a profound respect for his predecessor, in part because he was a 'real chief' (Campbell's emphasis), that is, Ellenborough had both commanding presence and ability. [32] Unfortunately, these attributes were combined with a bad temper and arrogance, which found expression in caustic criticism from the bench and a practice of ridiculing bad arguments and those who employed them. Nor was Campbell alone in finding fault with Ellenborough for his manner. The conservative prime minister Perceval once wrote that Ellenborough had 'great strength which he puts forth on occasions too trivial to require it. He wields a huge two-handed sword to extricate a fly from a spider's web.' [33] Ellenborough believed the English law superior to every other and not likely to be improved by comparison to the practices of other countries. His one act of legislation, 43 Geo. III c. 58, known as Ellenborough's Act, created nine new capital crimes. A more likely opponent for Romilly's bills could not have been imagined.

If inclined to object to all change, Ellenborough was not without conscience, nor was he incapable of considering moderate alterations, provided they came from those he trusted. He revealed some of the manner of his deliberation in a letter to Wilberforce about his views on the slave trade. The issue gave him real anxiety. He could not well believe that the slave trade was 'consistent with the will of God', and claimed that if he could be certain of this, he should and would oppose it, despite the policy of man. [34] At the same time, however, he admitted that as 'a man and a Christian, I am frightened at the consequences of any innovation upon a long established practice, at a period so full of danger as the present'. He would give as much weight as he could to Wilberforce's arguments, but he found it difficult to break his pattern of defending what was.

Still, Ellenborough was not entirely against making changes. The practice of the criminal courts required that when judgment was read against anyone convicted of a capital crime, the sentence of death had to be pronounced, even if the judge fully expected to recommend a pardon. Ellenborough at one point considered bringing in a bill to alter this requirement. Among his papers is a 'proposed act' which would have allowed a sitting justice to substitute another sentence when he knew the felon would not hang. Written in Ellenborough's own hand, it is undated, but the draft says it would have taken effect 10 April 1810.[35] It had to have been drafted prior to Romilly's great attack upon the criminal laws in that year. The act would 'remedy the mischief arising from the passing of sentence of death universally in cases of conviction for felony without benefit of clergy', because in cases when the sentence was unlikely or was not intended to be carried out, the pronouncement 'has a tendency to weaken the impression which ought to be made by the public passing of so awful a sentence'. The act would have allowed a judge to pronounce a sentence of transportation or imprisonment, as deemed appropriate. The bill never was introduced, and the reason for Ellenborough's hesitation remains uncertain. The introduction of Romilly's bills may have caused the Chief Justice to draw back, for fear that he would be seen as endorsing indirectly what he intended adamantly to oppose. Had he proceeded with the bill, Ellenborough's reputation would now be quite different. Clearly one cannot say he was unaware of problems in the administration of justice, cognizant that harsh language followed by soft actions took away much of the threat that the pronouncement of a death sentence was meant to convey. Had the Chief Justice brought in such a bill, it would have passed Lords and Commons almost without comment, but this particular amendment had to wait for the reforms of Sir Robert Peel in 1823. Ellenborough chose to be remembered as the enemy of mitigation, so that he might not risk being remembered as one who helped usher in an upheaval of the law.

Eldon's reasons for opposing legal reforms were similar to Ellenborough's, but included other elements. His objections were based as much in real intellectual skepticism as in personal inclination or social orientation. Again, his response to Wilberforce's solicitation in the anti-slavery campaign was revealing.[36] Eldon wrote that he thought he perceived, in himself and in the House of Lords, 'a strong inclination, if Abolition be Justice, to do Justice in a most unjust trade', but he was not fully convinced. 'I wish my mind had been so formed as to feel no doubts on this awful and fearful business', but such was not the case. Indeed, Eldon's mind was formed in exactly the opposite direction, to feel doubts and sense distinctions to which others were oblivious. Campbell faulted him for delaying Chancery decisions because he could not reconcile himself to an outcome which might be less than flawless.[37] Even Eldon's official, and sympathetic, biographer Horace Twiss admitted that the tendency to hesitate so long was a fault for one in high judicial station, a fault 'much exaggerated indeed by his political adversaries, but still a defect'.[38] Much evidence supported Twiss's interpretation that Eldon's delays were more a result of an active mind and a perhaps over-scrupulous concern in deciding upon the rights of others, than of incompetence or laziness, as his harsher critics contended. Romilly, who was himself often vexed by the Chancellor's indecision, still admired him for the amount of work he could carry on in the face of an expanding load in the courts of equity.[39]

With regard to mitigating the capital statutes, Eldon, who had daily contact with Romilly, most fully acknowledged the humane concerns behind the latter's bills; he simply thought it misdirected and doubted that amelioration would lead to the kind of certainty of punishment and prevention of crime which proponents declared to be their objects. Eldon could not believe that restricting the death penalty by statute would accomplish anything beneficial. He told the Peers,

> My Lords, as the law at present exists, you have in effect what is sought by this Bill. If the principle is not the same in each, the practice is similar. It is needless, my Lords, for us to differ about theories, if our practice is in unison.[40]

Eldon would not allow that amendment might bring greater humanity to the law; instead, he saw in it many sources of doubt, which led him to preserve the status quo.

Though their characters differed, both Ellenborough and Eldon basically agreed in their approach to existing laws and their administration, and on one thing in particular: that the majesty of the Crown was enhanced by the exercise of mercy in capital cases, and that the king and his ministers should take an interest in the cases brought to their attention. For most of the country the king's pardon was handled by the Home Office in conjunction with the judges of assize sessions, though the monarch might take an active interest in an exceptional case from the shires. By traditional right the king exercised his prerogative in London directly. Meeting 'in council' with several of his ministers and other Privy Councillors, the king reviewed all cases of those capitally convicted at the Old Bailey, whose jurisdiction covered crimes committed in Middlesex and the City of London.[41] These cases were presented by the Recorder of London, who, along with the Common Serjeant, and the Serjeant-at-Law, tried up to five hundred cases in each of the eight sessions held at the Old Bailey each year. Since the Old Bailey was the busiest of all courts in England, the King in Council had a heavy load whenever the Recorder presented his report.

When Eldon attended the council for the first time, he was shocked by what he perceived as 'the careless manner in which...it was conducted'.[42] Though called to decide upon the very lives of men and women, the king and his council seldom had more than a few scanty notes from the Recorder and the judge's opinion by which to determine who would receive mercy, and who would suffer the full penalty of the law. Eldon resolved never to attend a Recorder's report 'without having read and duly considered the whole of the evidence of each case'. Given his scrupulousness in other matters, one need not doubt his truthfulness when he claims he never did.

The chief law officers could take advantage of the council to encourage the exercise of mercy, but also to delineate some rules upon which to base the decision. Eldon himself told the story of when he was the only one at a council meeting opposed to hanging a man convicted of street robbery in Bedford Square. He told George III that a distinction should be made between those robberies which involved violence, and those which did not. Since the case at hand had no attendant violence, Eldon thought the man should be pardoned and given a lesser sentence. The king observed wryly, that 'since the learned judge, *who lives in* Bedford Square, does not think there is any great harm in robberies there, the poor fellow shall *not* be hanged'.[43] At other times, Eldon would not appear to have been so lenient, but he did believe that the use of the king's prerogative made the operation of English law more humane than its detractors acknowledged, and therefore, while the principles of law might have differed between himself and those in favor of reform, the 'practice was in unison'.

Conclusion

The belief in the efficacy of the Crown's prerogative of mercy underlined the fact that the defense of the criminal laws was connected with the preservation of a system of deference. As it stood, the administration of justice left much in the hands of those whom Frankland called the 'wise and the good'. The system assumed aristocratic benevolence, but also had the advantage of protecting privilege and helping to maintain hegemony over standards of respectability – a convict was far more likely to receive a pardon if he had well-heeled advocates in his county or in London.[44] For this reason, Radicals would be among the first to enlist in the campaign against the Bloody Code, which they saw as a tool of the elite long before Douglas Hay so identified it; but also because of this reason, any substantive change would require advocates of mitigation to win a rhetorical battle over what respectability needed for security.

The rhetorical battle was not one of merely rational argument; it had as much, perhaps more, to do with the emotional sensibilities of the participants.[45] Sympathy, an identification with and an emotional attachment to the convicted felon, was an important motivator for many involved in penal reform. Though defenders of the laws manifested compassion for the condemned at some level, their arguments declared sympathy for the victims of crime, and anger toward those who would destroy or take another's property. And their insistence on the law's duty to protect persons and their property was anything but calm. Crime was an evil to be fought: its causes to be found in greed and immorality. They did not believe it necessary to inquire further about it. Ellenborough could easily imply that those desiring to mitigate the penal code favored the guilty criminal over the innocent victim, even if such a charge had little support in actual practice.

The basic difference between the conservatives and the reformers still boiled down to the fact that the law's defenders accepted that some ought to hang for forgeries and larcenies as examples and warnings to others; reformers believed that it was both immoral and impolitic to hang men and women for non-violent offences. But the conservative justification of the penal statutes demanded that those who would alter or abolish them prove not only that they were contrary to the revealed laws of God (had not Paley implied as much?) but that they were ineffective in protecting property and that civil society therefore did not require extensive use of the punishment of death to protect itself – in essence, that the legal structures could afford to be more humane. The social and economic dislocations in the decade following Romilly's first bills, together with the entrenched suspicion of innovation, made the reformers' effort almost quixotic. As much as Romilly might have helped define and focus humane sentiment on capital punishment, the conservatives still set the conditions for public debate and for the measures that could actually be introduced. As will be seen, the language of the Evangelical revival and the support of Evangelical politicians helped overcome these conditions.

7
Mobilizing Opinion, 1811–18

The debates of 1810 had revealed the basic political and rhetorical battle lines of penal law reform as they would stand for the next decade. Those in favor of Romilly's proposals emphasized the unwillingness of crime victims to prosecute for relatively minor offenses because an offender might be hanged, but also deplored the irrationality of a system where judges commonly recommended mercy more often than they let a death sentence stand. All agreed that the practice of the courts was more humane than the law they claimed to administer, but Romilly's supporters concurred with Sir William Grant's assessment that the practice was right and the statutes were wrong. The opposition was just as persistent, however, and while Government spokesmen in the Commons soon found they could not control the vote there, they continued to speak against Romilly's bills, while Lords Eldon and Ellenborough dominated the upper house. A few measures did make it through both houses between 1810 and 1818, though they hardly rewarded the strenuous fight. But the parliamentary debates served, and were intended to serve, as a means of bringing the hanging statutes regularly before the public, and thereby to educate, or create, public opinion, which would in time push the limits of what was politically possible. The incorporation of language emphasized by Evangelical politicians and activists also pushed these limits, adding an appeal to ultimate ends to the practical utility of penal reforms. One could perceive a slow change in the style of the Government's opposition as a result of this pressure.

'Public opinion' had a fluid definition in the early nineteenth century, but it would never have meant 'popular' or 'mass' opinion. Enough has been written about the popularity of hangings to make one doubt that the masses were anxious to see capital punishment too much limited, even if crowds were sometimes hostile in situations where they thought the felon deserved better.[1] By 'public opinion', Romilly, Horner, and the members of the Capital Punishment Society meant the views of those whose opinions and votes mattered to members of Parliament. This group included the educated classes of landowners, professionals and substantial merchants, who were most likely to have been affected by new ideas of sensibility and sympathy with those less fortunate.[2] But they were also the ones who benefitted most, and suffered least, from the system as it was, so their support of criminal law reform could not be taken for granted. The perception of the collective views of these classes was what constituted the public opinion most important to legal reformers.

Parliamentary moves, 1811–18

Though faced with a determined opposition, Romilly showed little inclination to desist from pushing his measures forward. On 21 February 1811, he again brought in the three larceny bills introduced the previous year. He was confident that the public was with him and pledged that he would persevere unless his proposed measures were defeated by a much larger majority than had rejected them in the previous session.[3] Romilly again emphasized that he did not propose a general reform of the penal laws, but hinted that he might bring in something further 'of inferior magnitude' in a few days. As expected, Perceval and Plumer spoke their opposition to the measures, while not opposing their introduction. In response to the Government's opposition, Romilly felt obligated to tell the Commons that in bringing in these measures, he 'had no pretensions to more humanity than others; he had never proposed the measure merely on the ground of humanity; and he claimed no merit but that of doing his duty'. This disclaimer was clearly addressed to the conservative opposition; Romilly attempted to present his proposals within the rhetorical limits set by the crown's ministers and judges.

Romilly revealed the measure of 'inferior magnitude' a week later. On 27 February he brought forward two petitions, one from the owners of bleaching grounds in northern Ireland, and the other from several calico printers in England.[4] Two eighteenth-century acts made stealing from bleaching grounds a capital offence when the value of the cloth exceeded five shillings in Ireland or ten in England. The petitioners claimed that this 'protection' hindered prosecutions by its severity, making victims lenient in prosecuting, juries unwilling to convict, and thus 'secured impunity to offenders, and operated as an encouragement to the commission of crimes'. Romilly thought that the petitions provided

strong illustration of his earlier claims, 'not opinions drawn from speculative and theoretical reasonings, but the explicit declarations of
experienced men, pointing out the inefficacy of laws made expressly
for their protection'. On 4 March he introduced two bills to repeal the
statutes specified in the petitions. Romilly wrote to Lord Holland that he
had not planned to bring in such bills before he was approached by the
petitioners; significantly, he recorded in his diary that both 'these petitions were set on foot and promoted by Quakers'.[5]

The bleaching grounds bills prompted no debate in the Commons,
though his other proposals sparked some fire. At the second reading of
the bills on 29 March, William Frankland delivered his full-blown apologetic for the existing laws, which was longer even than Romilly's in
1810. Romilly excused himself for not replying to Frankland directly
because 'the greater part of his speech was so dark and abstruse' that
'he did not understand it'.[6] The broader purpose of the speech was
revealed when it was reprinted as a pamphlet for wider circulation.[7] In
one section Frankland passed on the opinions of the Recorder and
Common Serjeant of the City of London upon questions he had put to
them. The position of these law officers carried some weight, since they
presided at the Old Bailey, where a quarter of all felony trials in England
and Wales were heard. Their opinions dealt with whether crime was
increasing or decreasing, the effect of the repeal of capital punishment
from pick-pocketing (Romilly's 1808 bill), whether the law officers had
seen any reluctance to prosecute, or jurors to convict, and whether it was
advisable 'or safe' to remove capital punishment from shoplifting and
stealing from ships or dwelling houses. Predictably, the Recorder and
Common Serjeant thought that crimes had increased since the repeal in
1808, they had seen little reluctance to prosecute, and they believed that
the changes proposed by Romilly's three bills would bring only mischief
and insecurity. The Recorder did, however, entertain the possibility of
adjusting the *value* of goods determining when a crime became capital, a
position with which Frankland concurred.[8]

Whether his speech persuaded many in the House may be doubted, for
most who spoke after Frankland favored the bills. Lord George Grenville
demonstrated that the severity of the law was inconsistent with Christian morality; Sir John Anstruther supported Romilly for desiring to
'bring back the written to the practical law'; and James Abercromby
appealed to the expediency of relieving juries and prosecutors of the
necessity of twisting the facts to make crimes fit under non-capital
statutes.[9] Perceval attempted some rebuttal, but when the division
came, the dwelling house bill passed in a vote of 79 to 53; all the bills

passed their third reading in the Commons on 8 April, with 50 for and 39 against.[10]

The struggle now moved to the Lords. Romilly again asked Lord Holland to take charge of the bills.[11] Holland was pleased to do so, but wondered if they had a chance. He requested background information on the acts to be amended and inquired what arguments might be raised against amelioration. Romilly in fact thought they had a good chance in the Lords, if the friends of reform would turn out for them. He noted that Perceval had 'made as strenuous an opposition to them as he could' in the Commons, sending out Treasury letters requiring an attendance at the third reading, and dispatching messengers to bring in votes while the debates were going on, and 'yet with all this only 39 members were found to divide against the bills'.[12] Providing background on the acts to be amended was difficult; Romilly knew of no record of any debate on them. The shoplifting act dated from the reign of William and Mary, before transportation was an option, and simply removed the benefit of clergy from an action for which any illiterate person could have been hanged anyway. Of this context Romilly made much, implying that the expectations of his and Holland's times were different, in part because they had other options. Suggesting strategies for meeting the opposition to the bills was also a challenge. He had no hope of mitigating Lord Ellenborough's hostility, because there was 'no argument whatever' in the Chief Justice's position. Of his opponents generally, he complained, 'They assert, they do not argue.' They simply declared that terror prevented crimes, and since crimes prevented could not be counted, it was an argument that admitted no proof. But what evidence in favor of the bills he could provide, Romilly did, including the expanded second edition of his *Observations on the Criminal Laws* which had been printed in February. He also recommended Montagu's accounts of the 1810 debates.

Besides Lord Erskine, Romilly knew that the Duke of Gloucester wanted to support the bills, and he asked Holland to bring them on when it was mutually convenient, but early enough for them to pass in the current session. On 24 May Holland moved the second reading.[13] Without a large showing of Opposition or independent peers, the bills stood little chance of passing, and there were few of these in the House when Holland made his motion. He put forward a telling argument, but not telling enough to faze Lord Ellenborough. The Chief Justice again tried to minimize the reformers' options: either the laws must give the judges maximum discretion, or 'there must be a graduated scale of punishment proportioned to all the shades and difference of crime'. This ploy was nullified, however, by his own ally, Lord Eldon, who defended the author of the bills for having 'allowed the judges great latitude of discretion' in measuring out the punishments offered in place in death. Eldon repeated his simple belief that the threat of death was necessary to deter criminals. Ellenborough also rehearsed his views on 'speculation and modern philosophy', but did not apply these to the bills regarding theft from bleaching grounds, 'on account of the petitions from those who were to receive the protection of the law'. None of Romilly's opponents clarified why the principles espoused in the bleachers' petitions were inapplicable to other crimes, but they had no need; they had the votes to defeat the bills. Only ten voted for Holland's original motion, while 27 voted in favor of Ellenborough's amendment that 'the Bill be read this day six months', effectively killing Romilly's original three bills; but those on bleaching ground thefts passed.

By one measure, Romilly's efforts had again failed in their object. But much had in fact been accomplished in the 1811 debates. Though not in his original plan, the bills removing the death penalty for thefts from bleaching grounds and cloth printers became law (51 Geo. III c. 39 & c. 41, respectively), based on the very principles Romilly had been urging with respect to his other bills. Further, this reasoning and the interests it represented had taken all the bills through the Commons, despite organized Government opposition. This achievement gave the reformers solid grounds of confidence in declaring that public opinion was on their side. Romilly also won a measure of concession from his opponents, when the Home Secretary Richard Ryder admitted that the administration of the law needed some amending, though he would confine this to raising the value for which larcenies could become capital, and removing the necessity of judges passing the sentence of death upon those 'who were not intended to be executed'.[14] The Government was not united in this opinion (Gibbs, the Attorney General, soon after expressed his support of passing sentence in all cases), but it revealed movement on some of the less central points. Ryder may have thought that by acceding to smaller changes he might turn the larger assault, but this was a tangible change from the declared position of the Government the year before. The campaign of 1811, therefore, had yielded measurable advances, even if the main objective had not been reached.

In 1812 Romilly refrained from reintroducing his larceny bills, in the hope that the hostility in the Lords might subside. Instead he turned his attention to another law that had outlived its usefulness, an act from the

39th year of Queen Elizabeth that made it a capital offense for soldiers or sailors to beg or wander the streets without a pass from their commanding officers.[15] The law, which had not been enforced since the reign of Charles I, was one which Blackstone had singled out as a 'disgrace'; Romilly suggested the Commons would not 'deem it expedient to continue acts which, in the present times, never could be acted upon'. Having moved his bill on 7 February, he might well have been surprised to see Frankland rise and second his motion. Frankland supported the repeal of the Elizabethan statute, but thought it prudent to explain at length why such a statute might at one time have been necessary. In response, Romilly noted other acts of Elizabeth that were as old and disgraceful as the one he proposed to remove, such as keeping company with persons denominated Egyptians and communing with the Devil, concluding simply that 'men's lives should not be subject to such laws'. The bill passed the Commons without further debate, and passed through the Lords with only a small amendment: Ellenborough had objected to the phrase that it was 'highly expedient' to remove the old statute, and the 'highly' was struck, because, in Eldon's words, 'A statute inflicting death may be, and ought to be, repealed, if it be *in any degree* expedient.'[16]

If the campaign against the capital statutes gained a little ground in 1812, it also lost a little when the Government passed a measure to deal with the Luddite riots in the neighborhood of Nottingham. Home Secretary Ryder carried a bill which made frame-breaking capital, an increase of punishment from a previous statute of George III which had made the crime a felony punishable by transportation for 14 years. This earlier enactment, Ryder declared, 'had proved completely insufficient to deter the commission of the offense', though he did not offer more than rhetoric and his own reputation as proof of the law's insufficiency.[17] Many in the Commons spoke against creating a new capital crime, and Ryder himself was defensive about this addition to the statute book; he claimed he was no friend to the increase of capital punishments, and was openly apologetic to Romilly, although Romilly was absent at the bill's introduction. Wilberforce too was absent, but the opponents of the Bloody Code had able representation. Samuel Whitbread spoke against the bill, as did Richard Brinsley Sheridan and C. W. W. Wynn. The Evangelical Thomas Babington also objected to the measure and to the manner in which the Government was proceeding with it; he urged the 'importance of a committee, that posterity might know with what due deliberation the House had proceeded, before it determined on taking away the lives of any of the subjects of the crown'. Others agreed with this idea, but a motion for a committee was defeated 40 to 15. Babington also proposed that if the law must pass, it ought to be only temporary, an idea that did meet with general approbation.

The Government argued that the new frame-breaking legislation was needed to suppress an organized and sustained conspiracy to thwart the law and disrupt legitimate manufacturing, and not merely an economic protest. Upon the grounds of this stated purpose Romilly attacked the measure when the bill reached its second reading.[18] The bill as it stood said nothing about conspiracies or flagrant disregard for civil authority, which the ministers claimed they desired to prevent. Instead, it was directed entirely at 'individual depredation'. Romilly believed that the new law would soon be a dead letter with regard to suppressing conspiracy, but would remain a dangerous rock upon which any young apprentice might be wrecked, who momentarily lost his temper with his master and blindly battered a piece of machinery. Opponents of the measure were disappointed by its passage, but they could take some encouragement from the admission by one of the bill's more reluctant proponents, that aversion to increasing the number of capital punishments 'was generally prevalent in the House'. All who supported the bill did so on the grounds that only the extremity of the current *political* situation could justify it; as Babington had suggested, the act was given a two-year limit, a concession of some significance.

Romilly gained sufficient encouragement from the apologetic tone and rhetorical retreat of the conservatives in 1812 to reintroduce the bill to remove the death penalty from shoplifting in the next session. He omitted the bills regarding stealing from dwelling houses and on board vessels, because these 'had excited much more opposition than that relating to shops'.[19] The shoplifting bill easily passed the Commons on 26 March 1813, by a vote of 72 to 34, but its fate in the Lords was the same as its predecessors'.[20] Romilly tried again in 1816 and 1818, each time moving the bill quickly through the Commons without even a division being taken on it, only to be brought to a halt in the House of Lords by Eldon and Ellenborough. During these years, Romilly bolstered his argument with new examples and statistics, and further citations from Blackstone, adding comments from Edmund Burke, who also had disparaged penal laws which were not regularly enforced. By 1818 the conservatives in the Commons pressed no arguments against the bill, though the Attorney General objected to the assertion in the preamble that extreme severity 'was calculated to obtain impunity for crimes'.[21] Romilly insisted on the wording, contending that this principle was 'the very foundation of the bill', because it was manifestly clear to everyone that 'extreme severity' rendered conviction more difficult. By this time the Government members were no longer united. Irish Secretary Robert Peel rose to wish Romilly well during the second reading of the bill, promising to introduce similar legislation for Ireland if the measure was successful in the other House. Peel had already introduced a measure to change the Irish law on pick-pocketing, and Romilly warmly welcomed his endorsement.[22] The bill easily passed in mid-April, and Holland moved for the second reading in the Lords in early June. His efforts were countered by the Lord Chancellor who simply told the House that his opinions on the subject had not altered, which was sufficient to stop the proposal again.[23]

In the years of popular protests and disorders following peace with France, defenders of the hanging statutes tried to paint any claim that the laws were inhumane or unjust as an attack not only on the written code, but on those who administered it as well. Proponents of reform were therefore careful to separate their cause from other issues of the day. Since all parties acknowledged that the judges were quick to exercise mercy in most cases, one gained nothing by appearing to attack them. The result was an indirect argument that capital punishment made for bad criminal law, because it was out of tune with the predominant sentiments of the country. Rather than arguing that the laws *were* inhumane, reformers asserted that the people *perceived* the laws as inhumane, which meant that they could not effectively be enforced. This rhetoric was a less radical course than accusing the Government of supporting an immoral code, but the relationship between sound policy and humane and moral laws was always an integral part of the debate. Many echoed Lord Grenville's simple formulation that the only question of consequence was whether the offense of shoplifting was 'one to which the punishment of death ought to be annexed, or for which it was fit?', and if not, the law should be changed.[24] Wilberforce's support revealed the interweaving of moral conviction, humane sentiment and concern for good public policy. In 1818 he reproached the Commons for failing 'to render the penal code of this country less bloody'.[25] He was bolder than Romilly in declaring his conviction

> that the entire penal code ought to be revised, that punishment ought to be apportioned to the crime, and that their united efforts ought to tend to the grand object of free and just legislation – that of adopting all possible means of preventing crime, and of checking it in its early stages.

Wilberforce made no distinction between what was humane and just and what was sound and practical legislation. In this sentiment he was not alone, though he was exceptionally clear in asserting the connection in Parliament.

Romilly's shoplifting bill failed repeatedly to pass the House of Lords, but this was not the only measure of his impact. We have already noted his interest in prison reform, a concern which enjoyed considerable support from Evangelicals like Wilberforce and George Holford. Romilly also focused debate on the punishments meted out for high treason, which brought some moderate changes in the law.[26] On the issue of imprisonment for debt Romilly supported Lord Redesdale's bill, which curtailed the power of a creditor to keep a debtor in prison for life, and he was responsible for removing the proposed clause which would have made it capital to hide assets from a creditor.[27] But more importantly, Romilly's agitation perennially focused attention on the question of capital punishment. He provided the public ground, albeit narrow and relatively conservative, upon which others could rally. And outside Parliament a critical effort had begun to form a public outcry against the Bloody Code.

The campaign beyond Westminster

1) Periodicals and other voices of the press

While Romilly's exertions in Parliament met with continual rebuff in the Upper House, outside Westminster his words were encouraging others. Dugald Stewart had told him that his arguments would make 'a very strong impression on public opinion'.[28] Romilly's *Observations on the Criminal Law of England* received wide attention. Many periodicals used their review of this pamphlet to endorse the proposals to reform the 'bloody code'. Among these were the *Monthly Review*, the *European Magazine*, and even the *Quarterly Review*; others, such as the *Monthly Magazine*, published letters from readers enthusiastic about restricting capital punishment.[29] The *Anti-Jacobin Review* was unusual in its hostility to Romilly's measures, though its strongly conservative bent made this no surprise.[30]

For some periodicals, like the *Edinburgh Review*, reform of the penal laws became a part of their general campaign for improving the structure of government. The *Edinburgh Review*'s article appeared in 1812, after the bills had twice passed the Commons and failed in the Lords, and it was unreservedly in favor of Romilly's proposals. The author, Henry

Brougham, who had supported Wilberforce's anti-slave trade campaign and would later become a law reformer himself, laid out the whole spectrum of necessary legal changes, of which the criminal law was only a part. Brougham countered the charge of innovation by urging that those who opposed the amendments were the very ones who 'for the last twenty years have been tampering with every principle and bulwark of the constitution' by their suspension of Habeas Corpus, their Gagging Acts, etc.[31] Brougham's article set the tone for the *Edinburgh Review*, and he reiterated his arguments in later articles.[32]

Support for penal law reforms would have been expected from the whiggish *Edinburgh Review*, but the endorsement from the more conservative *Quarterly Review* was somewhat surprising. The author had mixed feelings about the criminal statutes, but was warmly in favor of the removal of the punishment of death for shoplifting and thefts from homes or boats. The article did, however, express an abiding conservative concern: 'The salutary mistrust of innovation is a feeling we do not wish to see impaired.'[33] Every proposed alteration required not only the strongest practical recommendation, but evidence that it was 'safe by its agreement with what we already enjoy'. Romilly's particular proposals met that test, because they would be conforming written law to the way law was actually practiced.

Although the bishops had voted against Romilly's bills in 1810, other religious groups quickly voiced enthusiasm for the reforms. The *Eclectic Review*, affiliated with Evangelical Dissent, reviewed Romilly's pamphlet and welcomed its evidence for restricting capital punishment. The author's conclusion was unequivocal: Romilly's publication would convince 'any intelligent and reflecting person, that the profuse enactment of capital punishments ... is, in every view of it, impolitic, inhuman, and unjust'.[34] Like the *Edinburgh Review*, the *Eclectic* followed and continued to support criminal law reform in articles on other topics, but with greater concern for the moral and spiritual issues involved, as would have been expected from a magazine whose founders desired to 'blend with impartial criticism an invariable regard to moral and religious principle'.[35] This emphasis could be seen in their promotion of Lord Erskine's 1809 bill for preventing blood sports and cruelty to animals, which the *Eclectic Review* reported would 'greatly contribute to the improvement of the moral sense of mankind'.[36] The concern for moral issues was also evident in their criticism of Bentham's *Théorie des peines et des récompenses*, which the reviewer praised for its intent, its support of penal law amelioration, and its depth of reasoning, but chided for its abstraction, its bewildering and multiple divisions, and its exaltation of the 'bare doctrine of utility' over 'the moral feelings of mankind, over those universal perceptions of right and wrong, which are the most certain test of its value and amount, and which therefore can never be safely disregarded'.[37] The *Eclectic Review* was always favorable to utilitarian principles, as long as these were seen in light of what the contributors considered the moral and spiritual reality of the matter at hand.

Wilberforce's Saints had their own organ in the press, the *Christian Observer*, founded in 1802 after a meeting of the Eclectic Society considered a proposal for a review to present a critical and Evangelical view on public events and other publications.[38] In 1810, Wilberforce's good friend Zachary Macaulay edited the journal, though many people (Wilberforce included) contributed articles and reviews. Macaulay did not review Romilly's *Observations*, but the *Christian Observer* followed the politics of criminal law reform in its 'Public Affairs' section. The editor sounded overly optimistic in his first notice of Romilly's bills in 1810, where he wrote that these 'humane and enlightened exertions to amend our criminal code' would 'be attended with success', but then, he was accustomed to long battles from the antislavery campaign.[39] The *Christian Observer* also published portions of the criminal returns, and from 1818, it regularly included large sections of the reports from the Prison Discipline Society.[40] Though not so great a priority as antislavery, amelioration of the criminal laws fitted naturally with the *Christian Observer*'s emphasis on moral reform. Its support of restrictions on the penalty of death would have reached a large section of the Evangelicals in the Established Church, as well as many beyond it.

The Monthly Repository of Theology and General Literature, a Unitarian magazine, also became a criminal law reform advocate. An article on 'Capital Punishments' in 1811 supported Romilly's proposals and framed an approach to the death penalty which again combined moral concerns with practical issues of law and order, fully confident that these were compatible and indeed complementary impulses. A letter in the same issue declared penal law reform to be second only to religious liberty among the pressing issues of the day.[41] Like the *Christian Observer* and *Eclectic Review*, the *Monthly Repository* followed the campaign for amelioration through the decade, and while capital punishments never became the central issue for any of these journals, it was an abiding concern. It was, furthermore, an issue clearly linked in the various reviews and articles with the cause of moral reform and the inevitable improvement of human society. The authors were not shy in declaring commitment to 'advanced' causes, to 'improvements' which bettered the overall conditions of the ordinary man and woman. In these periodicals articles on law reform stood next to those on the poor laws and pauper relief, religious liberty and toleration, the abolition of slavery, and the improvement of living conditions in prisons and gaols. One could see the shape of a reforming mentality in all these, but also a sense that all change had to be brought gradually and within set limits for it to succeed. These were respectable periodicals, appealing to a respectable, educated audience, not overtly whiggish in the political sense, but undoubtedly critical of the establishment in so far as it resisted moderate improvements, especially when they answered the call of conscience and Christian duty. While their readers never formed a majority of the British population as a whole, nor even of the middle classes of which they were members, these periodicals did speak to many who were active and articulate in forming public attitudes, and in that sense could be said to have shaped and directed public opinion. Their role in promoting criminal law reform was crucial, therefore, even if criminal law reform was but one of their many concerns.

In addition to these regular periodicals were dozens of pamphlets which in one way or another dealt with the issue of capital punishment. Many rehearsed the arguments of Romilly and other parliamentary advocates, but a handful deserve further attention to show the range of the discussion. Among the most sanguine, and indeed almost utopian, was a short piece published in 1814 in the *Pamphleteer* on the 'Right, Expedience, and Indiscriminate Denunciation of Capital Punishments'.[42] The *Pamphleteer* was a periodical composed mostly of reproductions of previously published pamphlets. In this case, the editor advertised that the article was 'original', though anonymous. The writer began with an examination of one 'of the most formidable obstacles to the progressive improvement of our nature', the 'horror of innovation' found in every discussion of reform. The writer's response was not to denigrate the past, but to insist that had veneration for the past triumphed, it would have resulted in a halt to the 'progress of civilization at any stage of its career', at the first cottage, for instance, and would have precluded the whole range of rightly praised improvements of the previous century. One might honor the past by paying attention to it, but in fact, the author continued,

> The frame of civil society is a chain of innovations – all great men have been great innovators – and nothing but the reduction of the earth to its original barbarism could satisfy so fond a regard for what is old, if consistency were a virtue of the opponents of reform.

The author's arguments for restricting the death penalty combined predictable lines of moral and pragmatic concern with a vision of the upward spiral of civilization and spiritual progress, in which the laws of man must conform more and more to the combined mercy and justice of God. 'Mercy, or rather beneficence', the author declared, 'is the foundation of his designs; Justice, or discipline preparatory to happiness, the means of their success, and the pioneer of their triumph.' Few statements so seamlessly wed utilitarian visions of human happiness to confidence that God's providence was behind every improvement; God was on the side of amelioration because bad human laws prevented a true understanding of God himself. By defining justice as reformatory rather than retributory, the author attempted to reconcile punishment to tender feeling and hoped for a day when capital punishment could be abolished entirely.

Not all articles in the *Pamphleteer* were as ornate and optimistic as the 'Right, Expedience, and Indiscriminate Denunciation of Capital Punishments'. Two years later it reproduced a much less speculative piece by John William Polidori, MD. The article contained the usual praise for the frame of the English constitution, while at the same time insisting that the 'multitude of crimes' and the behavior of both judges and juries pointed to 'the existence of some radical error in the very foundation of our criminal laws'.[43] Polidori's program of reform was anything but radical, however. He endorsed Romilly's proposals, and even more his cautious method, as well-suited to amending what was ill-framed to begin with. Nonetheless, the doctor's rhetoric went beyond changing a handful of laws, and he expressed the hope that Romilly would press on 'and gradually reduce our criminal law to a form for which we may need no longer to blush in the presence of foreigners who inquire into the administration of our justice'.

Another class of literature combined the hard facts of the administration of the criminal laws with the flavor of political radicalism. Narratives of condemned felons formed a popular genre, but the stories could also be a medium for challenging the existing order, particularly if a story told of a convict wrongly accused, ill-used by the judge, and unjustly condemned. A handful of such tales appeared in the decade of Romilly's campaign. One of the most famous and illustrative of these stories was that of Eliza Fenning, executed at Newgate in 1815 after being convicted of attempting to poison her employer's family.[44] Much weight had been given to the prosecution witnesses, and very little to the defense; other evidence was suppressed, including statements that pointed the blame elsewhere. Romilly thought the case very much less than proven and recollected it as an example of the 'savage conduct' of the Recorder of London, Sir John Silvester; he wrote an unpublished essay examining the scanty trial evidence, noting with grim irony that Fenning was prosecuted under a provision of Lord Ellenborough's Act.[45] Others made their disgust public, laying out a posthumous defense for Fenning that the cursory trial had not permitted. The *Examiner*, edited by the radicals Leigh and John Hunt, denounced the more respectable press which had shown such caution about 'exciting prejudice' against the law.[46] Besides the *Examiner* and other newspaper editorials, several pamphlets appeared on Fenning's case. The most persuasive was a collaboration between the radical William Hone and a Dissenting Evangelical writer named John Watkins, whose thorough examination of the evidence convincingly portrayed Fenning's case as a gross miscarriage of justice.[47] More stories of justice gone bad have been forgotten than have been remembered, but Fenning's case made a lasting impression.[48] V. A. C. Gatrell has rightly observed that Hone and Watkins' portrayal of Fenning's conviction struck 'the oligarchy's law on a vulnerable flank' by displaying the 'callousness of justice' in terms anyone could understand.[49] The sad fate of Eliza Fenning and its frequent rehearsal by the pens of the respectable and radical alike certainly revealed the growing unease about the English criminal law. Romilly and his allies could not attack the judges as directly as did the radical press without losing political credibility, but the radical attacks were part of the background against which they presented their ostensibly more dispassionate arguments.

2)   The Society for the Diffusion of Knowledge upon the Punishment of Death, and the Improvement of Prison Discipline

For the periodicals, mitigation of the capital statutes was but one among many issues, and usually not the biggest. For the Capital Punishment Society, the penal laws were the whole reason for its existence. The leading members of the Society were involved in many other issues, especially antislavery and philanthropic efforts, which led to an occasional blurring of focus.[50] Many, though by no means all, of the members were Evangelicals or had close Evangelical connections, and the Society was one conduit for introducing the religious arguments in favor of penal reforms. Although the Capital Punishment Society was an evolving organization, with some shifting edges, the core membership was constant, and its carefully controlled agitation was a necessary part of making criminal law reform politically plausible.

The Society was founded by the barrister Basil Montagu and the Evangelical Quaker William Allen in 1808. Montagu, an illegitimate but publicly recognized son of the Earl of Sandwich, had already won respect in the legal community for his writings on bankruptcy; he would become the leading publicist on criminal law reform between 1809 and 1830. He has been described as a disciple of Bentham,[51] but while he had great regard for the utilitarian philosopher, this designation obscures Montagu's original contribution, as well his evident piety. Montagu appreciated Bentham's systemization, but he seldom invoked the principle of utility directly, preferring to appeal instead to the 'progress of Knowledge and of Christianity', which he equated with the advance of humanity.[52] This manner of argument was much more in line with the language of Evangelicals like Wilberforce and Buxton than with Bentham or James Mill, though Montagu left too few clues of his religious beliefs to align him definitively with the Saints or any other party in Britain.

According to Montagu's own account, his interest in reforming the penal code began after he intervened in the case of two men convicted of sheepstealing in Huntingdon.[53] Montagu had received information that suggested the men were fit 'objects for mercy'. He immediately sought and gained a reprieve from the Home Secretary, and then took the first available post-chaise to Huntingdon, arriving only hours before the men would have hanged. After delivering the reprieve, he observed a crowd gathering from all directions. A friend suggested that it might be advisable for him not to be seen, as the mob was not pleased at their disappointment of a hanging. Montagu was unsure if his friend's perception was exaggerated, but the whole incident stuck with him. He began to put together a book of opinions on the death penalty, but needed assistance to finance it. For this he turned to his Quaker friend William Allen.

Allen already had a reputation for philanthropy in London and had been a supporter of the anti-slave trade campaign. The timing of Montagu's visit to him was propitious, for Allen had been reading a pamphlet on the Philadelphia Society for Alleviating the Miseries of Public Prisons. Impressed by the penal law reforms instigated in Pennsylvania by the society, Allen was eager to form a similar group in England. Allen recorded in his diary that he and a small group met in Montagu's chambers in Lincoln's Inn on 12 April 1808, for the purpose of forming 'a little society...to endeavour to diminish the number of capital punishments'.[54] They agreed to explore starting such an association, but their organizational efforts were delayed until the beginning of July, when they met as a committee to make more formal arrangements.[55]

Romilly was not privy to these meetings. The first predated his initial speech on the criminal laws by over a month. At the second, the committee directed Montagu to approach Romilly about working together. The Capital Punishment Society began independently, and while it supported his cause, Romilly was not a member of the governing committee; his name does not even appear on any of the published subscription lists, though he might have been among the anonymous benefactors. Meeting with Montagu later in July 1808, Allen learned of Romilly's delight 'with the idea of having coadjutors in this great cause' of mitigating the death penalty, and the CPS set 'to work immediately in diffusing information on the subject'.[56]

Allen pulled in other Quakers in the metropolis, including several from the Barclay banking family, but the membership of the CPS was eclectic. Thomas Clarkson was among the subscribers in 1812, as were the Rev. Francis Wrangham, the bookseller and Methodist MP Joseph Butterworth, the radical Samuel Whitbread and the civil lawyer Dr Stephen Lushington, who often hosted meetings of the CPS committee.[57] Thomas Fowell Buxton attended a meeting of the society as early as December 1808, and Wilberforce took interest in their activities.[58] Allen noted the attendance of Sir James Mackintosh at a meeting in late 1813.[59]

The first 'diffusion' resulting from this ambitious society was Montagu's collection of opinions on capital punishment in 1809.[60] He included quotations from Samuel Johnson, William Blackstone, the Marquis Beccaria, William Paley, Erasmus and even a translation from French of one of Bentham's works published by Dumont. While not all favored limitation on capital punishment, that was the predominant concern. Eventually Montagu published two additional volumes, one in 1812, the third in 1813, and from the start they enjoyed success as quick references for those needing arguments for criminal law reform. In addition to the *Opinions*, the CPS published accounts of the early debates on the criminal laws, beginning with the debates of 1810, which had been poorly reported in Hansard's official *Parliamentary Debates*.

Most discussions of English criminal law reform have referred to the Capital Punishment Society as a Benthamite or utilitarian organization. Montagu had a great admiration for Bentham, but in describing the origin and object of the Society, he quoted at length from one of Thomas Clarkson's works to explain the spirit in which it met:

It is much to be lamented that nations professing Christianity should have lost sight, in their various acts of legislation, of Christian principles...As Christians we should be influenced by Christian principles...But where are our forbearance and our love; where is our regard for the temporal and eternal interests of man; where is our respect for the principles of the Gospel, – if we make the reformation of the prisoner a less object than his punishment, or if we consign him to death in the midst of his sins, without having tried all the means in our power for his recovery?[61]

Although Montagu never identified himself as an Evangelical, he continually emphasized the importance of framing laws in conformity with Christian principle. His publications carried arguments with the same stress on moral and spiritual reform as those of the Evangelicals. And like the Evangelicals, he was quick to seize upon church tradition to support his cause. In the second volume of the *Opinions*, Montagu quoted a letter from Dr Forde, the Ordinary of Newgate Prison, in which the clergyman referred to the second prayer in the Anglican church service, which requested forgiveness from Almighty God, 'who desireth not the death of a sinner, but rather that he may turn from his wickedness and live'.[62] This phrase became the reformers' dictum, appearing again and again in Montagu's publications and in the speeches and writings of others. In another pamphlet, Montagu recorded it had been his habit to attend public worship in the chapel of Newgate at least once a year:

I have never heard this congregation acknowledging that they have 'erred and strayed like sheep,' or the christian consolation, 'who desireth not the death of a sinner but rather that he should turn from his wickedness and live,' without a deep feeling of our infirmities both in the depravities of sin and in the excesses of human power.[63]

Neither Clarkson, nor Wilberforce, nor Buxton ever put together a more concise and Evangelical expression of the sentiment behind their support for mitigation of the death penalty. Montagu's publications sponsored by the CPS were one means by which the language and optimism of Evangelicalism reached the wider public, and they helped to move the discussion of punishment beyond retribution and proportionality toward a goal of prisoner reformation and conversion.

In 1816 a second edition of the *Opinions* was published, and these, along with reprints of the Parliamentary debates, constituted the bulk of the Capital Punishment Society's efforts to that date. The Society published three additional tracts in 1817 and 1818.[64] The first tract described

the Society's reason for existence and its faith in public opinion, asserting that once the impolicy of capital punishments had taken strong hold
of the public mind, a 'collision' of sentiment, a confluence of ideas and
emotions, would 'naturally lead to the best substitutes, and the most
effectual remedies'.[65] The Society did not mean to leave the direction of
penal reforms to random collision, however, and suggested many examples that might be followed. One was William Penn's statutes for
Pennsylvania, a 'code of penal law built upon the Christian principle
of the reformation of the offender', and the Society identified as its
model an association formed in Philadelphia in 1787, which improved
conditions in the city's jails and eventually helped pass a law restricting
the death penalty to the crime of murder.[66] The reformation of offenders
was the theme of tract number two, which gave a detailed description of
the Maison de Force at Ghent, a prison that exemplified humane prison
discipline, including practical education and religious instruction, solitary cells for reflection and sleep, healthy food and living conditions, and
a strict work regime to train the prisoners in habits of industry rather
than idleness.[67]

A third tract appeared in 1818, which pulled quotations from the
Opinions into an organized argument, adding sections drawn from recent
parliamentary debates, and providing statistics on the increases in
crimes, especially forgery, despite the high number of hangings. 'The
frequent recurrence of these spectacles', the tract suggested with studied
restraint, 'and still increasing number of offenders, shows that the
remedy is not altogether efficacious.'[68] Most distressing was the public
execution of women for forgery, because the obvious inequality of punishment to crime provoked only sympathy for the convict and heaped
ridicule upon the law. Throughout, the tract stressed the need to make
moral reform and spiritual regeneration a goal in dealing with offenders.
As it was, they were dispatched into the next life with little preparation
or, worse, hardened because offenders believed that dying for a forgery or
the theft of a few dozen shillings provided more than sufficient atonement for all their sins.

Montagu had compiled the third tract, but it received numerous addi-
tions and amendments before the Committee of the Society was satisfied
with it.[69] He also published a separate pamphlet in 1818.[70] Some
redundancy of argument was natural, but Montagu's tract had a different
feel and organizational approach. The structure was more clearly laid out
than in any of the other CPS publications, and reflected Montagu's
familiarity with Bentham's work. Earlier tracts had quoted Bentham,
but this time Montagu adopted some of Bentham's language and style

in the way he structured his argument. For example, Montagu argued that the indignation against crime, which was necessary for its prevention, arose out of the

> joint action of three powers: By the fear of the disapprobation of the community or the moral sanction: and by the fear of future punishment, the dread of the disapprobation of the Almighty, or the religious sanction: and by the fear of the punishment awarded by the law, or the legal sanction.[71]

Montagu gives full credit to Bentham for this 'mode of considering the effect of punishment' in a footnote, and the passage was indeed a paraphrase of statements in Bentham's *Introduction to the Principles of Morals and Legislation*.[72] Montagu's regard for Bentham did not, however, preclude his deployment of other arguments in making the case for mitigating punishments. Montagu went much further than Bentham in clarifying the 'religious sanction', giving it positive as well as negative content. He declared that it was a duty of sound government to employ the death penalty only in extreme cases, particularly in a society professing Christianity. Christians were taught to have compassion and to 'have a tender forbearance one with another and to regard each other as brethren'. In another section he considered the Christian teaching, 'Be angry, and sin not,' as an injunction against punishment as retribution. Montagu urged that those who took their religion most seriously should avoid the capital statutes, either by finding alternative laws under which to prosecute, or by dropping prosecution altogether. Montagu took more seriously than secular utilitarians the importance of religion in molding human sensitivities and legitimating human laws.

Besides influencing the CPS publications, William Allen sponsored a periodical called *The Philanthropist* from 1811 to 1819. Allen claimed his sole purpose in publishing this collection of stories, editorials, and analyses of events was 'to stimulate to virtue and active benevolence'.[73] Along with antislavery, prison reforms, educational expansion, and charitable service to the poor, the *Philanthropist* advocated limitations on capital punishment. Every year the magazine carried lengthy articles on penal matters, at least one on prisons and one on the criminal laws, sometimes more. Since James Mill is known to have authored most of the longer articles on penal matters, the praise of Bentham was not surprising.[74] Once again, however, though Mill was undoubtedly the closest to Bentham of all those involved in the Capital Punishment Society, his articles drew from many sources and, perhaps in deference to the editorial board, the *Philanthropist* articles displayed a greater piety than one might otherwise have expected from the author. For example, the review of Bentham's *Théorie des peines et des récompenses* reminded the reader that in considering Bentham's ideas, one ought always to measure them against the laws of God.[75]

Publication had been the main activity of the CPS until 1817, when the governing committee decided to broaden its tactics. Though with evident hesitation, the members resolved to encourage and to associate with societies formed for the same purpose outside London. Some feared that 'improper characters might obtain admission into provincial societies'.[76] The peace following Waterloo brought social unrest to much of Britain, and extreme, even revolutionary, agitators were said to have joined and even to have taken over some of the previously 'respectable' organizations advocating political and humanitarian reforms in the provinces. To avoid gaining a radical reputation, members of the CPS governing committee had been carefully selected, 'so much so', its secretary recorded, 'that even Subscribers did not for that reason become entitled to any share in its management'. After nine years of diffusing information, some on the Committee still thought careful screening of the membership necessary 'since too great caution could not be exercised when any alteration of an existing code of laws was sought to be effected'. Only after much debate did they resolve to 'view with pleasure the establishment of separate Societies in provincial towns'.[77] Besides diffusing information, the new groups would be encouraged to collect and document details of noteworthy cases and prisoners.

This new promotion of their cause resulted in a host of correspondents from various areas of England. In January 1818, the Committee put together a circular letter for these provincial correspondents in which they promised to send them 'facts and observations as may keep alive the sympathy and attention of the Public', and requested the recipients to 'disperse them as widely as possible by obtaining their insertion in the daily, weekly, or other periodical publications throughout the kingdom'.[78] At least a few of the recipients took them up on this suggestion.[79] One, J. E. Bicheno, went so far as to publish a full-length book on the philosophy of criminal jurisprudence in 1819.[80]

The activities of the CPS dovetailed with those of the Prison Discipline Society (PDS), organized by Buxton and Samuel Hoare in 1816. The membership lists of the two societies overlapped and the two effectively merged after 1819. The Capital Punishment Society was perceived to have had great influence, and it did help create the impression that public opinion had got firmly behind the reform of the penal code.

Gatrell has argued that the reality was far less certain, pointing out that the participants spent far less on the CPS than they did on antislavery efforts or the British and Foreign Schools Society. Gatrell has contended that even for most Quakers, whom he considered the most sympathetic to the claims of the CPS, the issue of capital punishment was not particularly pressing.[81] But given the Quaker suspicion of government action, and their communal injunction against holding public office, their very involvement in this cause, like that of the antislavery, indicated its importance to them as a group. More importantly, the governing committee of the CPS was not dominated by the Quaker participants, and to consider it as merely a Friends' society would be to distort the facts. But whether or not the influence of the CPS was as wide-reaching as its members might have claimed, it clearly was believed in its own time to have been speaking for a considerable portion of the population, and that is what established it as one of the shapers of public opinion. The proof was in the politics: the overwhelming support in the Commons for Romilly's measure in 1818 showed that the elected House of Parliament and, by implication, the electorate (the most solid indication of public opinion there was) now believed in amelioration.

The promises of 1818

Despite the defeat of Romilly's shoplifting bill in the Lords in 1818, most events of the year portended well for the proponents of penal law reform. Peel's stated interest in reforming the criminal laws of Ireland suggested that the younger members of the Tory ministry might be more willing to entertain reform than their elders. In addition to the general attack on the capital statutes, Sir James Mackintosh had initiated an inquiry into the operation of the laws against forgery. On the basis of its findings, he contended that the Bank of England was itself partly responsible for the number of forgeries perpetrated against it each year, since the officers of the Bank refused to implement methods to make the forgery of bank notes more difficult, and also resisted all attempts to return to cash payments.[82] This inquiry followed a public uproar over the hanging of two women for forgery in February.[83] While Mackintosh's arguments were ostensibly aimed at reforming the currency of the realm, much of what he said savored of a general attack on hanging for forgeries. His whole purpose was to show that the ridiculously high numbers of forged banknotes were proof that the capital punishment of the crime was no deterrent. His proposals were not accepted, but he had effectively broadened the debate on the criminal laws and had begun the difficult task of dismantling the forgery statutes.

Besides these parliamentary efforts, the work of Elizabeth Fry and the Ladies Committee of Newgate had captured the public attention in London by their successful efforts to comfort, educate, and reform women confined in that dreadful place. Her brother-in-law, Thomas Fowell Buxton, had taken this further in his publication on prison discipline.[84] He followed his inquiry with election to Parliament in June 1818. In that same election, Romilly was elected for Westminster. This achievement was the more significant because Romilly, who finished at the head of the poll, never campaigned for the seat and visited the hustings only after the voting was over and his election was clear. All these factors boded well for the repeal of the capital statutes in the Parliament to come, and none would have anticipated the changes that sudden tragedy made inevitable before the year's end.

8
The Partnership: Mackintosh and Buxton, 1819–22

Tragedy and new leadership

Romilly's wife Anne had suffered bouts of illness in early and mid 1818. During September her condition was precarious. Sir Samuel found much of his personal contentment in Anne's company. The extent of his emotional investment in his wife became clear as his own health deteriorated from worry and lack of rest. Anne showed signs of recovery in early October, but then deteriorated rapidly. She died on 29 October. Her death proved too much for the lawyer who had withstood so many public confrontations. Etienne Dumont, who stayed with Romilly following Anne's death, later attested to the signs of Romilly's internal agony, but he could not have conceived the 'melancholy catastrophe' which ensued.[1] On 2 November, while momentarily unattended by family or physician, Romilly locked his bedchamber door and slit his throat. Although the butler and his doctor reached him before he died, nothing could be done. The Coroner's jury met the next day and quickly reached the verdict that 'the deceased cut his throat while in a state of mental temporary derangement' brought on by his wife's illness and death.[2]

The tragedy struck those on both sides of the criminal law question deeply. The conservative Lord Eldon, upon taking his seat in the Court of Chancery the morning after, noticed the vacant space where Romilly had been accustomed to sit. 'His eyes filled with tears. "I cannot stay here," he exclaimed; and rising in great agitation, he broke up his Court.'[3] The Saints also mourned. James Stephen, who lost his first wife in 1796, and his second in 1816, wrote Wilberforce a letter full of self-reproach for having delayed a visit to Romilly; he empathized deeply with Romilly's violent emotions, and felt that perhaps he might have comforted him. Wilberforce responded briefly, that Romilly's death gave him much to say, yet rendered him incapable of saying it.[4] Stephen considered Romilly's death a severe loss to the antislavery movement as well as to law reform, one bereft even of the comfort of knowing that Romilly's spiritual state was secure. The *Christian Observer* called Romilly 'one whom we most highly venerated', and his death reminded one of the vanities of life and the need to make known the promises of the gospel, especially to the suffering.[5] The Evangelicals were not alone in drawing religious lessons from Romilly's death. The leading Unitarian minister, Thomas Belsham, published a sermon prompted by the suicide, which found the mortality of man strikingly exemplified by the removal of 'the wise, the venerable, and the good'.[6]

Looking back on the period of the Regency from mid century, the Duke of Buckingham and Chandos recalled, 'No death excited so profound an impression, as that of Sir Samuel Romilly ... he was a great loss to the party, and as a legal reformer, a loss to the nation'.[7] Few barristers of the period received as many posthumous accolades and public declarations of remorse at their passing as Romilly. Certainly the death of Lord Ellenborough a few weeks later failed to produce such a sympathetic public effusion. Romilly's persevering initiative in bringing forward bills to amend the hanging statutes between 1808 and 1818, as well as his influence on prison reform, have made it natural for historians to use him as the focus in discussing the political battle over the criminal laws. The reform of the penal code was certainly larger than Romilly, but it may well have been Romilly's death which quickened the enthusiasm of those interested in restricting the death penalty. Lessening the severity of the Bloody Code was no longer the hopeful wish of a small minority; it had become the expectation of a large enough portion of politicians and their constituents that it was now a mainstream idea, if not yet a majority opinion. In these same years, the pressure of numbers on the courts made it necessary to pardon an increasing portion of offenders, generating further inconsistencies and making the existing statutes appear all the more unreasonable to the partisans of reform.

In the immediate aftermath of Romilly's death, it was unclear who would rise up to press the cause. Romilly's closeness to the Whig leadership, indicated by the presence of Henry Brougham and Lord Lansdowne among the bearers at his funeral,[8] suggested that penal reforms might become more of a party issue than Romilly would have wished. Though devoted to the Whigs through friendship and commitment to the ideals of civil and religious liberty, Romilly never considered his cause an exclusively Whig interest. His recurrent stimulation of the issue, however, always contained an inherent criticism of the party in power. Unless an independently minded member took up the cause, the Whigs seemed the likely source of direction. Had Buxton already been in the Commons, he might well have taken up the cause, as he would the abolition of slavery when Wilberforce retired in 1825. But his newness to the Parliament, and the fact that he was not a lawyer, precluded his candidacy. Wilberforce himself seemed a natural candidate. As he introduced a petition calling for changes in the criminal code in early February 1819, Wilberforce eulogized Romilly and called upon the public to rally behind repealing the hanging statutes.[9] Some of his supporters took him to mean he was taking the issue upon his own shoulders. The influential Evangelical clergyman Charles Simeon wrote that he rejoiced 'that the revision of our laws is, as far as the bringing of it before parliament goes, committed to you'.[10] Simeon knew that Wilberforce had none of Romilly's legal expertise, but felt he had more practical wisdom in politics, and thought his leadership would not 'give undue advantage to licentious Jacobins', since the statesman's conservative social attitudes were well known. Simeon's enthusiasm was proof that law reform had the support of many Evangelical clergymen, but Wilberforce's reply revealed that he knew his own limits well. He told Simeon that he was not equal to the task; his eyes were getting worse, and he could write but little.[11] His speech was intended to help another come forward, though Wilberforce's support for penal reforms never wavered.

In the event, the only real candidates did indeed come from the ranks of the Whig faithful. The two most obvious were Brougham and Sir James Mackintosh. Both had participated in the debates on the penal laws; both had written about the importance of legal reform. Of the two, Brougham was the more politically ambitious, which made Mackintosh hesitate before pursuing the issue; Sir James feared that asking Brougham about the matter 'might suggest to him what he had not before thought of'.[12] But Mackintosh was for many reasons a better choice for leadership. He had a claim to longer familiarity with Romilly's plans, their friendship dating back to the early 1790s, and so could provide a sense of continuity. He had, furthermore, not only practiced law in the criminal courts, but had served as a judge, albeit in the distant colonial courts of Bombay. Mackintosh had also broadened the debate on capital punishments by his inquiry into the prevention of forgeries in 1818. Finally, his style in debate was less polemical, or at least less blatantly partisan, than Brougham's; he tried to find common ground to build on. The matter was not settled until January 1819, after Mackintosh had been queried by Henry Grey Bennet, an MP who was pressing for prison reforms, in a way that required 'at least a specific answer'.[13] With the encouragement of Lord Holland, Mackintosh 'answered Bennet's call almost expressly in the affirmative'.[14] By the beginning of February, others beyond the Whig leadership also expected Mackintosh to come forward, as Wilberforce told Simeon that he anticipated his call would be answered by Sir James. As Mackintosh was preparing to bring the matter forward, events outside Parliament nearly overtook his actions and made them appear more like a response to popular demand than Romilly's ever had.

Petitions for change

Beyond the halls of Westminster a petition campaign was begun by the Corporation of the City of London, though the mobilization effort showed more than a little influence from members of the Capital Punishment Society. In 1818 Samuel Hoare, Jr., had asked some fellow bankers and commercial leaders to consider putting forward petitions. The CPS leadership then decided to encourage all members to pursue this end.[15] It was a strategy that had worked well in the anti-slave trade campaign, but until 1817 the CPS had not had the resources to promote such an effort. When the leadership started encouraging provincial associations in 1817, it greatly extended its powers of agitation. When petitions for criminal law reform poured into Parliament in 1819, many came from localities with provincial societies.

The London petition was prompted by a speech by Samuel Favell to the Court of Common Council on 10 December 1818. Favell was a member of the Council and a recognized leader of orthodox Dissent.[16] He had called for the meeting expressly to consider a petition regarding the criminal laws. Favell's language suggested he was sympathetic to Evangelical views, and he confidently declared that the laws, 'being opposed to religious consideration and moral feeling', became inoperative because the actions of prosecutors, judges and juries circumvented the statutes.[17] Echoing Romilly's arguments, Favell insisted laws should be enforced as they were written, and mitigation 'should be rare'. This could only happen if the sanctions of the written code coincided with the general temper of the population. Favell went beyond Romilly's targets, proposing an overall revision of the criminal code. The speech also contained examples of opinions and facts from various CPS publications, especially Montagu's collection of *Opinions* and Buxton's inquiry into English prisons, and he acknowledged his debt to both authors, as well as to Stephen Lushington and Thomas Forster, also members of the Capital Punishment Society, in the published version of his speech.[18]

The London petition, presented to the House of Commons on 25 January, was less specific in its proposals than Favell's address, but it incorporated some of his examples and arguments.[19] It asked Parliament to bring the laws more into line with the 'moral and religious sentiments of the nation', lest crime should increase because of a 'tenderness for life ... originating in the mild precepts of our religion'. As things were, the state of the law produced 'evasions dangerous to the community', and would continue to produce them, because the evasions were not based simply on the sentiments of individuals, but

> upon certain and general principles of our nature, upon the advanced state of civilisation in the country, and upon the diffusion of Christianity, by which we are daily taught to 'love each other as brethren, and to desire not the death of a sinner, but rather that he should turn from his wickedness and live'.

The appeal to the 'state of civilisation' and the 'diffusion' of Christianity had a distinctly Evangelical sound, reminiscent of Wilberforce's address in 1810 in support of Romilly's shoplifting bill, while the reminder to love one another and desire not the death of a sinner echoed the morning and evening prayers of the Anglican prayer book.[20] The petitioners thereby linked the practical need for law reform to the appeals of Christianity, portraying the hanging statutes as relics of the barbaric and pagan past, which the progress of civilization and true religion had rendered obsolete. The petition did not specify alternative punishments, asking the House merely to adopt whatever measures it deemed appropriate, but its expectations were for sanctions which, because they were milder, might be more regularly enforced. From one viewpoint, then, the request from London was for more punishment, in the hope that more temperate penalties would lead to the correction and rehabilitation of the offender.

The petition from London's Common Council opened the way for others. Between 25 January and 1 June, 76 additional petitions pleading for revision of the criminal laws were received in the House of Commons.[21] Some came from small towns and parishes like Ross in Herefordshire or Madeley in Shropshire; others arrived from larger boroughs and cities, like Norwich, Portsmouth, and Bristol. The signatories ranged from the 'Mayor and Inhabitants' of Guildford or Bedford, to 'Merchants and Manufactures' of Bradford, to 'divers Freeholders and other Inhabitants of the County of Essex'. A second petition from Bedfordshire was sent to Parliament signed by the Grand Jurors at the Lent Assize, held in

March 1819. The variety of professional backgrounds and the geographical range of the sources of the petitions defied simple categorization, and no one group could have been credited, or blamed, for their initiation. That Quaker and Evangelical correspondents of the Capital Punishment Society were behind some of them is certain; but the origins of many others remain unclear.[22] Most of the new petitions declared belief in the principle of certainty over severity, and their wording often reflected other portions of the London petition as well. They tended to fall into two groups: those stressing moral or religious objections to the existing statutes, and those simply objecting to the severity of the written law because it did not promote good order. Law and order issues easily merged with concern for religion and the humane treatment of convicts; good moral order and humanity were both assumed to be part of civil society. Not surprisingly then, many petitions expressly put forward the reformation of offenders as preferable to their extermination.

One of the more controversial petitions, and the only one besides London's to be reported in full by Hansard in 1819, came from the Quakers. It had originated in the annual meeting of the Society of Friends, and J. J. Gurney had prevailed on Wilberforce to present it in the House of Commons, which he was glad to do on 9 February. The petition was similar to London's in insisting that the frequency of the punishment of death was 'repugnant to the mild and benevolent principles of the Christian religion'; it was controversial because of its optimism in proclaiming that 'were these principles received and acted upon to their full extent, were the genuine spirit and precepts of the gospel of our Lord Jesus Christ implicitly obeyed, way would ultimately be made for the abolition of this practice in all cases'.[23] The petition's request was more circumspect, though still ambitious: it prayed that 'such a change may be effected in our penal code, as may, whilst it shall secure the ends of justice, imprint on it the characters of Christian mercy, righteousness, and love, the firmest bulwarks of society and government'. Some chose to hear the more extreme of these two statements, portraying the petition and the cause it promoted as visionary and unrealistic. Mackintosh later declared that the petition had 'been hardly dealt by' because of its speculation about a future in which the death penalty might be dispensed with: 'The hope thus expressed, has exposed these respectable petitioners to be treated with levity.'[24] The suggestion that the petition caused laughter or lessened the momentum begun by the Corporation of London must be balanced by the fact that Wilberforce's commendation of the Quakers' promotion of 'any cause favorable to the interests of humanity' received a warm response in the House. Wilberforce also used the opportunity to deliver a short but powerful eulogy on Romilly, which provoked cheers from all sides of the Commons. Although he recorded in his diary that 'my plan did very ill', he reported to J. J. Gurney that he nonetheless found 'a very sympathising audience'.[25] Another diarist present at the debate was Charles Greville, who wrote that Wilberforce's speech 'reminded one of the better days of the House of Commons'.[26] Had the effect of the speech and the petition been as negative as some historians have claimed, one as sensitive to political winds as Mackintosh would not have chosen to follow Wilberforce's speech with a notice of his intention to make a motion on the criminal laws.[27]

Wilberforce's speech revealed more of his perspective on penal matters. He lamented that so little improvement had been accomplished since the days of John Howard, despite much writing on crime and punishment. He then tried to focus the issue at hand:

> It had not been sufficiently considered that the moral improvement of offenders ought to be the first great object, and that capital punishment would be rendered less frequent most effectually by diminishing the disposition and the motives to crime.[28]

This statement echoed his comments to Wyvill in 1787, that the most effective way to prevent greater crimes was to punish the smaller, but he now provided an enlarged explanation. For Wilberforce, the reformation of manners in 1819 meant not only instruction in what is right, but addressing the circumstances that led to doing wrong, 'diminishing the disposition and the motives to crime'. His participation in numerous 'bettering' societies, and his concern for vocational as well as spiritual training in the prisons, showed the nature of Wilberforce's ideas. He was not an advocate of alteration in the social system, but his assessment contained a more complex understanding of human motivation than those who held that 'terror' was sufficient to discourage crime. If both views accepted a man's ability to calculate the potential outcome of his deeds, Wilberforce was more sensitive to habits and environments which fostered criminal activity. His reasons for desiring a more certain, less severe, infliction of punishment related to his belief that sinners could 'turn from their wickedness and live'. The ideal 'turning' was repentance and spiritual revival, but for Wilberforce and his followers the reformation of manners, with or without conversion, held certain advantages for this world which execution obviously removed. In his February address Wilberforce also accepted his share of the shame of having neglected what he now saw as an imperative reform of the English legal system. But he was not alone in this shame; the 'legislature had been criminal itself' and 'had abandoned its duty' by failing to address the obvious inadequacies of the penal system. Guilt had grown, 'and the only atonement which [the legislature] could make to the country was by seriously applying itself to the subject, and endeavouring to diminish the evils which had grown up under the present melancholy system'. These were strong words, evidence of why some, then and since, have described Wilberforce as the voice of the country's conscience in the Commons.

The flow of politics

The influx of dozens of petitions intensified public attention on the efforts to ameliorate England's penal system. Toward the close of the previous session, Lord Lansdowne had moved for papers respecting the state of prisons to be prepared and presented to the House of Lords. Early in 1819 the Home Secretary Lord Sidmouth intimated that a committee for consideration of the returns would be appointed. In January George Canning had given notice on behalf of Lord Castlereagh that copies of the prison papers would be laid before the Commons as well; Castlereagh also planned to move for the appointment of a committee of inquiry.[29] Canning, who had spoken in support of Romilly's bills on several occasions, was now a member of the Cabinet, and his presence meant the Government could no longer oppose criminal law reform. Its next best move was to control the direction and extent of reform by taking up the issues in committees under their control. On 25 February, Sidmouth made his motion in the Lords for the appointment of a select committee to consider the papers on the prisons and gaols. Castlereagh made his motion in the Commons on 1 March.[30]

Castlereagh intended to persuade the Commons that the full range of issues connected to amending the penal laws should be dealt with by one committee, so that the several parts of the penal system might be made a more harmonious whole. Debate of Mackintosh's motion for a select committee to consider the criminal laws had already been scheduled for 2 March, but Castlereagh hoped to remove the argument for a second committee. He repeatedly asserted that there was no material difference between his goal and Mackintosh's and went so far as to state his confidence that the committee should, with the help of Sir James, Gray Bennett, Buxton and others, 'be enabled to devise the means of improving the merciful character of our laws, and promoting the salutary diminution of punishments'. A second committee, Castlereagh claimed, looking only at the criminal laws, would make the work of the judges more difficult by raising doubts about the existing laws, and might lead to outright denunciation of those laws were it not first shown that secondary punishments could be made available and effective. While willing to accept reformation of offenders as a goal for prison discipline, he still asserted that the 'great, the only object of punishment was to deter'. Castlereagh's speech was an implicit admission by the conservative ministry that the penal system was flawed, though the he never explicitly admitted that the capital statutes themselves were part of the problem. Indeed, his repeated reference to the gaols, prisons and transportation as forms of 'secondary' punishment proved he still considered hanging a primary deterrent against crime, rather than a sanction of last resort.

Castlereagh presented practical explanations for facts recorded so plainly in the Home Office returns. He attributed the increase in crimes following peace with France to the decrease in demands for commodities used in war, which left many unemployed, and to the return of thousands of soldiers, including many who had served for a decade or more, whose habits were no longer those of civilians involved in commercial trade. The reformers accepted that the conditions Castlereagh described contributed greatly to the problem of crime, but this did little to preserve the conservative view of the laws. Castlereagh had noted that while crimes against property had increased, crimes of violence had in fact lessened, a division which seemed to argue for a similar division in the categories of punishment. Further, since the increase in crimes was traceable to factors other than the laws themselves, one could not very well argue that the increase was a reason against the revision of the capital code or that such revision would necessarily produce a further rise in crime.

Those most in favor of reform found many other points of discord with Castlereagh. He had portrayed them as pursuing impractical ends and accused them of defining the sources of crime too narrowly, which they denied. Buxton objected strongly to the accusation that he saw, or had ever described, the failures of prison discipline as the *chief* reason for the increase in crimes. The proponents of reform readily admitted the importance of alternative punishments, though they deferred offering lengthy comments until the next day, when Mackintosh would bring forward his motion. Castlereagh's committee included most of the major players, including Mackintosh, Buxton, Wilberforce, Bennett, and Brougham. Among the supporters of the Government, the committee included the Attorney General, Canning, Sir William Scott (Lord Eldon's brother), and George Holford. Castlereagh's allies outnumbered the ardent reformers, but their presence meant that the committee would get the most persuasive evidence for the amelioration of prison discipline.[31]

Much of what Castlereagh said for his committee on 1 March was really directed against Mackintosh's motion for a separate inquiry on the criminal laws on 2 March. Mackintosh had long pondered his approach to the motion for a committee on the criminal laws. He had prepped and marshalled the Whig MPs, who certainly showed more support for him than they had for Romilly. To avoid making the issue look partisan, Mackintosh consciously sought help outside the party. The most obvious and influential source of support was the Saints, now including Buxton. He solicited and received Wilberforce's promise to second his motion for the committee.[32] Wilberforce's commitment gave the motion two added sources of strength. Mackintosh was known for his philosophical lectures and writing, and this would have tended to make the speculative element in penal reform seem more prominent than he desired. Wilberforce was known for his conservative social view, and his second diminished any charge of social innovation levelled against the committee. At the same time, Wilberforce's moral and humanitarian concerns added an appeal which few politicians could afford to dismiss outright. Wilberforce genuinely liked Mackintosh, and was eager to see the committee established. His assistance also served to bring Buxton more quickly into a leading position.

Having secured an appropriate second, Mackintosh was provided tactical entry for his motion on 2 March when Charles Wynn asked whether Lord Castlereagh intended to subdivide his committee, which he seemed to have intimated the night before, but which was contrary to the rules and practice of Parliament. Castlereagh quickly denied any intention to break with custom, but stated that his committee would be arranged in a manner best suited to the inquiry. Wynn pressed the matter and appealed for a discussion on procedure. The Speaker concurred that the charge to a committee was a charge to every member on it, meaning that one could not split a committee up into smaller groups, each responsible only for a part of the orders given the committee as a whole.[33] The ruling having been heard, Mackintosh stood up immediately to move for a separate committee on the criminal laws. He gave two reasons for the second committee. First, it would be physically impossible for Castlereagh's committee to carry out both the inquiry on the prisons and that on the reform of the penal code, and return a full report in a reasonable time. Second, the charge to the prison committee did not include what Mackintosh had in mind: 'to consider so much of the

Criminal Laws as relates to Capital Punishment in Felonies, and to report their observations and opinion thereon to the House'.[34] Mackintosh took the wording almost verbatim from a resolution of the House of Commons in 1770, whose precedent Mackintosh hoped would shelter his proceeding.[35] The scope of the committee was therefore limited, and its goal could be accomplished in a limited time. It differed from Castlereagh's broader and purposely hazier objective, because it focused exclusively on the efficacy, or inefficacy, of capital punishments.

Mackintosh thanked Castlereagh for his comments the preceding day, which relieved him of proving that an investigation into the operation of the criminal laws was necessary. Instead, Mackintosh listed the parliamentary precedents for an inquiry and discussed the opinions of the great legal writers of the eighteenth century, who had all favored amelioration. The proliferation of capital statutes in the same period was evidence of the one inconvenience of the triumph of parliamentary government in 1688: the ease of making new laws. As Mackintosh put it, a member of Parliament could often indulge his whims and caprices, 'and if he could not do any thing else, he could create a capital felony'.[36] Yet the evidence of the returns showed that in the same period, juries and judges were sending fewer and fewer to execution. Mackintosh repeated Romilly's charge that the practice of the law was contrary to the written statutes, because the statutes were contrary to the dominant opinion of the country. He was personally appalled that anyone could be executed for forgery, or any crime simply against property, and agreed that these offenses proliferated precisely because victims of crime, judges and juries were similarly appalled. The Commons was quite familiar with this Blackstonian argument by now, and Mackintosh assured his listeners that he had no intention of considering the abolition of capital punishment. Rather, he proposed to break the capital laws into three classes: those like murder and assault, which entailed a clear threat to human life; those like arson, highway robberies and piracies, which, while primarily offenses against property, carried with them the implicit threat against the person; and those that formed the majority of capital statutes, ranging from frauds to specific forms of larceny to 'the most frivolous and fantastic' of crimes, mentioning in particular crimes from the Black Act, like breaking down the banks of a fish-pond, or bearing arms at night while in black face. Mackintosh desired no change of punishment for the first two classes, nor thought it prudent even to consider. But the third class, where the punishment of death was pronounced yet seldom carried out, presented many opportunities for amendment.

Castlereagh praised Mackintosh's temperate presentation, and tried to blunt its impact by repeating his concerns for the judges' ability to implement the laws were the second committee appointed and for the need to have effective secondary punishments in place *before* the repeal of capital statutes – he blamed the failure of Romilly's bills in the Lords on their lacking a sanction as effective as the 'terror occasioned by the infliction of the capital penalty'. But Castlereagh's repeated agreement that laws needed investigation, and his willingness to consider changes that might lead 'to the improvement of morals, and to the diminution of crime', weakened his case. His support was further undermined by Buxton, who rose next to speak. This was not his first speech in the Commons, but this was his first real opportunity to lay before the House his facts and arguments in complete array; he felt much of his future service rested on whether he succeeded in moving his listeners.[37] Compared to the smooth current of Mackintosh's speech, Buxton's was a waterfall, powerful and full of the fury of enthusiasm and hard evidence. He set out to show 'that one source of crime, and a most prolific one, is our criminal laws'.[38] He had three basic arguments: first, that most of the capital statutes were of recent creation, and therefore could not be defended as part of the 'ancient law of England': second, that most of these laws were at variance with natural justice and revealed religion; and third, that they were practically inoperable, and therefore impolitic. Mackintosh had used anecdote to illustrate the passage of hanging statutes; Buxton counted the statutes and put them into time periods. This more than proved his ally's assertion that most capital crimes had become so since the Revolution. Out of 223 crimes from which the benefit of clergy had been removed, 156 had been enacted since the accession of the House of Brunswick. The only innovation he proposed, Buxton declared, was 'the old law of England!' His moral arguments rested on a simple query which conceded that in cases of murder, the natural and biblical mandate for punishment would be death, but on what principle could one base an argument for execution in other crimes? Proportionality of punishment to the severity of a criminal act seemed to him almost instinctive. When a murderer was hanged, the public felt that justice was done; but when a forger or petty thief suffered the same, the crowd reacted with a cry of murder. Buxton agreed:

> – they express my feelings at least, for I deny the justice of that warrant – I impeach the equity of that sentence; I acknowledge, that legislators may determine upon property and possessions, and ten thousand other circumstances; but life is sacred, and may not be invaded without the express permission of Him who gave it.

He commented that ideas so novel, 'or, more properly, antiquated' as his might not quickly persuade the gentlemen who heard them, but he thought the House would be convinced by the facts against the policy of the laws. To the evidence of partial verdicts and frequent reprieves for crimes without violence, Buxton added examples from his personal experience with juvenile offenders in the London jails. He answered those who asserted the deterrent value of the supposed terror of the punishment of death with examples to the contrary. He knew of a gang, one of whose members had been caught and sentenced to death. The other members showed no sign of fear, and they were eventually arrested for a larceny committed within two weeks of their acquaintance's hanging. The lack of sobering effect could also be inferred by the absence of solemnity during any public execution.

Buxton's speech contained little speculation, and his anxiety about his competence to speak proved unjustified. Several praised him for his practical research. John Smith, a Nottingham banker and Wilberforce's cousin, called the arguments 'unanswerable'. William Smith wrote that Buxton 'had acquitted himself to universal satisfaction', and that few had made such an impressive début.[39] Wilberforce also praised the speech, and observed the changed tone of debate from that which he had heard a decade earlier; gone were those arguments against any and every alteration of old laws and customs. Only Canning gave anything approaching a defense of the Ministry's plan. He pointed to his consistent, often ardent, support of Romilly's measures as reason for trusting that Castlereagh's committee would deal adequately with the issue of capital punishments, but he defended the notion that such punishments did deter crime and rearticulated the conservative position that changes ought to be gradual, practical, and linked with the reform of secondary punishments. He failed to persuade the House, though, which voted 147 to 128 in favor of Mackintosh's motion. Twenty-two members were appointed to the committee, seven of whom also served on the prison committee, including Mackintosh, Buxton, Wilberforce, Holford and Brougham. The committee had a whiggish tilt and included some younger members, like Lord John Russell and Viscount Althorp, whose efforts in matters of reform would become more evident in the 1820s and 1830s.

Mackintosh's committee lacked a member who could guarantee the Government's support of their findings and recommendations. Speculations in counter-history often carry an element of the wistful, but one must ask whether the Government would have felt a greater obligation to carry penal law reform earlier had the inquiries remained in one committee. For all the strong words and arresting rhetorical examples, the battle over the committee on the criminal laws was not really about separating the inquiry into effective secondary punishments from the inquiry into the supposed ineffectiveness of the capital statutes. The reformers' participation on both committees proved that. The essential points at issue were who would control the investigation into the capital statutes themselves, and how would the questions be put? Would it be a Government known to favor the preservation of as much of the existing system as possible, or those who favored real restrictions on the ultimate sanction? One might argue that Castlereagh's proposal could have led to a larger systemic change than the specific challenge to the capital statutes, because he proposed to implement a coordinated structure. Furthermore, without Government support, the committee on criminal laws stood little chance of success in the upper house. But had Mackintosh accepted Castlereagh's arguments for one inquiry, the investigation into the capital statutes would likely have been muted. For many conservatives, the 'terror' of the threat of death was still a given, and to question its effectiveness was to challenge its legitimacy in all cases. The effectiveness and the legitimacy of the punishment of death were separable questions, however, and the committee on the criminal laws limited itself to the first. Still, its appointment in 1819, with the help of conservative Evangelical moral reformers, inherently questioned the reasonable extent of the state's authority over life and death. Whatever the outcome of its investigation, the existence of the committee on the criminal laws represented a major shift in the battle over the capital statutes.

The Report of the 1819 Committee

By the end of the first week of March 1819, Parliament had three inter-related inquiries underway into the operation of the penal laws of Great Britain, two in the Commons and one in the Lords. Expectations were high. The *Christian Observer* considered the vote for Mackintosh's committee on the capital statutes proof that the question was above party, and that the substantive reform 'so universally desired by the nation' might soon become reality.[40] The *Edinburgh* and *Eclectic Reviews* published articles asserting the strong claims the subject had on the 'deliberate consideration of Parliament' and looking forward to the 'great Inquest of the nation'.[41] Hoping to guide that inquest, new authors joined the pamphlet war. Former Whig MP and promoter of the arts William Roscoe published a small book on penal law and the reformation of offenders. Roscoe's work went through two editions in 1819 (and would have a third in the 1820s) and was notable both for its review of the successes and failures of the emerging penitentiary system in America and for its absolute rejection of capital punishment. Since the only 'proper object of human punishment is the reformation of the offender,' Roscoe reasoned, 'it will follow as a necessary consequence that it is not allowable under any combination of circumstances to put a fellow creature to death.'[42] This language was even stronger than the Quakers' petition, and few followed Roscoe's extreme line. J. E. Bicheno, a barrister of the Middle Temple and correspondent of the Capital Punishment Society, hoped to apply the 'principles of political economy' to the criminal law and acknowledged inspiration from both Bentham and the Evangelical minister Thomas Gisborne, whose *Principles of Moral Philosophy Investigated* he quoted extensively. Like Gisborne, Bicheno doubted the morality of punishment as an example and argued that only the right of self-defense could support the punishment of death, which restricted it 'to the fewest possible cases'.[43] In addition to these, Buxton's speech was printed and circulated by the friends of reform.[44]

The pamphlets and articles, along with the petitions laid almost daily before the Commons, raised the expectations for criminal law reform greatly. Such hopes could hardly be met, but the desire not to disappoint them entirely compelled the Select Committee on the Criminal Laws to bring forth an agenda as soon as practicable. When Mackintosh presented the Report on 6 July 1819, he declared that the committee had been thorough in their investigations, but not exhaustive; the work had really just begun.[45] Aside from the Report itself, little has been left for the historian to evaluate the operation of the Select Committee on the Criminal Laws. Mackintosh served as faithfully as he could as its chairman, but he was troubled by health problems, and in early June Buxton had taken the chair to question the remaining witnesses. If anything, Buxton was more enthusiastic for the inquiry than Mackintosh, and his personal involvement with prisoners convinced him of both the inefficacy of the penal laws and the urgency of their reform. As the committee got started, Buxton wrote,

> I conjecture that no man on the committee goes so far as I go – namely, to the abolition of the punishment of death, except for murder; but all go a very great way, and if we merely make forgery, sheep and horse stealing, not capital, it is an annual saving of thirty lives, which is something, and satisfies me in devoting my time to it.[46]

Devote time he did, to both the committee on the criminal laws and to Castlereagh's committee on prisons and jails; he wrote to a friend in Ireland that he gave a full three mornings a week to each.[47]

The Report of the Select Committee on the Criminal Laws made recommendations for reform based upon the committee's examination of sixty-one individuals and an unprecedented array of criminal statistics, but its proposals were far more conservative than the rhetoric which put them forward.[48] The investigation had definite strengths and weaknesses. The committee broke new ground in many ways, and its methods suffered from the lack of precedent. At the same time, committee members had greater freedom to display opinions than would later be possible when the gathering of evidence had been more fully taken over by specialists and bureaucrats. The heavy presence of witnesses from commercial backgrounds was justified by the argument that those involved in trade, whether as merchants, brokers or bankers, were the ones most able to describe the effect of the laws with which the committee proposed to deal. But these were not the only witnesses. Eleven of the sixty-one giving evidence were court clerks or government officials summoned to verify and complete the returns requested by the committee; these were published in the appendices to the Report and contained all the available information on the commitments, convictions and executions in England and Wales since the middle of the eighteenth century. These statistics documented both the growth of the Bloody Code and the changes in the patterns of punishment.[49] They provided the empirical basis for the committee's recommendations regarding obsolete and little-remembered statutes.

Other witnesses included clerks from various magistrates' offices in the metropolis. London had stipendiary magistrates, but their legal expertise was still relatively low. It was the clerks of the Lord Mayor of London and the sitting magistrates in Guildhall, Worship Street, and Whitechapel who held the 'institutional' knowledge about the practice of law enforcement; they were among the first to know of crimes and were responsible for beginning the record of prosecutions. When a victim suspected someone, or brought the suspect to a magistrate, the clerks were the ones responsible for clarifying the laws and recording what the charge would be. It was at this point that a victim would most likely weigh the question of whether to prosecute capitally or otherwise, or not at all. Other witnesses who could testify about the early stages of criminal prosecutions included T. W. Carr, the Solicitor for Excise, William Lewis Newman, Solicitor of the City of London, and Patrick Colquhoun, who had served as magistrate in Westminster since the early 1790s. Colquhoun had advocated police reform for over 20 years and his writings had been quoted by Montagu. Even among the men of commerce, several had served as sheriff, magistrate, or grand juror and a few had been petty jurors also; one, Sir Richard Phillips, a bookseller with a radical leaning, had at some point been all of these, and based his testimony on his frequent appointment as a juryman at the Old Bailey. Thus, while the selection of witnesses was by no means exhaustive, any accusation that they had little background in the actual functioning of the laws was off the mark.

The charge of 'lack of expertise' was raised because the Select Committee chose not to interview any sitting justices of the Crown. The Report explained that the committee did not call them because it

> appeared unbecoming and inconvenient that those whose office it is to execute the Criminal Law should be called on to give an opinion whether it ought to be altered. As the Judges could not with propriety censure what they might soon be obliged to enforce, they could scarcely be considered as at liberty to deliver an unbiased opinion.[50]

Mackintosh knew the absence of judicial testimony would weaken the Report, and in his summary to the House of Commons he tried to fortify the explanation for excluding the judges: 'Not being free to condemn [the law], their commendation, had they commended it, would have had no weight; for what value can attach to praise when there is no liberty to censure?'[51] The *Quarterly Review* later called this a 'a mistaken delicacy' and considered the omission of the judges' opinions a major flaw.[52] The appearance that the committee heard only those who already agreed with them was hard to overcome; in 1821 the Solicitor General charged that the 1819 Committee had failed to seek the testimony of 'persons of opposite opinion'.[53]

Perhaps the best justification for excluding the judges was not their possible conflict of interest, but one put forward by one of the witnesses, George Boulton Mainwaring, a magistrate for the county of Middlesex. Mainwaring argued that magistrates and their clerks had better opportunity to observe the influence of the laws on the minds of prosecutors 'than those who see the cases in their last stages, where the parties are compelled to proceed'.[54] This explanation was well supported in the testimony to the committee, which centered less on the administration of the criminal laws and more on the state of public opinion about how the capital statutes affected the prosecution of offenders. This was the Report's greatest strength. Bankers recounted incidents where prosecutions for forgeries had been avoided because of the victims' discomfort at exposing the known perpetrator to capital punishment. Men involved in trade described their reluctance to bring thieves before the magistrates because of the harshness of the laws. Others spoke of more domestic crimes: Dr Stephen Lushington told the committee that he refrained from prosecuting a servant he knew to be stealing from him, because he 'could not induce [himself] to run the risk of taking away the life of a man' for thievery.[55] Certainly the individuals who gave such testimony had not been randomly selected; at least 9 of the 61 witnesses had been supporters or organizers of the Capital Punishment Society; two others were leading members of the Prison Discipline Society.[56] They were none-the-less respected and often well-known members of their professions; their evidence enabled the committee to point to real individuals and specific instances, in which the harshness of the laws prevented prosecutions. The press, both popular and 'respectable', seized upon these examples, which gave weight to the argument against severity as a deterrent, and deployed them against those who denied the frequency of jury verdicts contrary to the evidence.[57]

Given the strong language of the Report, its actual recommendations were rather timid. The Report listed twelve felonies the committee considered obsolete, obscure, or aimed at purely local abuses.[58] These it proposed should be removed altogether or, if still a public nuisance, made simple misdemeanors at common law. In addition, the Report identified fifteen offenses 'never fit to be punished with Death' that were 'yet so malignant and dangerous as to require the highest punishments except death', and recommended transportation or imprisonment with hard labor as fit alternatives.[59] In the area of larceny, the committee upheld Romilly's intention to repeal capital punishment for theft from shops, homes and river vessels, but also suggested that the laws regarding larceny needed a comprehensive overhaul. The laws on forgery created the most conflict for the committee. Because of the testimony of bankers and merchants regarding forgery prosecutions, the Report recommended replacing the capital punishment with transportation or imprisonment on a first offense, but proposed retaining the death penalty for repeat offenders.[60] The forgery of Bank of England notes, however, would remain 'on the same footing with the metallic currency', an exception the committee recommended with 'great pain and reluctance' and with a plea for a more complete review, consolidation and amelioration of all the forgery laws.[61]

The Report constituted no plan for radical reform, and Mackintosh continued to pursue a moderate course. Although ten of the twenty-seven offenses specified as obsolete or overly harsh arose from 9 Geo. II c. 22, the infamous 'Black Act', the Report resisted recommending its simple repeal. Such caution kept the Report 'respectable' precisely because its proposals could be implemented without any extensive restructuring of the laws.[62] The leaders of the committee knew the Report would come too late in the year to consider bills that session, and Mackintosh told the Commons he would introduce legislation early in the next.[63] Although these measures would include multiple offenses in comparison to Romilly's practice of one amending statute for each impractical capital statute, the method was basically the same – an incremental and specific alteration of the laws, rather than a complete reordering and categorization of criminal offenses. Critics of the Report might pick at its specifics, but the recommendations presented little that had not been considered before and were certainly less than some on the committee would like to have seen.

The politics of implementation

The Report generated much interest in the weeks after its presentation, but the momentum it gained for the reform effort was mitigated by the events in Manchester in mid August and the subsequent debates on 'Peterloo' which followed. Most issues of reform suffered under the weight of the Six Acts. Buxton's conclusions were typical of the Evangelical leaders. He wrote to J. J. Gurney, 'I voted with the ministers because I cannot bring myself to subject the Manchester Magistrates to a parliamentary inquiry; but nothing has shaken my conviction that the Magistrates, Ministers & all have done exceedingly wrong.'[64] Evangelical support for the ministers at this time, even if reluctant, seriously damaged the Saints' reputations as partisans of reform; Wilberforce's support of the Government prompted William Hazlitt's oft repeated remark, 'What have the *Saints* to do with freedom or reform of any Kind?'[65] Nonetheless, Wilberforce and his allies looked forward to pursuing penal reform; Buxton in particular listed as primary among his goals for 1820 'to assist to the best of my ability in Parliament to amend our Criminal Code' and 'to amend our Prisons'.[66] The death of King George III and the subsequent dissolution of Parliament and new elections stayed the execution of these plans. Not until the beginning of May was Mackintosh able to bring forward motions to reconstitute the Select Committee on the Criminal Laws and to reintroduce the three bills Romilly had regularly carried through the Commons.[67] Mackintosh also obtained leave to bring in a fourth bill, to consolidate the laws on forgery, which he introduced a few days later, along with the Capital Felonies Punishment bill and the Capital Felonies Repeal bill.[68] The punishment bill included all the statutes deemed in the 1819 Report 'never fit to be punished with death;' the repeal bill dealt with the acts for obscure and obsolete crimes deemed 'so nearly indifferent as to require no penalty' or which could be punished as misdemeanors at common law. Mackintosh soon suspended consideration of the forgery bill and the dwelling house and river vessel robbery bills, because he learned that the law officers intended strongly to oppose them.[69] Instead, he focused his efforts on the shoplifting and capital felonies repeal and punishment bills, which passed their third reading in the Commons on 4 July 1820, with only minor amendments. They would not fare so well in the Lords.

On 17 July, the Marquis of Lansdowne moved the third reading of the Shop-lifting bill.[70] Little was said against it, but Lord Eldon objected to the bill being brought on when the justices were out of the House and insisted that instead of repealing the capital punishment, the value which made a theft capital be raised to £10, which eventually became £15 by the final version of the bill. Objections to the other bills abounded, with particular emphasis placed by Eldon and Redesdale on the continuing need for many of the provisions of the Black Act. The debate was carried over to 18 July when Eldon simply stated his absolute opposition to the inclusion of references to the Black Act, which the Lords agreed to delete from both the repeal bill and the now renamed capital felonies commutation bill. Eldon raised other quibbles, which met with concession, so that of the original eleven statutes listed for repeal, only five survived. With Eldon's amendments, the bills were returned to the Commons and were passed on 24 July, receiving the royal assent the following day. The *Quarterly Review* considered the modifications in the bills so extensive as to render the reforms 'virtually postponed'.[71] Disappointed by the amendments, Mackintosh could still claim more of a victory than the conservatives wished to admit. At one point, concerning fraudulent bankruptcy, Eldon positively stated that 'he had no doubt there were cases in which, on account of the capital punishment, prosecutions had been prevented'.[72] Here was the admission of the basic principle upon which Mackintosh had argued most of his measures, and for the first time the Lord Chancellor had granted the essential point. Rhetorically it would now be hard to backtrack.

Buxton and Wilberforce were relatively quiet in 1820 discussions of the criminal law, though both again served on the select committee.

Buxton's time was sapped by personal tragedy: between 20 March and 1 May, his eldest son and three of his daughters died. In such a circumstance, his energies naturally turned toward the needs of his wife and four surviving children. While his support helped pass reform measures through the Commons, he could do little to affect the outcome in the Lords. As it turned out, Wilberforce's major efforts in 1820 dealt with the affairs of Queen Caroline. George IV had good reason to suspect his estranged wife of infidelity, though his affairs were also well known. The King's efforts to gain a divorce and prevent Caroline's coronation provoked the airing of royal follies in the 'trial' of the Queen in the late summer and autumn, exposing the monarchy to public criticism and unpopularity unequaled until the late twentieth century. Wilberforce sought points of conciliation between the parties and led the Commons in formulating an address to the Queen that would provide a basis for compromise between the royal antagonists. Led to believe the Queen would accept his proposal, Wilberforce was greatly humiliated by her public rejection of the terms, and he received immense abuse from the popular press. Nonetheless, leaders on both sides of the Commons recognized the importance of what the Evangelical leader had tried to accomplish. Lord John Russell published an open letter to Wilberforce in *The Times*, calling him the only man in England who might arbitrate the issue and prevent the trial of the Queen.[73] Russell acknowledged the decisive middle-ground held by the Saints, which allowed them to tip the scales in issues such as penal law reform. Had the matter been one of merely partisan conflict, Russell's call might have worked; unfortunately, this matter involved two uncompromising personalities, and subsequent efforts could not prevent the trial and its consequences. Though relieved by her 'acquittal' in November, Wilberforce lamented the mess the 'Ministers and the Queen's Advisors and the House of Lords altogether made of this sad business'.[74]

The acts passed in 1820 were considerably less than most members of the criminal law committee desired. They had managed to enact about half of the recommendations of the 1819 report, but the dwelling house and navigable river robberies bills remained uncarried, the repeal of the Black Act and the issue of forgery unaffected. By early 1821 the reformers were again mustering. As in 1819, petitions began to flow into the Commons.[75] Following the advice of the committee of 1820, the reformers focused on the punishment for forgery. Mackintosh called for the second reading of the Forgery Punishment Mitigation bill on 23 May, 1821. Buxton presented the initial defense.[76] He employed the findings of the 1819 Report liberally and presented a general examination of the supposed efficacy of capital punishment before focusing on forgery. He began with the issues of deterrence and the 'innovation' of the capital statutes. Noting, with poignant illustration, the varied offenses which could be punished with death ('... kill your father, or a rabbit in a warren, the penalty is the same!'), he tested the conservatives' assertion that the capital statutes prevented crime, which they had themselves proposed was their only legitimation. 'Has crime decreased?' Buxton queried. 'Has it remained stationary? Certainly not. Has it increased? It certainly has, and at a prodigious rate. Why, then, your system has failed!' Buxton illustrated the increase from the collected statistics, countering Castlereagh's arguments by adjusting for the economic conditions following the peace of 1815. He compared statistics for two periods: 1798–1801 and 1814–18. He took four crimes carrying the penalty of death in both periods – highway robbery, burglary, horse stealing and stealing from a dwelling house – and one whose death penalty had been amended in 1811 – stealing from bleaching grounds. The evidence revealed that stealing from bleaching grounds alone of the five crimes had not increased in the intervening years: it had actually decreased by two thirds. In contrast, theft from dwelling houses was ten times more frequent in the later period than in the earlier.

From statistics Buxton moved to a well-developed comparison of contemporary English penal laws with those of other countries, with earlier criminal codes of the Saxons, Danes and Normans, and even with the earlier practice of the common law. The comparison portrayed England's extensive capital statutes as innovations, which forced juries unwilling to see a criminal executed to declare 'their belief in things, not merely very strange or uncommon, but actual physical impossibilities, absolute miracles, wilder than the wildest legends of monkish superstition'. Buxton went further to ask 'what impression on the public mind must be made, if not this – that there are occasions in which it is not only lawful, but commendable, to ask God to witness palpable and egregious falsehood?' Buxton's religious sensitivities recoiled from this, but he told the House he would rather agree with the juries than send men to death for stealing 40 shillings or a sheep. He concluded with an appeal to the mild spirit of the Christian religion, which did not seek the death of the criminal, but his reformation, 'that he should turn from his wickedness and live!'

The power of Buxton's speech was acknowledged by every side. Even the conservative John Miller agreed that Buxton's was 'one of the most powerful and eloquent speeches ever addressed ... in favor of extreme mitigation of punishment', though Miller remained convinced that he was too 'sanguine and enthusiastic'.[77] The *Christian Observer* praised the 'great research and invincible argument' and expressed the hope that Parliament was 'strongly inclining to what has for some time been a very general feeling through the county, respecting the duty of mitigating the severity of the criminal code'.[78] Buxton's use of evidence and good sense convinced Wilberforce that he was the right man to be his confidant and successor in the fight against slavery, as well as carrying on the battle to amend the penal code.[79] For the moment, Buxton's speech helped carry the vote on the bill's second reading in the early morning hours of 24 May, 118 to 74.

On 4 June, two petitions against the bill were presented, signed by bankers in London, Westminster and Bristol.[80] There had been no petitions against any of the previous bills and the timing was crucial – the third reading was scheduled for later in the day. The debate went late into the night and brought several amendments. Some advocates, including Buxton, believed the Ministers had remolded the bill to their liking and left the House thinking that further discussion would be put off until the next day. Unexpectedly, Castlereagh pressed for a vote, 'That the bill do pass'. The stratagem greatly frustrated Mackintosh and his friends, but they could not stay the vote long enough to muster their supporters; the bill failed by six, 121 to 115.[81]

Many observers were disappointed, but most felt the question delayed rather than truly defeated.[82] Indeed, Castlereagh's maneuver had to be seen as a staying action, for the Government knew it would have been defeated in a more straightforward vote. Penal law reform was now a respectable issue, and in pamphlet form Buxton's speech and a new essay by Montagu kept it before the public. These pamphlets mixed the statistics from the Government's own criminal returns with arguments for proportionality and appeals to the teachings of Christianity to make the powerful case that neither reason nor revealed religion supported the existing system. As Montagu put it succinctly, 'The progress of Knowledge and of Christianity has destroyed, and will continue to destroy these mistaken enactments; and the law, however reluctantly, must follow their commands.'[83] His optimism sounded very much like Wilberforce's connection of the spread of Christianity and the refinement of manners, which he had argued in his *Practical View* in 1797. Together with Buxton's appeal to the 'mild spirit of the Christian religion', Montagu's rhetoric revealed just how far the language of the Evangelical revival had shaped the notions for improvement in the penal law. It also gave the reformers a sense that Providence was on their side and that no parliamentary stratagem was sufficient to prevent their eventual victory.

In 1822 the Liverpool Government was reconstructed, but the law officers remained strongly opposed to further criminal law amendments and the right time for new legislation never appeared. Mackintosh and Buxton decided to change tactics. Instead of a specific bill to reform a particular abuse, they sought a more general resolution. On 4 June, a year to the day after the defeat of his forgery bill, Mackintosh moved, 'That this House will, at an early period of the next session, take into their most serious consideration the means of increasing the efficacy of the criminal laws, by abating their undue rigour: together with measures for strengthening the Police, and for rendering the punishment of Transportation and Imprisonment more effectual for the purposes of example and reformation'.[84] Mackintosh appealed to Fox's 1806 motion on the slave trade as a precedent. Predictably, Ministry supporters were unhappy. The motion was opposed by the Attorney General, Sir Robert Gifford, and by Sir Robert Peel, the new Home Secretary, both of whom disliked the resolution's lack of specificity. The motion's second clause acknowledged that the removal of capital punishment had to be linked to the revision of secondary punishments, but Mackintosh decided it made the resolution too broad and dropped it. The defeat of the Government in this vote, 117 to 101, illustrated the importance the Commons now placed on the issue. Just as important, the debate revealed that the new men in the Ministry might well be more willing to entertain reforms than had earlier members. In response to Mackintosh's motion, Peel had informed the House that if the reformers brought forth specific proposals in the next session, they would find in him no 'predetermined opponent'. Whether he would prove an ally had yet to be determined.

9
Consolidation, Mitigation and Conclusions

The vote on the 1822 resolution convinced Sir Robert Peel that ministerial opposition to criminal law reform helped the Whigs and the Radicals portray the Government as out of touch with the wishes of the country. Peel viewed public opinion as a volatile and shifting standard, but he did not think it something political leaders could ignore altogether. At the same time, amending tangled laws appealed to his desire for order and efficiency; he had already indicated his willingness and ability to make reforms as Irish Secretary. Peel's intentions were surely complex, made more so by his practice of hiding his personal beliefs within the boundaries of his political advice. The attempt to understand Peel and his purposes has generated a large and controversial discussion, one which has informed this study, but which is also to the side of the main purpose here.[1] For one of Peel's goals in taking penal law reforms into the Government's hands was to take it out of the realm of public debate. When that happened, the dynamics of reform began to change. This chapter reviews Peel's reforms, but its focus is to draw attention to the reaction to his amendments, when the politics reemerged and public agitation pressed for even greater amelioration. This will lead us to a concluding analysis of the factors that made criminal law reform as much an Evangelical issue as a utilitarian one.

Peel takes charge

When Lord Liverpool notified Peel of a mid-November cabinet meeting to discuss subjects 'likely to be brought forward in [Parliament]', Peel used the opportunity to write down all the issues in which the Home Office had an interest, but especially penal reforms. Peel called it a matter 'which it would be proper for the Government to take into their own hands'.² As he had previously told the Scottish law officers and judges, the climate of opinion made it 'vain... to defend what is established merely because it is established'. One had to have sound arguments, to weigh both sides, and if current practice was found wanting, the best policy was 'to take to ourselves the credit of the Reform, and that by being the authors of it, we should have the best chance of prescribing limits to the Innovation'. The most constructive way for the Ministry to meet Mackintosh's resolution was to consider the question 'in its details', not to argue 'as if there was some criminal code which must be maintained in all its integrity'. Instead, Peel advised that the Government look at all the offenses punishable by death, select those which could be 'safely visited with a mitigated Punishment', and be prepared to defend those for which the death penalty should be maintained. Peel contended that little separated the 'reasonable advocates' of reform from the 'reasonable Defenders' of the laws, and he suggested that those who desired a code of strict proportionality, like those who insisted that no parliamentary act be touched, were 'very limited in number'.

Peel's willingness to look into reforms in part represented the generational change in the Ministry. Castlereagh's suicide in August 1822 added to these changes and might have given Peel broader liberty in considering legal reforms. While he might have empathized with the appeals to humanity, Peel never argued his case for amelioration upon them. His confident and cautious handling of the matter succeeded with Liverpool, and rumors of the Government's decision to sponsor criminal law reforms began to circulate in early 1823. But the specifics were vague; how far were the Ministers prepared to go? Not knowing the answer to this, Mackintosh rose on 21 May to fulfill the previous year's resolution. He spoke at length in introducing nine proposals he intended to serve as foundations for future bills.³ These included repeal of the Black Act, abolition of capital punishment for shoplifting, for theft from houses and ships, for horse, sheep or cattle stealing, and a revision of the forgery laws; another provided for judges to withhold pronouncement of the sentence of death when they did not intend it to be carried out. Peel rose next to give the Government's response. True to his advice to Liverpool, he reviewed the matter in its details. He could not agree with all the proposals, but he conceded 'the necessity of some amendment... the real question between them was only as to degree'. He agreed with the repeal of the Black Act and of many of the larceny laws, and he also approved of giving judges discretion in pronouncing a sentence. However, Peel considered revision in the laws on cattle, sheep and horses 'unwise'. Neither would he support mitigation of the forgery laws, claiming he had reached that conclusion 'from the great number of exceptions' which Mackintosh had 'himself thought necessary', although Mackintosh had allowed them only in the hope of making his proposal more palatable to conservatives. Peel carefully defended judicial discretion and sought to rescue the criminal law from general abuse by portraying the statutes needing amendment as anomalies in an otherwise prudent and coherent system.

Differences emerged quickly over what ought to be considered anomalous statutes. Buxton was disappointed and thought Peel's proposals would 'most imperfectly redeem' the recorded pledge of the house; their operation would not save 'one human life in the course of ten years'. He had dissuaded many persons from sending petitions because he had hoped the ministers would go farther. Conversely, James Scarlett, who had helped draft the 1821 *Forgery Punishment Mitigation Bill*, expressed satisfaction that Peel 'confessed himself a convert to the opinion that severity of punishment was not the most expedient method of repressing crimes', especially when that severity stood against the predominant feelings of the people. While Peel's 'confession' did not convince the Whig and Radical supporters of penal law reform to drop Mackintosh's proposals, it did persuade sufficient numbers of independents and backbench Tories to side with the Ministers. The resolutions were defeated, 76 to 86.

Despite the vote, the debate elicited a pledge from the Home Secretary to ameliorate the laws, and the Government had admitted the need for mitigation. A battle had been lost, but the war over the principles argued by the reformers had essentially been won. Concrete measures were already in the works, and within a week Peel brought in four bills to begin to redeem his pledge.[4] The Felonies bill repealed the Black Act; the Larcenies bill removed capital punishment from shoplifting and several other forms of theft; the Capital Punishments Repeal bill removed death as a penalty from localized abuses, such as fraudulent pensions in Greenwich or frame breaking; and the Sentence of Death bill gave judges the freedom to pronounce a judgment they believed would be carried out. A fifth bill allowed for those sentenced to transportation to be sent to the colonies to labor on public works. These proposals sailed through the Commons with hardly a word of discussion, and through the Lords with only a little more; all received the Royal Assent by 8 July. What was more, Peel indicated that he intended further enactments. This possibility greatly affected public opinion; the *Christian Observer*, which held that Peel's first bills did 'nothing more than [repeal] those penalties which had, in point of fact, become merely nominal', expressed the expectation 'that every new session will witness other ameliorations' until the criminal code became 'what policy and Christianity alike demand that it should be'.[5] Whether optimistic or uncertain, reformers outside the Government were forced into a 'wait and see' posture and entered a period of relative quiescence.

From the political standpoint, therefore, Peel had removed a thorn from the Government's side, at least temporarily. He also gained the opportunity to implement a more complete overhaul of England's criminal laws than any MP had previously dared advocate in public. Between the end of 1823 and the start of 1830, in addition to the famous act creating a metropolitan police force, Peel carried seven bills consolidating and mitigating the penal laws, three affecting the administration of those laws, and three improving the prisons and jails. Furthermore, he succeeded in passing legislation to amend the jurisprudence of Scotland and to reform the Courts of Chancery, while maintaining the support of the Scottish legal establishment and the Lord Chancellor. These were impressive feats, and their accomplishment has deserved notice. Yet Peel's measures fell short of removing capital punishment for all non-violent crimes, the goal envisioned by reformers such as Romilly and Buxton. Peel's caution would lead to a renewal of the mitigation campaign in 1828. If the limits of Peel's legislation illustrated how far he thought expediency should take him, the storm that followed proved that the politics of criminal law reform was about more than mere utility.

Peel's limits and the demand to go beyond

The apparent ease with which Peel's measures passed through the Lords in 1823 proved the advantages of having the Home Secretary initiate reforms. But it would be wrong to assume that Peel had easily accomplished the adhesion of conservative hardliners like Lord Eldon. The history of one measure, the 1823 Gaol Act, illustrated that the Lord Chancellor could be as obdurate with fellow members of the Ministry as with the Opposition. The draft bill had been prepared by the prison committee in 1820 at the desire of the Home Secretary Lord Sidmouth. William Courtenay had charge of the bill in the Commons, but it was rejected in the Lords. Peel, who had been an active member of the prison committee, had understood at the end of the 1822 session that Eldon intended to bring in a revised bill at the reassembling of Parliament and asked his Under-Secretary Henry Hobhouse to remind the Lord Chancellor of this. Eldon responded that he could 'not think of attempting' to push the current bill through the Lords.[6] He thought the judges mostly ignorant of it, believed the Attorney and Solicitor Generals had had little to do with it, thought he had heard some Lords express aversion to it, believed that the distressed state of the landed classes would mean that the country would not bear the burden it would impose, and, finally, knew that he, the Lord Chancellor, could not,

> with the insupportable burthen of my other official business, undertake the conduct of *any important Bill* thro' the House, and certainly [could not] do so with respect to any Bill, materially affecting the Justice to be administered in the country, brought to the bar of the House of Lords before the Chancellor even heard that any body thought of such a bill.

Such words reminded the young Home Secretary, in no uncertain terms, of the old Lord Chancellor's belief in the importance of obtaining judicial opinions on all legal reforms. Peel's next move was conciliatory, but firm. He rehearsed for Eldon the bill's history, and politely informed him that the Solicitor General had early been involved with the bill.[7] Furthermore, since the bill had been supported by every member of the Government in the Commons and 'the faith of Government was pledged' before he had entered office, Peel thought that some bill 'for the consolidation of Prison Laws, and the Improvement of Prison Discipline' had to be brought in, but he assured Eldon that he would not place the burden of its passage on him.

The conciliatory approach worked, and the Gaol Act passed, but the episode cautioned Peel about the challenges of reforming legislation. He would not rush to initiate penal law reforms, but worked closely with those whose approach he could support. In March 1824, Dr Stephen Lushington, who had been active in both the Capital Punishment and Prison Discipline Societies, moved for a committee 'to consider of the expediency of Consolidating and Amending the Criminal Law of England'.[8] Lushington said his intention was to arrange the existing criminal laws as to type, and then to unite each of these classes into one statute. He gave examples of placing all the laws dealing with larceny into one general statute and of uniting all the acts dealing with forgery. Once this consolidation had been accomplished, the House would be in a better position to judge the 'principal existing defects'. Lushington was a longtime friend of Buxton, and known to be sympathetic to the Whigs, so the audience might easily have imagined which imperfections he would have listed first.[9] Peel found it expedient to serve on this select committee, along with the Attorney and Solicitor Generals, and the

President of the Board of Trade, William Huskisson. The committee also included Buxton, Mackintosh and Wilberforce's cousin John Smith.[10] The 'prearrangement' of the select committee was suggested by the fact that Lushington brought in the report on 2 April, less than three weeks after its appointment. The formal report was a single-page statement consisting of four resolutions for the consolidation of the criminal law and for the consideration and correction of 'certain omissions and anomalies'; following this page was a lengthy appendix prepared by the barrister Anthony Hammond.[11] Hammond's document began with an introductory statement of principles to guide statute consolidation, followed by extensive observations and details about the contemporary state of the forgery laws and a draft bill to consolidate them. The report generated no immediate legislation, but did provide a plan for the public discussion of consolidation, which Peel utilized selectively over the next two years.

During this same period, the Home Secretary was making himself invaluable to the stubborn Lord Chancellor by his careful investigation of the workings of the Court of Chancery. Eldon had considered the calls for inquiry into the delays of cases a personal attack upon him and his abilities, but Peel was able to handle the matter in such a way as to recognize Eldon's considerable efforts, while preparing reforms which would alleviate the backlog and streamline future appeals.[12] By autumn 1825, the resistance was gone from Eldon's correspondence with Peel, and he was encouraging him to send drafts of his penal law reform bills to the judges, even expressing a willingness to follow up on them himself.[13] Peel was conscientious in getting Eldon's views as well as the opinions of the Crown judges prior to introducing legislation. As he brought in his consolidation bills in 1826, he particularly thanked Justices Bailey, Hullock, Holroyd, Burrough, and Gaselee for their suggestions, a move that at once reassured his conservative listeners and informed the Whigs and Radicals that Peel had the backing of the legal establishment.

The 1826 bills consolidated the laws dealing with theft and amended certain aspects of the administration of justice. Addressing the Commons, Peel traced the calls for removing obsolete and unnecessary statutes back to a committee in 1666. Nothing had come of this inquiry, and Peel, like Romilly and Mackintosh before him, criticized the proliferation of penal laws in the eighteenth century because of the 'desultory and unconcerted speculations of every man who had a fancy to legislate'. Peel gave credit to Charles Abbott for beginning the process of restoring order to the statute book in 1796, but it was left to Peel to break 'this sleep of a century' by uniting in one statute 'all the enactments that exist, and are fit to be retained, relating to the crime of theft'.[14] The measure removed ninety-two statutes and replaced them with one thirty page document. Moreover, the language of the new law was designed to catch those criminals whose guilt was manifest, but who escaped punishment because of technical omissions in the common law or existing statutes. Peel's second measure, on the administration of justice, also erected safeguards against prosecutions being thrown out on purely technical grounds. The bill reorganized judicial procedures, from the coroner's inquest in cases of murder or manslaughter, to the procedures at assize sessions. Though it passed by the end of April, the bill provoked discussion and led to a further Criminal Justice Act in 1827, which rearranged the jurisdiction of the assize and quarter sessions and improved regulations affecting the investigation of crimes.[15] Most symbolically, the 1827 act abolished the age-old benefit of clergy and declared that no felony was capital unless explicitly made so by act of Parliament.

Peel had postponed full consideration of his larceny bill until 1827, to work out difficulties regarding the malicious destruction of property. In February he brought in three bills instead of one bill. The first consolidated the larceny laws, as he had intended the year before, but Peel placed acts of malicious violence against property into the second bill; the third repealed the existing statutes made obsolete by the new bills, as well as a few that Peel thought the country could do without.[16] These acts reduced 146 laws to 2 and also provided a substantial mitigation of punishment; the removal of the distinction between grand and petty larceny alone eliminated dozens of capital crimes, though in fact very few convicts had been hanged for theft in recent decades. The new laws made the standard punishment for a felony seven years' transportation or two years' imprisonment, a very real reduction that ten years before had been construed as too lenient by the Government's law officers and the Crown's leading judges. Peel also drafted a bill consolidating over fifty statutes for crimes against the person, which passed in 1828.[17]

Peel proclaimed that his bills not only created no new capital offenses, but greatly reduced the number of crimes that put an offender's life at risk. He repeatedly defended gradual change by reminding his fellow MPs that it 'was necessary to carry along with him all the instruments engaged in the administration of justice', or no benefit would be gained.[18] He had expected his reforms would win him some recognition for improving England's judicial institutions, but Peel also hoped the alterations would placate those pressing for greater mitigation.[19] Indeed, many commentators were pleased. The *Christian Observer* called Peel's 1826 plan 'admirable', and was delighted with the reduction of capital crimes in 1827; the editor was particularly happy to see the abolition of 'the preposterous plea of benefit of clergy'.[20] But not all were satisfied. In its 1827 report, the heavily Evangelical Prison Discipline Society broke with its earlier policy of avoiding political comment. While acknowledging the benefits of Peel's exertions, the report declared that there was a growing conviction in the public mind 'of the injustice and impolicy of capital punishments' and that despite the changes in the law brought by the Home Secretary's bills, much had yet to be done 'to ameliorate its spirit and refine its character'.[21] The clamor for criminal law reform had abated only temporarily, and public concern was still real.

In 1828 the Capital Punishment Society was reorganized and by early 1829 had sent out a circular advocating the abolition of capital punishments for all crimes short of murder. The circular argued that capital punishment did not diminish crimes, and that in countries 'where punishments are mildest there are generally the fewest atrocities'.[22] Echoing Wilberforce's words in 1787, the circular also asserted that since the 'sanguinary method' had been tried for ages, 'with little apparent success', it was now time to try the other method, which the CPS identified as imprisonment with a regular and severe course of labor and 'a season for reflection and reformation'. These recommendations echoed those of the Prison Discipline Society, and for good reason: Allen, Hoare, Buxton, and Lushington served on the steering committees of both societies.

As Peel prepared his bill to consolidate the laws of forgery, then, those very forces he had sought to square were reorganizing to challenge the Government's sincerity again. Scarlett, who had earlier supported Romilly and Mackintosh, had been appointed Attorney General. He provided a draft bill for Peel's consideration in August 1829, but Peel drew more heavily on the assistance of the barrister W. Gregson, who had done much of the writing of the consolidation bills in 1827.[23] His measure, introduced in the early morning hours of 2 April 1830, proposed to consolidate 120 statutes on forgery into one.[24] Sixty of the old statutes were capital, and while the bill repealed them all, it retained the death penalty for some specific offenses, including the forgery of negotiable and transferable securities and of printed notes used as money. In retaining capital punishment for these forgeries, Peel was putting the forgery of paper money on the same footing as coinage, a principle he derived from the report of the 1819 Committee. Indeed, as Peel himself claimed, in regard to the offenses still punishable by death, there 'was no very material difference' between his proposal and Mackintosh's bill of 1821.

The proposal would eliminate dozens of capital crimes; others would be removed as individual departments, like the Excise, the Post Office, and the Navy and Army, brought in the reports requested by Peel for the consolidation of the forgery statutes in their respective areas. Peel told the Commons that he was now 'a strong advocate for the mitigation of capital punishments', and that he wished to remove them 'in all cases where it was practicable', but it was better to proceed cautiously, lest any increase in crime be attributed to the mitigation of punishment. All who responded spoke with admiration of the recent reforms, and praised the mitigation in the forgery bill, even if they were disappointed that it retained hanging for some offenses. But while Peel had finally brought the Government up to the point where the reformers had been in 1821, most of the old reformers had moved toward more extensive restrictions on the death penalty. Buxton hoped Peel was serious in his intimations of further reforms in time – Peel had told him privately that he agreed with Buxton and his allies, but that he needed time to bring others around to their view.[25] But Buxton also had cause to doubt how far Peel would go – the Home Secretary had a record of stubborn insistence on the letter of the law when it came to the Crown's right to pardon or commute capital sentences, which hardly suggested a strong opposition to the punishment of death.[26] So Buxton praised Peel for the improvements he had introduced, while making it clear that he did not think they went far enough. Indeed, by retaining the death penalty for any case of forgery, Buxton suggested that Peel had not 'acted up to his own principles, still less to those of Lord Bacon', whom he had quoted liberally. Buxton also told the Commons that Mackintosh intended to bring in a bill to repeal the punishment of death for forgery entirely. The lines of confrontation had once again been drawn.

Those against the death penalty for forgery had already begun to stir public opinion. J. Sydney Taylor, a member of the CPS, published essays in the *Morning Herald* newspaper, while other Society members encouraged Basil Montagu to write another pamphlet.[27] Once again, an organized campaign besieged Parliament with petitions, and most were signed by bankers and merchants calling for the abolition of the death penalty for forgery. Peel actually presented such a petition from the Society of Friends in Ireland, though he was quick to note his disagreement with the extent of their proposed mitigation.[28] Buxton dictated the text of another petition, to underline his conviction that the punishment of death did nothing to protect commercial transactions.[29] Signed by over a thousand bankers in 214 towns, and presented by Brougham, the petition claimed that experience had proved that 'the infliction of death, or even the possibility of the infliction of death, prevents the prosecution, conviction, and punishment of the criminal', thus endangering the very property the law intended to protect.[30] On the same day, forty other petitions were laid upon the table of the House of Commons, joining the hundred or more previously presented. The number and geographical sources of the petitions defied easy categorization and suggested that rather than turn the pressure for reforms, Peel's previous measures had raised the public's expectations. A proposal that ten years earlier was considered too radical for the Government to accept, was considered by many in 1830 as falling short of the mark.

A deliberate effort was made to keep the language of these petitions simple and straightforward – Brougham observed that the petitioners 'did not go upon any abstract principle of religion, or upon any view of humanity; they came forward as practical men', to object to a punishment 'injurious to their trade and interests'.[31] The language of humanity and religion was not entirely absent from the petitions, however – one signed by bankers and merchants in Darlington and Kingsbridge specifically asserted 'that the Creator, the Lord and Giver of Life, had not given to any Monarch or Legislature...the right to exercise unlimited discretion, and inflict the punishment of death for every offence it might think fit'.[32] Also, much of the public discussion continued to be framed in religious terms. Montagu's *Thoughts on the Punishment of Death for Forgery* was full of allusions to the mild spirit of Christianity and how it affected public opinion and the function of England's laws. Speaking on Mackintosh's proposal, Buxton declared he would forego discussion of the unfitness of the punishment of death for forgery, and put 'out of view the precepts of humanity and religion' in such a manner as to bring them all more clearly into focus.[33] But these ardent reformers had learned from experience, in antislavery as well as criminal law, that those who were unpersuaded by appeals to Christianity and human feeling would listen to more worldly reasoning, such as the appeal for the better protection of property and social order.

Against this background the Commons took up Peel's bill on 24 May. Instead of introducing a separate bill to remove capital punishments, Mackintosh brought in a motion to amend Peel's. His arguments built on the petitions: since the 'object of all punishment was, to protect the life and property of all', he challenged the assertion that the threat of death protected against forgery.[34] Mackintosh appealed to the character of those who had signed the petitions for mitigation, practical men of business, bankers and merchants from around the country, upon whom the laws depended because they not only furnished the evidence and the prosecutions, but also served on the juries. They, not he, testified that the death penalty deterred them from prosecuting, no matter the evidence against the alleged culprit. Peel's own statistics discounted the 'threat' from the capital sentence, since they proved that once convicted, a forger still had a one-in-eight chance of escaping execution. Mackintosh proposed to replace the punishment of death with transportation or imprisonment up to 14 years, or both in truly extreme cases. Peel successfully defended his bill in committee, but Mackintosh reintroduced his amendment on the measure's third reading, and in the early morning hours of 8 June he succeeded in removing the punishment of death from the forgery consolidation bill by a vote of 151 to 138.[35] Peel relinquished the bill to Mackintosh, since he could no longer support it, but agreed not to 'take advantage of any thing like a thin House tomorrow to rescind the vote of that night'.

   Peel had repeatedly claimed that his bill was not to be viewed in partisan terms, but all the office holders and their friends voted with the Ministry while the bill was in committee, with only a few more joining them on the third reading. The amendment succeeded not by making converts, but because Buxton and Mackintosh effectively whipped up support in the two weeks between the committee and the third reading of the bill. They gained a few votes by agreeing to retain the death penalty for the forgery of wills, and Peel jumped on this exception as proof of inconsistency, but Brougham defended it as dealing in practical compromise, since the exception affected very few cases. Peel told the cabinet it would be difficult to find juries to convict capitally on forgery charges, now that the Commons had agreed with Mackintosh's amendment. Wellington, however, refused to acquiesce, believing that the Government's reputation would be tarnished if it gave in because of a majority of only 13 in the Commons; he and Lord Ellenborough thought a 'contrary vote of the House of Lords' might turn public opinion back 'into its former course'.[36] The Ministry did overwhelm the amended bill's supporters, and a motion to remove the amendment was passed by a vote of 77 to 20, a large enough majority to prevent any further discussion in the Lords.[37] Although the Forgery Law Consolidation Act received the Royal Assent on 23 July 1830, in substantially its original form, Peel's suspicion proved correct, and the point of the more ardent reformers had been won – no one has since been hanged for forgery in England or Wales.

Peel's approach to reform had reflected Lushington's proposal that the criminal laws first be consolidated, so that their glaring defects might be seen and remedied more easily. Peel had a clear grasp of the broader political realities affecting such an amendment. Though his father had strong religious commitments and often supported Evangelical initiatives, Peel was not an Evangelical.[38] Neither was he a doctrinaire utilitarian, and though his efforts incorporated aspects found in both movements, his plans really went in a different direction.[39] His reforms stayed within the common law tradition by emphasizing efficiency and by sticking closely to the actual practice of the courts and the opinions of the judges. Yet his conservative reforms did what no frontal assault on the criminal law had accomplished in the fifteen years following the Napoleonic Wars: Peel broke Parliament's habit of rejecting virtually any change as 'dangerous innovation'. Peel's object had been to minimize inconsistences in the administration of justice and mercy. The second Lord Ellenborough thought both public opinion and human decency demanded that not all who were sentenced to death should be so punished; the consequence was that it was 'not the law but individuals who decide whether a man shall suffer or not, a very difficult and painful duty', which unfortunately fell to the King's ministers to execute.[40] Peel's consolidation of the laws removed the vast majority of awkward cases from the Recorder's Reports and the petition appeals to the Home Office, by regularizing the punishment and reserving the death penalty for convicts of undisputed guilt, in cases judged to threaten social and commercial stability. Peel was willing to let offenders hang, despite royal desires to commute their sentences, because he thought a more regular system for exercising the prerogative of mercy could be arranged, and the laws brought into order with it.[41] While fighting Mackintosh and Buxton over the punishment for forgery, he never gave the Ministry reason to believe he fundamentally disagreed with assigning the death penalty to certain varieties of that crime, even if his private conversations with Buxton suggested otherwise. Nor, for all his anxiety over hearing the Recorder's reports, did Ellenborough consider that the solution was the removal of the death penalty from crimes against property alone; rather, like his father, he still believed that the threat of death prevented non-violent crimes.[42] Peel appeared to agree.

But the political dominance of this conservative view would not stand for long. In autumn 1830, William IV invited the Whigs to form a ministry. This alteration almost guaranteed that Peel's limits on penal law reform would soon be exceeded. Indeed, the changes came faster than Peel had expected, despite his consistent attempts to slow them. In

1832 the death penalty was removed from forgery, and by the end of 1833 most of Peel's penal legislation had been revised or superseded.[43] By 1839, only nine crimes were punishable by death, and only one of these (embezzlement by an officer or servant of the Bank of England) did not involve an attack upon the physical safety of an individual or group.

Evangelicalism and the politics of criminal law reform

Boyd Hilton has reminded us 'how surprising it was that – without any political revolution or noticeable transfer of power – one of the bloodiest codes in Europe was transformed so quickly into one of the mildest'.[44] He has made a plea for retaining an important place for 'liberal Tories' such as Peel in that transformation, in contrast with V. A. C. Gatrell's view that Whig politicians played the crucial role. Gatrell's sense was that the politicians were responding primarily to practical needs and the pressure of numbers on the institutions of justice, implying that these were greater factors in reforming the criminal laws than ideological beliefs or the agitations of extra-parliamentary pressure groups.[45] Certainly the number of capitally convicted felons was a bother to those in power, but one wonders whether Peel's formulation of better criteria for the exercise of mercy would not have served the Whigs as well as the Tories, if other influences had not come to bear. That the changes in England's penal laws were ultimately a matter of politics, under the direction of one party or another, is not in question; but it is evident that among the factors shaping the politics were a group of politicians neither particularly Tory nor Whig, nor Radical, and a set of expectations that guided them to press for the restriction of capital punishment to the fewest number of crimes necessary. One returns, therefore, to the role played by ideas and pressure groups on reform-minded politicians, which leads immediately back to the central question of this study: what was the real impact of Evangelicalism on criminal law reform?

Answering this question should not detract from the importance of utilitarian ideas; the goal has not been to supplant the principle of utility, but to understand the presence of Evangelicals and their reasons in the support of the criminal law reforms. But as we have found, the language of the debates did not break neatly into discrete categories of 'utilitarian' and 'religious' arguments, nor even 'pragmatic' and 'humane'. Indeed, the evidence explored in the preceding chapters suggests at least one certain point: the contrast between 'humanitarian impulses' and 'practical concerns' in the reform of England's criminal laws is a false dichotomy. The concept of civil society propagated by the reformers did not distinguish between humane and pragmatic as such, but assumed that in a truly civilized society, policy would and should be in line with humanity, and both would reflect true religion. That being said, one can easily observe that Evangelical political activism played a crucial role in passing penal law reform measures through the Commons, which forced the Lords to deal with the issue ever more frequently, until it was clear that the public had accepted the reformers' version of penal matters. Secondly, because they occupied the crucial middle-ground, but also were active in leading the issue, the expectations and language of the Evangelicals shaped the options for reform. This last point may be illustrated with regard to secondary punishments. Absent from the debates in 1830 was discussion of prison reforms, because the reformation of the criminal while incarcerated was one intended outcome of Peel's earlier prison legislation, despite Peel's private skepticism.[46]

Historian Robert Hole has observed a shift in the way ministers and clergymen discussed the relevance of religion to larger society in the early nineteenth century, and by his definition, most arguments for criminal law reform sounded secular rather than religious.[47] That is, to our modern ears, the arguments do not appear to require an appeal to God to be understood today. Those in the early nineteenth century heard at least a few things differently. Both in Parliament and out, arguments often rested on Christian values refined through church history and reinjected into public discourse by Evangelical politicians and their allies. This was especially true for arguments based on belief in the progress of civilization, a belief which in this debate was almost always connected to the growth of Christianity, as both Wilberforce and Montagu made explicit in their publications. In his final pamphlet, Montagu wrote that he made three assumptions: 'that it is the nature of time ever more and more to disclose truth'; 'that humanity advances with knowledge'; and, finally, 'that humanity advances with Christianity'.[48] Sanguinary statutes had to fall before this progress. Montagu concluded,

> In vain, from henceforth, will be any resistance but the resistance of reason. 'If this counsel or this work be of men, it will come to nought: but if the desire, that a sinner should turn from his wickedness and live, is of God, it cannot be overthrown'.[49]

When speaking of the role of Evangelicalism in effecting and legitimating the reform of the penal code, we are talking about a movement that boldly asserted the relevance of God's providence to everyday affairs. We are speaking of politicians and reformers who wanted the secular to conform to the spiritual. They made secular arguments religious, either by redefinition or by finding in their traditional beliefs a basis for such arguments, and they made traditional religious arguments secular, by adapting them to address the social and political situation of their times. Contemporary social developments quite likely affected their 'sensibilities', but that should not detract from their contribution. Indeed, it is not too much to say that Evangelicalism made Montagu's appeal possible by making religious discourse politically viable in early nineteenth-century Britain. It had reintroduced piety into public life.

Another reason for the Evangelical impact on criminal law reform came from the energy with which they attacked the issue. Men like Henry Thornton, Fowell Buxton and William Wilberforce were known not only for their seriousness in religion, but for their activism in business and society. Again, they may have reflected the new middle-class sensibility, but they did not leave matters at the level of internal feelings and impressions. Driven by the conviction that when one discovers an injustice, one must do what one can to make it right, they continually pressed the issue. Through such organs as the *Christian Observer* and *Eclectic Review*, the Saints and their allies kept their priorities before the larger Evangelical community. Furthermore, they worked not as isolated individuals, but labored with others, forming societies and organizations reaching across denominational boundaries to help them accomplish their goals. The Capital Punishment Society, the result of the collaboration between Montagu and Allen, and the Prison Discipline Society, founded by Buxton and Hoare, included many from the Established and Dissenting churches, as well as the Society of Friends. We may note here that while Quakers played a great part in pressing for reforms and in circulating petitions, to say that they were the source of social agitation for criminal law reform is misleading.[50] Two things stand out in this regard. First, they always worked alongside others. Second, the Quakers most involved with penal law reform, as in antislavery, were not from the old line of quietists, but those whose religion had been shaped by the Evangelical revival, like Allen, J. J. Gurney, and Elizabeth Fry, who were comfortable making social contacts beyond their sect. They helped create a broad community of support for criminal law reform, which was at once more personal than that of a political party and better suited for the issue at hand. As we have seen, the reformers denied that criminal law reform was a partisan issue, and though the Whigs supported amelioration, the limits of their party discipline kept them from acting effectively on it.

The activism of the Evangelicals can best be seen if one overlays their involvement in criminal law reform with their antislavery efforts. When once the slave trade had been abolished in 1807, the campaign leaders turned to the criminal laws, and pressed that issue (while always keeping an eye on the slavery question) until Peel committed the Government in 1823. At that point Buxton began to lead the abolitionist movement, taking Mackintosh with him.[51] When Peel's consolidations fell short of their expectations, the reformers took up the criminal laws again. The change of Ministry in 1830 made further amelioration more likely, and also opened the possibility for the abolition of slavery in 1833. Both issues remained part of the public discourse after that point, but the nature of the discussion and of the reforms proposed was entirely different. In addition, after 1833 the increased sectarianism among the Evangelicals reduced their effectiveness to speak as a group on social issues.[52]

Evangelicals had hoped their new models of prison discipline would provide a way to bring order and legitimate opportunity into the lives of offenders, whose early experiences had led them only into chaos and ill-gotten gain. While defining the limits of acceptable behavior and delineating the means by which the community would enforce its standards on those whose actions trespassed those limits, reformers sought 'to strike a balance between encouraging self-discipline and responsibility in individuals and imposing discipline and good order on potential deviants'.[53] While this study makes no effort to evaluate the application or success of the new theories of prison discipline, it may be appropriate to note that as early as 1822, those who had preached the efficacy of combining a healthy diet and atmosphere with the active imposition of disciplinary employment, training, and separation for sleep and contemplation, were forced to back away from their more ambitious goals in the face of the complaint that such plans would provide a higher standard of living for society's criminals than was available to most of the honest working poor. The result was a harsher, leaner prison regime than envisioned by Buxton and other members of the Prison Discipline Society. In a very real sense, these reformers' plans were never tried. Furthermore, they had held that the system should be so structured as to promote private efforts alongside the public, so that non-professionals like Elizabeth Fry could still take a personal interest in the betterment and reformation of prisoners. Their vision was not, therefore, entirely in line with the more impersonal and bureaucratic models derived from later Benthamites, nor was criminal law reform in the period 1808–30 purposely or consciously about the centralization of authority or the increase in state power. If these things followed, it was as an unintended consequence of challenging the capital code and regularizing prison administration.[54]

The politics of criminal law reform in the first three decades of the nineteenth century were, therefore, as much a matter of religion as of utility. Issues of efficiency and expediency were always a part of the debate, but so were concerns of the spirit and of the structure of a society which would best enable human beings to exercise their liberties as God's creatures. The politics were about limiting government authority to take away life, even as they were about modifying its authority to impose discipline. R. K. Webb has described the gradual reform of the criminal laws through the 1820s as 'preparing the way for more far-reaching reforms by accustoming Parliament and public to the possibility of effective state action against inherited evils'.[55] Penal law reform, in essence, fueled hopes for other legal and political reforms. This study has attempted to recount the public debates on the criminal law in a way that reveals the mixture of energies and optimism at work in the early nineteenth-century reforms. Delineating the Evangelical involvement has allowed us to make better sense of the compromises made and of the measures actually implemented than reliance on utilitarian theories alone would allow. Wilberforce and Buxton never considered their efforts to be exclusively Evangelical concerns, and they were only too happy to work with Romilly and Mackintosh in criminal law reforms as they did in antislavery. The combination of the lawyer's rational critique of the criminal laws with that of religiously-motivated reformers was socially and politically more powerful than either set of criticisms alone. Evangelical support gave wholeness to the arguments and tied them into existing community values. Wilberforce and his allies showed that criminal law reform was not radical, but in harmony with a peaceful, lawful society. Nonetheless, they did challenge the social structures of their times and altered British expectations of what criminal justice should be. Henry Brougham once proclaimed that the 'age of Law Reform and the age of Jeremy Bentham are one and the same'. Judged from the politics of criminal law reform, it is at least as true to declare that the age of law reform was the age of Evangelicalism.

Notes

1 Mitigating the 'Bloody Code': an Introduction

1 'Benthamic' designates those reforms and the language that describes them or their theoretical basis that comes directly from Bentham's own writings, and ought to be distinguished from the language and purposes of those friends and followers of Bentham who have often been labeled 'Benthamites'; the Benthamites often went down very different paths from those which Benthamic discourse suggested.

2 Publication of Bentham's works has been a main occupation of the Bentham Project at University College, London

3 Jeremy Bentham, *An Introduction to the Principles of Morals and Legislation* (New York: Hafner Press, 1948; reprint of the 1823 edition), p. 2.

4 See Jefferson Selth's biography of Etienne Dumont, *Firm Heart and Capacious Mind: the Life and Friends of Etienne Dumont* (Lanham, MD: University Press of America, 1997), pp. 151–80.

5 Letter to Thomas Thomson, 15 August 1803, quoted *Memoirs and Correspondence of Francis Horner, M.P.*, edited by Leonard Horner (Boston· Brown and Company, 1853), p. 236.

6 See Romilly's 'Review of Bentham on Codification', *Edinburgh Review*, v. 29, pp. 217–37, and Chapter 3 below.

7 *The Works of Jeremy Bentham* (London, 1838–43), John Bowring, ed., v 10, p. 27

8 See Miriam Williford, *Jeremy Bentham on Spanish America: an Account of His Letters and Proposals to the New World* (Baton Rouge: Louisiana State University Press, 1980).

9 Brougham, *Speeches of Henry Lord Brougham* (Edinburgh: Adam and Charles Black, 1838), v. 2, pp 287–8.

10 See J. S. Mill, 'Bentham', in *Utilitarianism and Other Essays* (London: Penguin Books, 1987), pp 132–3.

11 W. Blake Odger, 'Changes in Procedure and the Law of Evidence', *A Century of Law Reform: Twelve Lectures on the Changes in the Law of England During the Nineteenth Century* (London: Macmillan, 1901), p. 232.

12 Mill, 'Bentham', pp. 138–9.

13 Sir James Fitzjames Stephen, *A History of the Criminal Law of England* (London: Macmillan, 1883), v. 2, p. 216, and Sir Henry Sumner Maine, *Lectures on the Early History of English Institutions* (NY: Kennikat Press, 1966; reprint of seventh edition, 1914) Maine, p. 397.

14 A. V. Dicey, *Lectures on the Relation Between Law and Public Opinion in England During the Nineteenth Century* (London: Macmillan and Co., Ltd., 1952; first edition in 1905), p. 63.

15 See Elie Halévy, *The Growth of Philosophical Radicalism* (translated from the French by Mary Morris, London: Faber & Faber Limited, 1948), and *A History*

of the English People in the Nineteenth Century, v. 1. *England in 1815* (translated by E I Watkın and D. A. Barker, New York: Barnes & Noble Inc., 1961).

16 Halévy, *Philosophical Radicalism*, p. 36.

17 Leon Radzinowicz, *A History of the English Criminal Law and its Administration from 1750*, v. 1, *The Movement for Reform*, 1750–1833 (New York: Macmıllan Company, 1948), p. 360.

18 Radzinowicz, p. 361.

19 See O. MacDonagh, 'The Nineteenth-century Revolution in Government', *Historical Journal*, v. 1 (1958), pp. 52–67; and D. Roberts, 'Jeremy Bentham and the Victorian Administratıve State', *Victorian Studies*, v. 11 (1959), pp 193–210. More recent studies include L. J. Hume, *Bentham and Bureaucracy* (Cambridge: Cambridge Universıty Press, 1981), and Helen Beynon, 'Mıghty Bentham', *Journal of Legal History*, v. 2 (1981), pp. 62–76.

20 D. J. Manning, *The Mind of Jeremy Bentham* (London: Longmans, 1968), p. 110.

21 H. L. A. Hart, *Essays on Bentham: Jurisprudence and Political Theory* (Oxford: Clarendon Press, 1982), p. 1.

22 Wilham Thomas, *The Philosophical Radicals: Nine Studies in Theory and Practice, 1817–1841* (Oxford: Clarendon Press, 1979), p. 4

23 Beynon, p. 70 More recent criticism of Bentham's ınfluence can be found C. J. W. Allen, *The Law of Evidence in Victorian England* (Cambrıdge: Cambridge University Press, 1997), and Rıchard A. Cosgrove, *Scholars of the Law: English Jurisprudence from Blackstone to Hart* (New York: New York Unıversıty Press, 1996).

24 Davıd Philips '"A Just Measure of Crime, Authorıty, Hunters and Blue Locusts": the "Revisionıst" Socıal Hıstory of Crime and the Law in Britain, 1780–1850', ın *Social Control and the State*, edited by Stanley Cohen and Andrew Scull (New York: St. Martin's Press, 1983), p. 65.

25 Randall McGowen, 'The Image of Justice and Reform of the Criminal Law in Early Nineteenth-Century England', *Buffalo Law Review*, v. 32 (1983), p. 95.

26 W R. Cornish and G. de N. Clark, *Law and Society in England, 1750–1950* (London: Sweet & Maxwell, 1989).

27 John Hostettler's *The Politics of Criminal Law: Reform in the Nineteenth Century* (Chıchester: Barry Rose Law Publıshers Ltd , 1992) also glosses over distinc- tıons

28 William Blackstone, *Commentaries on the Laws of England* (Oxford, 1769), v. 4, pp. 16–17.

29 Blackstone, pp. 18–19

30 Martın Wiener, 'The Unloved State: Twentieth-Century Politics in the Writ- ing of Nineteenth-Century History', *Journal of British Studies*, v. 33, no. 3 (July 1994), p. 284.

31 In addition, see David Taylor, *Crime, Policing and Punishment in England, 1750– 1914* (New York: St Martın's Press, 1998). Another helpful revıew ıs Joanna Innes and John Styles, 'The Crime Wave: Recent Writing on Crime and Criminal Justice in Eıghteenth-Century England', *Rethinking Social History: English Society 1570–1920 and its Interpretation*, Adrıan Wılson, ed (Manches- ter: Manchester University Press, 1993).

32 Douglas Hay, 'Property, Authority, and the Criminal Law', in Hay et al., *Albion's Fatal Tree: Crime and Society in Eighteenth-Century England* (New York Pantheon Books, 1975), pp. 17–63.

33   E. P. Thompson, *Whigs and Hunters* (New York: Pantheon, 1975), p. 262. The Black Act was 9 Geo. I c. 22.

34   See David Philips, *Crime and Authority in Victorian England, 1835–1860* (London: Croom Helm, 1977).

35   See Michel Foucault's *Discipline and Punish: the Birth of the Prison* (New York: Vintage Books, 1979; from the French, *Surveillier et punir; naissance de la prison*, Paris, 1975)

36   Michael Ignatieff, *A Just Measure of Pain: the Penitentiary in the Industrial Revolution, 1750–1850* (London: Penguin Books, 1978).

37   McGowen, 'Image of Justice', p. 96

38   See McGowen's 'The Changing Face of God's Justice· the Debate over Divine and Human Punishment in Eighteenth Century England', *Criminal Justice History*, pp. 63–98; 'The Body and Punishment in Eighteenth Century England', *The Journal of Modern History*, v. 59 (1987), pp. 651–79 and 'He Beareth Not the Sword in Vain: Religion and the Criminal Law in Eighteenth-Century England', *Eighteenth-Century Studies*, v. 21 (1987–88), pp. 192–211

39   Thomas Haskell, 'Capitalism and the Origins of the Humanitarian Sensibility, Parts I and II', *American Historical Review*, v 90 (1985), pp. 339–61, and 547–66.

40   Haskell, p. 342.

41   Haskell, p. 548.

42   David Sugarman, ' Law, Economy and the State in England, 1750–1914: Some Major Issues', in David Sugarman, ed., *Legality, Ideology and the State* (New York: Academic Press, 1983), p. 256.

43   Ignatieff, 'State, Civil Society and Total Institutions: a Critique of Recent Social Histories of Punishment', in Cohen and Scull, *Social Control and the State* (New York: St. Martins Press, 1983), p. 98.

44   Norman S. Fiering, 'Irresistible Compassion: an Aspect of Eighteenth-Century Sympathy and Humanitarianism', *Journal of the History of Ideas*, v. 37 (1976), pp. 195–218; Randall McGowen, 'A Powerful Sympathy Terror, the Prison, and Humanitarian Reform in Early Nineteenth-Century Britain', *Journal of British Studies*, v. 25 (1986), pp. 312–34, and V. A. C. Gatrell, *The Hanging Tree: Execution and the English People, 1770–1868* (Oxford: Oxford University Press, 1994), pp. 225–41

45   Robert Hole's *Pulpits, Politics and Public Order in England, 1760–1830* (Cambridge: Cambridge University Press, 1989) also illustrates ways in which religious language could both legitimate *and* challenge the social order.

46   See for instance Romans 1:1–6, Galatians 1:11–12, or Ephesians 3:2–7.

47   David Bebbington, *Evangelicalism in Modern Britain: a History from the 1730s to the 1980s* (London: Unwin Hyman, 1989), pp. 2–17.

48   A good example of the Evangelical priest can be found in Owen Chadwick's *Victorian Miniature* (Cambridge· Cambridge University Press, 1991; first edition, 1960).

49   This point is well illustrated by Harry Potter in *Hanging in Judgment· Religion and the Death Penalty in England* (New York Continuum, 1993), pp 30–45

50   See Sir James Stephen, 'The Clapham Sect', *Essays in Ecclesiastical Biography* (London Longman, 1850, second edition), pp. 287–383, and F. M. Forster, *Marianne Thornton: a Domestic Biography, 1787–1887* (New York· Harcourt, Brace and Co., 1956) Such is also the impression given by Thomas Fowell

Buxton's memoirs compiled by his son Charles; *Memoirs of Sir Thomas Fowell Buxton, Bart.* (London: John Murray, 1849).

51 Ernest Marshall Howse, *Saints in Politics: the 'Clapham Sect' and the Growth of Freedom* (Toronto: University of Toronto Press, 1952). See also Sir Reginald Coupland, *Wilberforce* (London: Collins, second edition, 1945).

52 Ford K. Brown, *Fathers of the Victorians: the Age of Wilberforce* (Cambridge University Press, 1961), pp. 348ff.

53 See Elie Halévy, *England in 1815* (New York, 1961), especially p. 590. See also E. P. Thompson, *The Making of the English Working Class* (New York Pantheon Books, 1963), pp. 42–6, 739–40

54 As seen in two biographies of Wilberforce: Robin Furneaux's *William Wilberforce* (London: Hamish Hamilton, 1974), and John Pollock's *Wilberforce* (London: Constable, 1977).

55 Ian Bradley, 'The Politics of Godliness: Evangelicals in Parliament, 1784–1832', (unpublished D. Phil. thesis, Oxford University, 1974), p. iii. See also his *The Call to Seriousness: the Evangelical Impact on the Victorians* (London: Jonathan Cape, 1976)

56 Bradley, *Call to Seriousness*, p. 143.

57 Halévy, *England in 1815*, see especially p. 583–7.

58 See also Kathleen Heasman, *Evangelicals in Action: an Appraisal of their Social Work in the Victorian Era* (London: Geoffrey Bles, 1962), which argues that Evangelicalism's emphasis on individual worth provided a humanizing element in the face of ever growing bureaucratic structures, p. 20.

59 Boyd Hilton, *Age of Atonement: the Influence of Evangelicalism on Social and Economic Thought, 1795–1865* (Oxford, 1988), p. 6.

60 See the essays in *The Enlightenment in National Context* (Cambridge: Cambridge University Press, 1981), Roy Porter and Mikulas Teich, eds.

61 Roger Anstey, *The Atlantic Slave Trade and British Abolition, 1760–1810* (Atlantic Highlands, NJ: Humanities Press, 1975); see especially pp 157–83. Criminal law reform shared many motivations with antislavery.

62 W. R. Ward, *Religion and Society in England, 1790–1850* (London: B. T. Batsford, 1972), p 17.

63 Bebbington, *Evangelicalism*, p. 61. See also David Bebbington, 'Revival and Enlightenment in Eighteenth-Century England', in *Modern Christian Revivals*, ed. by Edith Blumhofer and Robert Balmer (Urbana: University of Illinois Press, 1993).

2   Raising the Hue and Cry, 1808–10

1 See E. P. Thompson, *Whigs and Hunters: the Origin of the Black Act* (New York, 1975), pp. 219ff, for a revealing description of the expansive interpretation of the Black Act.

2 William Blackstone, *Commentaries on the Laws of England*, v. 4 (Oxford, 1769), p. 195.

3 5 Anne c. 6.

4 4 Geo. I c. 11 and 6 Geo. I c. 23

5 The most complete account of the early inquiries into criminal law reform is in Leon Radzinowicz, *History of the English Criminal Law and its Administration*

from 1750, v. 1, *The Movement for Reform* (New York: Macmillan, 1948), chapters 12 and 13.

6 See William Cobbett's *Parliamentary History*, v. 26 (1786–8), cols. 1056–9.
7 Sir William Holdsworth, *A History of English Law*, v. 13 (London: Methuen & Co., Ltd, 1952) pp. 259–63.
8 Romilly's speech appears both in Hansard, v. 11 (1808), cols. 395–400, and in *The Speeches of Sir Samuel Romilly in the House of Commons* (London, 1820), v. 1, pp. 38–47.
9 See Sir Samuel Romilly, *Memoirs of the Life of Sir Samuel Romilly*, edited by his sons (London, 1840), v. 2, pp. 44, 114ff and 428ff. Many of the biographical details come from this work.
10 See Robert and Samuel Wilberforce, *The Life of William Wilberforce* (London: John Murray, 1838), v. 3, p. 296.
11 Romilly, *Memoirs*, v. 2, p. 201.
12 See C. G. Oakes, *Sir Samuel Romilly, 1757–1818, 'Friend of the Oppressed'* (London: Allen & Unwin, Ltd., 1935), pp. 144f, for lucid discussion of this issue
13 Romilly, *Memoirs*, v. 2, p. 229.
14 25 Geo. II c. 36 was meant to encourage costly prosecutions which might not otherwise have taken place.
15 Romilly, *Memoirs*, v 2, p. 230 The passage on pious perjuries appears in Blackstone, v. 4, p. 239.
16 Romilly, *Memoirs*, v. 2, p 237.
17 See William Paley, *Principles of Moral and Political Philosophy*, seventh edition (Boston, 1811), p. 428
18 Romilly, *Speeches*, v. 1, p. 43.
19 Romilly, *Speeches*, v. 1, p. 40
20 See Hansard, v. 11, cols. 400ff.
21 Hansard, v. 11, cols. 400–1
22 See Romilly's *Memoirs*, p. 246f.
23 Letter to Romilly dated 17 May 1808, in Romilly, *Memoirs*, v. 2, p. 247.
24 See Hansard, v. 11, cols 877–86.
25 Romilly, *Memoirs*, v. 2, p. 246.
26 Romilly, *Memoirs*, v. 2, p. 252.
27 See Hansard, v. 11, cols. 1103–4
28 See Sir James Mackintosh, *Memoirs of the Life of Sir James Mackintosh* (Boston: Little, Brown and Co , 1853), v 2, p 112.
29 Letter to Sir James Mackintosh in Bombay, 22 June 1808, Mackintosh Papers, BL Add MS 52452, ff. 31–9.
30 Romilly, *Memoirs*, v. 2, p. 253. The completed work appeared in French in 1811, entitled *Théorie des peines et des récompenses*.
31 Recorded in the *Memoirs*, v. 2, pp. 253–4.
32 See Rev. Samuel Parr, *Characters of the Late Charles James Fox, Selected, and in part written by Philopatris Varvicensis*, in two volumes (London, 1809). In v. 2, he acknowledges the efforts of 'Sir Arthur Pigott, Sir Samuel Romilly, Sir James Mackintosh, Mr Serveant Lens, Mr. Robert Smith, Dr. Colquhoun, Mr. Francis Hargrave, and, above all, Jeremiah Bentham', in attempting to improve the penal laws of England (p. 524)
33 *Memoirs*, v 2, p. 291 The bills became 49 Geo. III c 6 and c. 121. For information on the bills' background and effect see Oakes, pp. 196–9

34 Hansard, v. 13 (1809), cols. 403ff.
35 Basil Montagu, ed., *The Opinions of Different Authors Upon the Punishment of Death* (London, 1809).
36 On the Capital Punishment Society and its role in building public opinion, see Chapter 7 below.
37 The quotation from Bentham is actually a translation from *Théorie de législation civile et pénale*, edited by Dumont. Montagu had been involved in translating Dumont's publication in 1807, but for some reason, the complete translation was delayed. See Montagu to Mackintosh, 26 August, 1807, Mackintosh Papers, BL Add. MS 52542, (temporary) ff. 17–22.
38 10 & 11 Will. III c. 23; 12 Anne St. 1, c. 7; and 24 Geo II c. 45, respectively.
39 Originally, Hansard's carried only a synopsis of the debates on Romilly's bills in 1810, in v. 15, cols. 366–74, and v. 16, cols. 767–80, 833–5, and 944–9. An enlarged record of the debates was later printed in the Appendix to Hansard, v. 19 (1811), cols. i–ccxxii.
40 Romilly, *Speeches*, v. 1, p. 108.
41 Samuel Romilly, *Observations on the Criminal Law of England, as it Relates to Capital Punishments, and on the Mode in which it is Administered* (London, 1810), p. 5.
42 See Romilly, *Observations*, pp. 9–10, for his statistics.
43 The details Romilly presented for London and Middlesex are given in the following table (adapted):

Date	Convicted	Executed	Proportion
1802	97	10	$c. \frac{1}{10}$
1803	81	9	$\frac{1}{9}$
1804	66	8	$c. \frac{1}{9}$
1805	63	10	$c. \frac{1}{6}$
1806	60	13	$c. \frac{1}{5}$
1807	74	14	$c. \frac{1}{5}$
1808	87	3	$\frac{1}{29}$

Reproduced in the *Speeches*, v 1, p. 112

44 John Beattie's study of the Surrey and Sussex assize records supports Romilly's general thesis; see *Crime and the Courts in England, 1660–1800* (Princeton: Princeton University Press, 1986), tables on pages 532–3 and 620, and p. 538, footnote 33
45 Romilly, *Observations*, pp. 14–15.
46 Romilly, *Observations*, p. 21
47 Paley, p. 427.
48 See Hansard, v. 19, Appendix col. xliii and following.
49 Since Chapter 6 examines the conservative defense of the penal laws in detail, only a brief description of the opposition to Romilly's bills appears here.
50 Hansard, v. 19, Appendix col. xlv.

51   Wilberforce, *Life*, v. 3, p. 439–40.
52   Francis Horner to Romilly, 10 February 1810, reprinted in *Memoirs and Correspondence of Francis Horner, M. P.* (Boston: Little, Brown & Co , 1853), ed by his brother Leonard Horner, pp. 4–5.
53   This pamphlet, *Debates in the Year 1810, upon Sir Samuel Romilly's Bills* .., was a more complete account of the debates than Hansard had published that year; it was the source of Hansard's appendix in v. 19 in 1811.
54   Letters from 'Anti-Draco' appeared in *The Times* on 16 February, 1 March and 9 March; from 'Publico', 19 March, 1810, p. 2, col. 5.
55   Parr to Romilly, 21 February, 1810, in *Memoirs*, v. 2, p. 303.
56   See Hansard, v. 19, beginning at Appendix col. li.
57   See Hansard, v. 19, Appendix cols. liv ff.
58   MS Wilberforce d. 54, f. 57. Wilberforce recorded that the debate lasted until 1:30 a.m.
59   Romilly, *Memoirs*, v. 316
60   *The Times* for 4 May 1810 confirmed Romilly's list.
61   *Speeches*, v. 1, p. 246.
62   Romilly to Lord Holland, 13 May 1810, Holland Papers, Add. MSS 51825, f. 26.
63   Romilly to Holland, 24 May 1810, BL Add MS 51825, ff. 33–5.
64   For the Lords' debate, see Hansard, v. 19, Appendix cols. lxxxvii ff.
65   Romilly, *Memoirs*, v 2, p. 325.
66   Romilly, *Memoirs*, v. 2, p. 335.
67   Romilly, *Observations*, p. 62
68   Hansard, v. 19, Appendix col. lxxix.

3   Romilly, Bentham and Utility

1   The three-volume *Memoirs of the Life of Sir Samuel Romilly, written by himself, with a selection from his correspondence* (London, 1840), edited by his sons, serves as the source of most of the information on Romilly's life.
2   See C. G. Oakes, *Sir Samuel Romilly, 1757–1818: 'Friend of the Oppressed'* (London: Allen & Unwin, 1935), pp. 7–13.
3   Romilly, *Memoirs*, v. 1, p. 32.
4   See the *Memoirs*, v. 1, pp. 43–5 and George Smeeton, *Memoirs of the Life of that Illustrious Patriot, Sir Samuel Romilly*, printed by Geo. Smeeton (London, 1818), p. 4.
5   Letter to Jean Roget, 1780 June 6, in Romilly, *Memoirs*, v 1, p 115.
6   Romilly, *Memoirs*, v. 1, pp 56–7. The second edition of Howard's *The State of the Prisons* appeared in 1780
7   Romilly, *Memoirs*, v. 1, p. 58.
8   The *Traités de législation* (1802) and the *Théories des peines et des récompenses* (1811).
9   Romilly, *Memoirs*, v. 1, pp 58–9.
10   Romilly, *Memoirs*, v. 1, p. 64.
11   Romilly to Jean Roget, 24 January 1782, *Memoirs*, p. 198.
12   Romilly to Jean Roget, 20 May 1782, *Memoirs*, v. 1, p. 226.
13   See Collins, *Sir Samuel Romilly*, p. 25 Two poetic tributes published after Romilly's tragic death confirm his charity; see M. R. Stockdale, *A Shroud for*

Sir Samuel Romilly (London, 1818) and Miss M. S. Croker, *A Tribute to the Memory of Sir Samuel Romilly* (London, 1818).

14 See the letters of 10 and 13 June 1783, *Memoirs*, v. 1, pp. 282–6.

15 Oakes, p. 343. This impression has persisted: see Linda Colley, *Britons: Forging the Nation 1707–1837* (New Haven: Yale University Press, 1992), p. 208.

16 Hansard, v. 22 (1812), cols. 935–947

17 Thomas Belsham, *Reflections upon the Death of Sir Samuel Romilly in a Discourse delivered at Essex Street Chapel, November 8, 1818*, (London, 1818), pp. 8–9.

18 *Memoirs*, v. 3, pp 76–7.

19 Oakes, p. 344.

20 Romilly referred to Hume's essay 'On Miracles' in an unpublished essay; Sir Samuel Romilly MS, Lincoln's Inn, MS Misc. 246, pp. 7–8.

21 Randall McGowen, 'The Changing Face of God's Justice: the Debates over Divine and Human Punishment in Eighteenth-Century England,' *Criminal Justice History*, v. 9 (1988), pp. 63–98.

22 Romilly, *Speeches*, v. 1, p. 137.

23 Romilly favored Paley's *Natural Theology* (1802); see *Memoirs*, v. 2, p. 103.

24 May 8 1783, reprinted in the *Memoirs*, v. 1, pp. 275–81.

25 Romilly, *Memoirs*, v. 1, p. 278.

26 This was the *Considérations sur l'ordre de Cincinnatus* published in London and Amsterdam in 1785.

27 *A Fragment on the Constitutional Power and Duties of Juries upon Trial for Libels.* Oakes, pp. 54f.

28 Martin Madan, *Thoughts on Executive Justice, with respect to our Criminal Laws, particularly on the Circuits. Dedicated to the Judges of Assize and recommended to the Perusal of All Magistrates; and to all Persons who are Liable to serve on Crown Juries* (London, 1785).

29 Samuel Romilly, *Observations on a Late Publication intituled Thoughts on Executive Justice, to which is added, a Letter containing remarks on the same work* (London, 1786), pp. 13–15.

30 Romilly, *Observations*, p. 27.

31 Romilly, *Observations*, pp. 1–3.

32 Romilly *Observations*, pp. 16 and 29–30, and William Blackstone, *Commentaries on the Laws of England, Book the Fourth* (Oxford, 1769), p. 17. David Lieberman's *Province of Legislation Determined: Legal Theory in Eighteenth Century Britain* (Cambridge: Cambridge University Press, 1989) has done much to recover Blackstone's original intention for his *Commentaries* as a primer for legislators.

33 Romilly, *Observations*, p. 25. Romilly's footnote on the laws of nature refers to Grotius

34 Romilly, *Observations*, p. 38.

35 Romilly, *Observations*, pp. 88–9.

36 Romilly, *Observations*, pp. 58–63.

37 Lansdowne to Romilly, 25 December 1785, reprinted in full in the *Memoirs*, v. 1, p. 328.

38 Romilly, *Memoirs*, v. 1, pp. 90 and 334. For Scarlett's introduction to Romilly, see Peter Campbell Scarlett, *A Memoir of the Right Honorable James, First Lord Abinger* (London: John Murray, 1877), p. 38.

39 *Memoirs*, v. 1, p 91.

40 Scarlett, p. 53.
41 Romilly, *Memoirs*, v. 1, pp vii–viii.
42 Romilly, *Memoirs*, v. 3, footnote on pp. 372–3.
43 MS Misc. 246 (also called 'Sir Samuel Romilly MS'), Lincoln's Inn, pp. 9–11 This manuscript appears to have been made from original documents and contains excerpts from several of the essays. It is uneven, and may have been compiled by one of his sons in the 1820s, since it refers at one point to Henry Brougham still as 'Mr Brougham'.
44 Romilly, *Memoirs*, v. 1, pp. 102–3 and 354–5.
45 Published in London in 1790.
46 Romilly *Probable Influence*, pp. 8–10.
47 *Probable Influence*, p. 12.
48 *Probable Influence*, p. 13 For the contrast, see his comments from his political journal of 1808 in *Memoirs*, v. 2, p. 247
49 *Memoirs*, pp. 107–12.
50 *Letters, containing an account of the late Revolution in France, and observations on the Constitution, Laws, Manners and Institutions of the English; written during the Author's residence at Paris, Versailles, and London, in the years 1789 and 1790*, translated from the German of Henry Frederic Groenvelt (London, 1792).
51 The book contained twelve 'letters' by Dumont, eleven from Romilly, and one from James Scarlett. See also Jefferson Selth, *Firm Heart and Capacious Mind: the Life and Friends of Etienne Dumont* (Lanham, MD: University Press of America, 1977), pp. 89–91.
52 Scarlett, p. 55. Scarlett moved into the Tory party in the 1820s, after Romilly's death.
53 Romilly's contributions to the volume bear the following titles: XIII On Lotteries, XIV On the Civil and Criminal Laws of England; XV On English Newspapers, XVI On the British Constitution, XVII On Elections of Members of Parliament; XVIII On Cruelty towards Animals; XIX On the Restraints Imposed by the English on Commerce; XX On Judicial Legislation, XXI On Literature and Literary Societies; XXII On Nobility; XXIII On the Attempts made in England to Abolish the Slave Trade
54 Scarlett, p. 55.
55 Oakes, p. 69
56 John Bowring, *The Works of Jeremy Bentham*, v. 10 (New York: Russell & Russell, 1962, reproduction of the Bowring edition of 1838–43), p. 186.
57 See the first chapter of Jeremy Bentham, *An Introduction to the Principles of Morals and Legislation* (London, 1789), for a more complete discussion of his definition and use of the 'principle of utility'.
58 Bowring in Bentham's *Works*, v 10, p 504 Dr Samuel Parr, who had become a great admirer of Bentham because of his plan for the Panopticon, met him at a dinner arranged by Romilly. See Romilly to Bentham, 13 February 1803, BL Add. MS 33544, f. 33.
59 See John Dinwiddy, *Bentham* (Oxford: Oxford University Press, 1989), p. 10; also Selth, pp. 151–80.
60 See Michel Foucault's *Discipline and Punish* (New York: Vintage Books, 1979; translated by Alan Sheridan from the French *Surveiller et punir; naissance de la prison*, Paris, 1975); Michael Ignatieff's *A Just Measure of Pain: the Penitentiary in the Industrial Revolution, 1750–1850* (London Penguin, 1989; first

published in 1978) provides further insight into Bentham's plan (pp. 109–13), but the first comprehensive attempt to reevaluate Bentham's scheme is Janet Semple's *Bentham's Prison: a Study of the Panopticon Penitentiary* (Oxford: Clarendon Press, 1993).

61 Bentham to Romilly, 27 November 1812, BL Add. MS 33544, f. 654.

62 5 April 1791, printed in the *Memoirs*, v. 1, p. 416.

63 Letter to Dumont, 9 January 1802, in *Memoirs*, v. 2, p. 75.

64 Bentham's contemporary Sydney Smith said he needed a 'middleman' to make his message understood; see his review of Bentham's *Book of Fallacies*, in the *Edinburgh Review*, v. 84 (1825), p. 367. The legal philosopher H. L. A. Hart has readily agreed with Smith's assessment; see Hart, *Essays on Bentham: Studies in Jurisprudence and Political Theory* (Oxford: Clarendon Press, 1982), p. 1.

65 Sir Samuel Romilly MS, Lincoln's Inn MS Misc. 246, pp. 14–15.

66 *Edinburgh Review*, v. 29, pp. 217–37.

67 Romilly, *Edinburgh Review*, v. 29, pp. 236–7.

68 See Bowring, ed , *Works*, v. 10, p. 450, regarding a letter from Romilly in 1810, urging Bentham not to publish his tract, 'Elements of Packing', which strongly condemned the practice in the courts.

69 Bentham to Sidmouth, 13 June 1812. BL Add. MS 33544, f 617.

70 The proposal appears in Bowring, ed., *Works*, v 10, pp. 468–71.

71 Madison was prevented by the hostilities between Britain and the US in 1812–15 from responding immediately, but he did reply in 1816 with a very gracious letter acknowledging receipt of the proposal and praising his efforts in legal theory, but gently turning down the offer. Pres. James Madison to Bentham, 8 May 1816, BL Add. MS 33545, ff. 222f.

72 Bowring, ed., *Works*, v. 10, p 469.

73 Romilly to Bentham, 12 September 1806, BL Add. MS 33544, ff. 209f

74 Romilly to Bentham, 1808, in Bowring, ed., *Works*, v. 10, p. 432.

75 On the theoretical import of Bentham's philosophy of positive law, see Gerald L. Postema, *Bentham and the Common Law Tradition* (Oxford: Clarendon Press, 1986).

76 *Groenvelt's Letters*, pp. 253–65, 276–83, and 318–28, respectively.

77 Lincoln's Inn MS Misc. 246, p. 17.

78 'Letters to C (1801)', *Memoirs*, v. 3, p. 382.

79 David Lieberman, *The Province of Legislation Determined: Legal Theory in Eighteenth-Century Britain* (Cambridge: Cambridge University Press, 1989), p 200.

80 Elie Halévy, *The Growth of Philosophical Radicalism* (London: Faber & Gwyer, 1928; reprinted in 1949 by Faber and Faber), p. 300. This is a translation by Mary Morris of Elie Halévy, *La formation du radical philosophique* (Paris, 1901).

81 Halévy, p. 299.

82 *Groenvelt Letters*, p. 237.

83 *Groenvelt Letters*, p. 239.

84 Jeremy Bentham, 'Law versus arbitrary power – or a Hatchet for Dr. Paley's Net', Bentham Papers, UC cvii 193–343. The unfinished manuscript is discussed in Fred Rosen, 'Utilitarianism and the Reform of the Criminal Law', *Cambridge History of Eighteenth-Century Thought*, and also in J. E Crimmins, 'Strictures on Paley's Net: Capital Punishment and the Power to Pardon', *The Bentham Newsletter*, no. 11 (June 1987), pp. 23–34. See also T. P. Schofield, 'A

Comparison of the Moral Theories of William Paley and Jeremy Bentham',
The Bentham Newsletter, no 11, pp. 4–22.
85 See Crimmins, p. 24.
86 *Observations on the Criminal Law*, pp. 28ff.
87 William Thomas, *The Philosophical Radicals: Nine Studies in Theory and Practice, 1817–1841* (Oxford: Clarendon Press, 1979), pp. 10–11.
88 Henry Brougham's recollections of Romilly and Bentham in his *Historical Sketches of Statesmen who Flourished in the Time of George III* (London: Charles Knight & Co., 1839) also treat Romilly as an independent benefactor of mankind; see pp. 290–8.

4   Evangelicalism and Penal Law Reform

1 The numbers varied over time. See Ian Bradley's unpublished dissertation, 'The Politics of Godliness: Evangelicals in Parliament, 1784–1832' (Oxford University, 1974), which is still the best study of Evangelical political attitudes Bradley's later book, *Call to Seriousness: the Evangelical Impact on the Victorians* (London: Jonathan Cape, 1976), allows later trends in English Evangelicalism to overshadow attitudes and purposes of these earlier politicians.
2 'Politics', p. 1; for the list, see Appendix 1, pp 271–88.
3 See Boyd Hilton, *Age of Atonement: the Influence of Evangelicalism on Social and Economic Thought, 1795–1865* (Oxford Clarendon Press, 1988), pp. 10–11 and 16ff. Hilton and Bradley both portray the Recordites as a vocal minority whose theological and political beliefs were a minority among Evangelicals.
4 Robert Isaac and Samuel Wilberforce, *The Life of William Wilberforce* (London: John Murray, 1838), v. 3, p. 60. See also John Pollock, *Wilberforce* (London: Constable, 1977), pp. 126–36; perhaps the most complete statement of Wilberforce's dislike of the party is the memorandum reprinted in the *Life*, v. 2, pp. 452–9.
5 Stephen to Perceval, 3 March 1809, Perceval Papers, Add. MS 49183, f. 112.
6 Undated letter (sometime in 1812), Thornton Papers, Cambridge University Library, ADD 7674, 1/67.
7 See Wilberforce, *Life*, v. 3, pp. 231 and 362.
8 Brougham to Wilberforce, MS Wilberforce, c. 3, ff. 86–7. See also Wilberforce, *Life*, v. 3, pp. 255–7
9 Thornton's *Enquiry into the Nature and Effects of the Paper Credit of Great Britain* (London, 1802) was praised in the twentieth century by both John Maynard Keynes and Friedrich Hayek, one of their few points of agreement; see Standish Meacham, *Henry Thornton of Clapham,1760–1815* (Cambridge, MA Harvard University Press, 1964), pp. 73ff.
10 Wilberforce to Cartwright, 18 March 1809, MS Wilberforce d. 56, ff 178–80.
11 Wilberforce to Cartwright, 30 December 1815, MS Wilberforce d 56, f. 82.
12 See David Bebbington, *Evangelicalism in Modern Britain: a History from the 1730s to the 1980s* (London: Unwin Hyman, 1989), pp. 5f, and 45f. While not without controversy, Bebbington has provided the best single overview of Evangelical theology and practice in Britain.

13 William Wilberforce, *A Practical View of the Prevailing Religious Systems of Professed Christians, in the Higher and Middle Classes in this Country, Contrasted with Real Christianity* (London, 1797), p. 127. The *Practical View* had four editions in its first year, and was reprinted several times the first three decades of the nineteenth century, with its 18th London edition appearing in 1830.

14 Wilberforce, *Practical View*, p. 128

15 Bebbington, pp. 42–60.

16 D. Bruce Hindmarsh, *John Newton and the English Evangelical Tradition* (Oxford: Clarendon Press, 1996), p. 64. See also *Thoughts of the Evangelical Leaders: Notes of the Discussion of the Eclectic Society, London during the years 1798–1814* (Carlisle, PA: Banner of Truth, 1978, reprint of the first edition: London, 1856), John H. Pratt, ed., pp 147f, 199f, 209f, 221f, 263f, 289f, 310f, and 500f.

17 Henry Venn, *The Complete Duty of Man; or a System of Doctrinal and Practical Christianity*, seventh edition (Bath, 1803), p. 126

18 See Bebbington, *Evangelicalism in Modern Britain*, pp. 47ff.

19 In *The Atlantic Slave Trade and British Abolition 1760–1810* (Atlantic Highlands, NJ: Humanities Press, 1975), Roger Anstey notes the especially strong regard for Thomas Reid among evangelical writers, p. 177.

20 Wilberforce, *Practical View*, p. 365.

21 Bradley, 'Politics', p. 13.

22 Wilberforce, *Practical View*, pp. 404–5.

23 Hannah More, *An Estimate of the Religion of the Fashionable World* (London, 1808 ed.), p. 146.

24 See Ford K. Brown, *Fathers of the Victorians: the Age of Wilberforce* (Cambridge University Press, 1961), pp. 317–60 for a list and discussion of the multitude of bettering societies.

25 Michael R. Watts, *The Dissenters; Volume II: The Expansion of Evangelical Nonconformity* (Oxford: Clarendon Press, 1995), p. 20.

26 For an example with regard to legal change, see W. R. Cornish and G. de N. Clark's *Law and Society in England, 1750–1950* (London: Sweet & Maxwell, 1989), pp 67–8.

27 Wilberforce, *Practical View*, p. 150.

28 See Pratt, *Thought of the Evangelical Leaders*, pp. 305–7. Wilberforce, Henry Thornton, and Thomas Fowell Buxton all kept notebooks to record both their activities and the relation of these to their spiritual state.

29 The much-used quotation comes from St. Paul's letter to the Ephesians 2:10.

30 See Bebbington, *Evangelicalism in Modern Britain*, p 45.

31 Wilberforce, *Life*, v. 3, pp. 79–80.

32 Abraham Kriegel quotes the phrase about winning heaven in the context of Evangelical emphasis on work in 'A Convergence of Ethics: Saints and Whigs in British Antislavery', *Journal of British Studies*, v. 26 (1987), p. 432. His statement is true, that the Evangelicals saw activity as important, but his reference to this particular passage is inapt.

33 Wilberforce makes this reference to Mark 9:24 in the *Practical View*, p. 128.

34 See Wilberforce, *Practical View*, pp. 190–2.

35 *Christian Observer*, v. 2 (1803), p. 44.

36 Consider Hume's famous comment from *A Treatise of Human Nature* (1738) that 'reason is, and ought to be the slave of the passions, and can never pretend to any other office than to serve and obey them', quoted from OUP edition (Oxford: 1951), v. 2, p. 282.

37 On Gisborne's influence, see Sir James Stephen, *Essays in Ecclesiastical Biography* (London: Longman, Brown, Green and Longman, 1850, second edition), v. 2, pp. 302.

38 Thomas Gisborne, *Principles of Moral Philosophy investigated, and briefly applied to the constitution of civil society; together with remarks on the principle assumed by Mr. Paley* (London, second edition, 1790), p. 17.

39 Gisborne, p. 21.

40 See *Christian Observer*, v. 4, 1805, pp. 363f. See also Wilberforce to Thomas Babington, 5 November 1799, Wilberforce, *Life*, v. 2, p. 351.

41 Gisborne, p. 17.

42 Pratt, *Thought of the Evangelical Leaders*, p. 364.

43 Wilberforce, *Practical View*, pp. 397, 402.

44 *Christian Observer*, v. 1 (1802), 'Prospectus', p. iii.

45 *Eclectic Review*, v 1 (1805), p 1.

46 See the *Eclectic Review* enthusiastic, though not uncritical, article about Bentham's *Théorie des peines et des récompenses*; v. 8 (1812), pp. 77–87.

47 *Philanthropist*, v. 1 (1811), p. 1.

48 Wilberforce to Grenville, 22 June 1804, Wilberforce, *Life*, v. 3, pp. 179–80

49 From the Diary, 2 July 1804, quoted in Wilberforce, *Life*, v. 3, p. 183

50 Hannah More, *Thoughts on the Importance of the Manners of the Great to General Society*, edition published together with *An Estimate of the Religion of the Fashionable World* (London, 1809), p. 25.

51 See Randall McGowen's 'The Changing Face of God's Justice: the Debates over Divine and Human Punishments in Eighteenth-Century England', *Criminal Justice History*, pp. 63–98, and Harry Potter, *Hanging in Judgement: Religion and the Death Penalty in England* (New York: Continuum Publishing, 1993), p. 15.

52 Both Hannah More's *Thoughts on the Importance of the Manners of the Great to General Society* and Wilberforce's *Practical View* offered a highly critical view of the value of earthly station and wealth.

53 Based on verses 1:18–32 and 8:18–22 of Paul's letter to the Romans.

54 See James Stephen, *Dangers of the Country* (London, 1807), regarding how the sin of slavery caused God's anger to burn against Britain; Wilberforce used the same general argument in favor of moral reform in the *Practical View*, p. 389.

55 See Bradley, 'Politics', pp 17–19.

56 Wilberforce, *Practical View*, p. 410.

57 See Robert Zaller, 'The Debate on Capital Punishment During the English Revolution', *American Journal of Legal History*, v. 31 (1987), pp. 126–44, and Nancy L. Matthews, *William Sheppard, Cromwell's Law Reformer* (Cambridge University Press, 1984), pp. 169–71.

58 Zaller, p. 136.

59 Basil Montagu, *Opinions of Different Authors upon the Punishment of Death*, in three volumes (London, 1809–13), avoided writers allied with the religious 'enthusiasts' of the Cromwellian era; Thomas Clarkson, however, conscientiously pointed to the historic Quaker opposition to capital punishment in

his *Portraiture of Quakerism* (1806) and *Memoirs of the Private and Public Life of William Penn* (1811).
60 William Blackstone, *Commentaries on the Laws of England*, v. 4 (1769), p. 237.
61 See Exodus, chapters 21–2.
62 21 Hen. VIII c. 11. Blackstone discusses this procedure, v. 4, pp. 355–6.
63 Gisborne, pp. 68–70.
64 Gisborne, p. 123.
65 Gisborne, p. 131.
66 Gisborne, p. 132.
67 See for instance the review of criminal law reform literature in the *Eclectic Review*, N.S. v. 11 (January–June 1819), p. 9.
68 Gisborne, p. 133.
69 Gisborne, p. 132.
70 Gisborne, p. 134.
71 *Eclectic Review*, N.S. v. 11 (1819), pp. 5–9.
72 Thomas Fowell Buxton, *An Inquiry Whether Crime and Misery are Produced or Prevented, by Our Present System of Prison Discipline* (London, 1818), pp. 9–13; see also pp. 65f.
73 Hansard, N.S v. 5 (1821), col. 906.
74 Hansard, v. 17 (1810), col. 339.
75 *The Book of Common Prayer* (Eubury Press, 1992), pp. 18 and 34.
76 Buxton, *Inquiry*, p. 14.
77 *Eclectic Review*, N S. 11, p 21.
78 Hansard, v. 17, col. 339.
79 Buxton, *Inquiry*, p 14.
80 Buxton, *Inquiry*, p. 52.
81 Buxton, *Inquiry*, p. 58.
82 Wilberforce, *Life*, v. 4, p. 370, from his journal for 13 February 1818.

5 The Evangelical Approach to Criminal Law Reform

1 See Robert Zaller, 'The Debate on Capital Punishment During the English Revolution', *American Journal of Legal History* v. 31, pp. 126–44.
2 Douglas Hay et al. in *Albion's Fatal Tree: Crime and Society in Eighteenth-Century England* (New York: Pantheon Books, 1975) and E. P. Thompson in *Whigs and Hunters: the Origin of the Black Act* (New York: Pantheon Books, 1975); even Leon Radzinowicz considered the Waltham Black Act an 'ideological index'; *History of English Criminal Law and its Administration since 1750* (New York: Macmillan Company, 1948), v. 1, p. 51.
3 See Michael Ignatieff, *Just Measure of Pain: the Penitentiary in the Industrial Revolution, 1750–1850* (London: Penguin Books, 1978), pp. 47ff.
4 John Howard's *State of the Prisons in England and Wales* enjoyed four editions between 1777 and 1792. See also Jonas Hanway, *Observations on the Causes of the Dissoluteness which Reigns among the Lower Classes of the People* (1772), *On the Defects of Police* (1775) and *Solitude in Imprisonment* (1776).
5 Basil Montagu, *The Opinion of Different Authors Upon the Punishment of Death*, in three volumes (London, 1809–13)

6   William Blackstone, *Commentaries on the Laws of England*, v. 4 (Oxford, 1769), William Eden, *Principles of Penal Law* (1771).

7   See Simon Devereaux, 'The City and the Sessions Paper: "Public Justice" in London, 1770–1800', *Journal of British Studies*, v. 35, pp. 466–503.

8   Robert Isaac and Samuel Wilberforce, *The Life of William Wilberforce* (London: John Murray, 1838), v. 1, p. 38.

9   Patrick Medd, *Romilly: a Life of Sir Samuel Romilly, Lawyer and Reformer* (London: Collins, 1968), pp. 47–50.

10 Sir Samuel Romilly, *Memoirs on the Life of Sir Samuel Romilly* (London: John Murray, 1840), v. 1, p. 90.

11 Frank McLynn, *Crime and Punishment in Eighteenth- Century England* (Oxford: Oxford University Press, 1991), pp. 271–4.

12 Wilberforce, *Life*, v 1, pp. 114–15; see also John Pollock, *Wilberforce* (London: Constable, 1977), pp 40–2, 47.

13 *Parliamentary History*, v. 26 (May 1786–February 1788), cols. 195–200.

14 For discussion of Pitt's proposed police reforms, see Stanley Palmer, *Police and Protest in England and Ireland, 1780–1850* (New York: Cambridge University Press, 1988), pp. 83–92.

15 Pollock, p. 59.

16 From Bishop Porteus's *Occasional Memorandum and Reflexions* (Porteus MS, Lambeth, 2103.8), quoted in Pollock, p. 60.

17 Wilberforce to Rev. C. Wyvill, 25 July 1787, MS Wilberforce d. 56, ff. 6–7, Bodleian Library.

18 Besides Pollock's *Wilberforce*, see also Sir Reginald Coupland, *Wilberforce* (London: Collins, 1923), and Robin Furneaux, *William Wilberforce* (London: Hamish Hamilton, 1974); also, Ford K. Brown's *Fathers of the Victorians: the Age of Wilberforce* (Cambridge University Press, 1961), and M J. D. Roberts, 'The Society for the Suppression of Vice and its Early Critics, 1802–1812', *Historical Journal*, v. 26 (1983), pp. 159–76.

19 Manchester to Wilberforce, 18 September 1787, Wilberforce Papers, Duke MSS, quoted in Pollock, p. 62.

20 Wilberforce, *Life*, v. 1, p. 237. See also pp. 243–4.

21 Wilberforce, *Life*, v. 1, p. 149.

22 William Wilberforce, *A Practical View of the Prevailing Religious Systems of Professed Christians, in the Higher and Middle Classes in this Country, Contrasted with Real Christianity* (London, 1797), pp. 143, 367, 399–404 and 410.

23 Hansard, v. 19, Appendix col lxxvi.

24 See Romilly's *Observations on a Late Publication*, pp. 30–1. On the growth of the sensibility adverse to public executions, see V. A. C. Gatrell's study, *The Hanging Tree: Public Execution and the English People, 1770–1868* (Oxford: Oxford University Press, 1994)

25 Pitt to Wilberforce, 23 September 1786, and 28 June 1788, in *Private Papers of William Wilberforce* (London, 1897), ed. by A. M. Wilberforce, pp. 16 & 21, respectively.

26 John Beattie, *Crime and the Courts in England, 1660–1800* (Princeton: Princeton University Press, 1986), pp. 569ff.

27 Beattie, pp. 574–5.

28 Janet Semple, *Bentham's Prison: a Study of the Panopticon Penitentiary* (Oxford: Clarendon Press, 1993), p. 106.

29 Quoted in Semple, p. 188.

30 Pollock, pp. 137–8.

31 Bentham to Wilberforce, 28 February 1797, MS Wilberforce d. 13, f. 41.

32 Bentham to Wilberforce, 5 May 1810, MS Wilberforce d. 15, f. 147.

33 Wilberforce to Bentham, 7 May 1810, Add. MS 33544, f. 461.

34 Semple, p. 273. The First and Second Reports of the Holford Committee appear in the Appendix of Hansard, v. 20 (1811), cols. lxxxix–cxxiii.

35 Bentham received £23,779 3s. as compensation in October 1813; Semple, p. 281.

36 See Samuel Crowther to Wilberforce, 8 January 1803, MS Wilberforce d. 17, f 127–8, and Wilberforce, *Life*, v. 3, pp. 82–84, and v. 4, pp. 256, 370.

37 The speech was reprinted by at least three groups; the 'official' version by the Spitalfields Benevolent Society was entitled *The Speech of Thomas Fowell Buxton, Esq., at the Egyptian Hall, on the 26th November, 1816, on the Subject of the Distress in Spitalfields* (London, 1816).

38 Most of the biographical details come from *The Memoirs of Sir Thomas Fowell Buxton, Bart.*, third edition, edited by his son, Charles Buxton (London, 1849).

39 Buxton Papers, MSS Brit. Emp. s. 444, v. 4, f. 379, Rhodes House, Oxford.

40 *Dictionary of Quaker Biography*, Friends House Library, under the listing for Buxton.

41 Buxton's *Memoirs* say nothing about his having joined the Friends, but do record his attendance of Josiah Pratt's ministry, p. 35.

42 *Dictionary of National Biography*, v. 16, pp. 293–4.

43 Buxton to Hannah Buxton, 22 October 1809, MSS Brit. Emp. s. 444, ff. 131–4.

44 *Dictionary of Quaker Biography*.

45 Buxton *Memoirs*, p. 27.

46 Buxton refers to it in a workbook containing drafts of speeches in 1820 and 1821, Buxton Papers, Rhodes House, MSS Brit. Emp. s. 444, v. 8, f. 57.

47 See William Thallack, *Peter Bedford, the Spitalfields Philanthropist* (London, 1865), pp. 36–51. Bedford was a Quaker and also attended the Devonshire House Meeting.

48 Buxton to Hannah Buxton, 9 November 1816, MSS Brit. Emp. s. 444, v. 1, ff. 171–4.

49 Buxton, *Speech*, p. 4.

50 Letter to Hannah Buxton, 27 November 1816, MSS Brit. Emp. s. 444, v. 1, ff. 183–6.

51 Quoted in Buxton, *Memoirs*, p. 53.

52 Letter to Mrs Hannah Buxton, 28 November 1816, MSS Brit. Emp. s. 444, v. 1, f. 187. We are not alone in finding this last an odd compliment – the lines have been drawn through in the original letter.

53 Quoted in Buxton, *Memoirs*, p. 52.

54 Buxton described the formation of the Society in a notebook left for his children. MSS Brit. Emp. s.444, v 4, ff. 381–2.

55 Letter to Hannah Buxton, January 5, 1817, MSS Brit. Emp. s. 444, v 1, ff 195–8.

56 Buxton's high view of independence meant 'that he was neither a threat to the government nor a source of strength to the opposition'. See F. C. Stuart, 'A Critical Edition of the Correspondence of Sir Thomas Fowell Buxton, Bart.,

with an account of his career to 1823,' (MA thesis, University of London, unpublished, 1957), p. 151.
57 Thomas Fowell Buxton, *An Inquiry Whether Crime and Misery are Produced or Prevented, by Our Present System of Prison Discipline* (London, 1818), pp. 83–9.
58 Quoted in Buxton, *Memoirs*, p. 65.
59 Letter to Jonathan Hutchinson, 3 December 1818, Gurney MSS, Temp. MSS 434, 3/331, Friends House Library, London.
60 Letter to Hannah Buxton, 6 December 1818, MSS Brit. Emp. s. 444, v. 1, ff. 235–8.
61 David Turley, *The Culture of English Antislavery, 1780–1860* (London: Routledge, 1991), pp 111ff.
62 Turley, p. 135.
63 Turley, p. 234. A provocative discussion of humanitarianism, capitalism and the British middle-class appears in *The Antislavery Debate: Capitalism and Abolitionism as a Problem in Historical Interpretation* (Berkeley: University of California Press, 1992), ed. by Thomas Bender.
64 Boyd Hilton's *Age of Atonement* (Oxford: Clarendon Press, 1988) overcomes some of this bias, but still portrays political economy as the 'dismal science'. A definitive study of Evangelical views of commerce and its place in civil society has yet to be written
65 Versions of this argument appear in Michael Ignatieff, *A Just Measure of Pain*, Randall McGowen, 'Image of Justice', and Clive Emsley in *Crime and Society in England 1750–1900* (London: Longman, 1987).

6   The Conservative Resistance

1 William Paley, *Principles of Moral and Political Philosophy* (London, 1785). Quotations in this study come from the seventh American edition (Boston, 1811).
2 Paley made his agreement with Burke clear in a letter to Edward Law soon after Burke's book appeared; Paley to Law, 28 November 1790, PRO 30/12, 17/ 4, ff. 33–5.
3 Paley, p. 422.
4 Paley, p. 423.
5 Hansard, v. 19 (1811), Appendix col. lxxxviii.
6 Hansard, v. 19, Appendix col. lviii. Compare to Paley, p. 424.
7 Paley, p. 426.
8 Hansard, v. 19, Appendix cols. liii., lxiv, lxxxvii, lxxxix, and cxii, respectively.
9 Hansard, v. 19, Appendix col. lxx.
10 Quotes from Hansard, v. 19, Appendix cols lxxi and cxiii-iv
11 We are in no better position to judge this either; see Clive Emsley, *Crime and Society in England, 1750–1950* (New York: Longman, 1987), pp. 18ff, or David Taylor, *Crime, Policing and Punishment in England, 1750–1914* (New York: St Martin's Press, 1998), pp. 7ff., for the difficulties of criminal statistics.
12 Hansard, v. 19, Appendix cols. lxxviii and cxiv
13 See Windham's or Ellenborough's comments in Hansard, v. 19, Appendix cols. lx and cxxii.

14 R. G. Thorne, *History of Parliament: the House of Commons, 1790–1820* (London: Secker & Warburg, 1986), v. 3, pp. 830–2.
15 Hansard, v. 19, col. 646.
16 Hansard, v. 19, col. lxxiv.
17 Paley, p. 434.
18 Randall McGowen's 'The Image of Justice and the Reform of the Criminal Law in Early Nineteenth-Century England', *Buffalo Law Review*, v. 32 (1983), pp. 89–125.
19 Paley, p. 426.
20 Hansard, v. 19, Appendix col. xlv.
21 Hansard, v. 19, Appendix cols. lxxxviii, xc, and cxviii.
22 Recorded in Sir Samuel Romilly, *Memoirs of the Life of Sir Samuel Romilly* (London: John Murray, 1840), v. 2, p. 331.
23 Hansard, v. 19, Appendix col. cx.
24 Hansard, v. 19, Appendix col. lxx.
25 Hansard, v. 19, Appendix col. lxxiv.
26 Hansard, v. 19, Appendix col. xliv
27 Hansard, v. 19, Appendix col. lxxxi.
28 Hansard, v. 19, Appendix col. lxv.
29 Hansard, v. 19, col. 622.
30 John Lord Campbell, *Lives of the Chief Justices of England From the Norman Conquest till the Death of Lord Tenterden* (London: John Murray, 1857), v. 3, pp. 109–42.
31 Hansard, v. 19, Appendix cols. lxxi, lxxxii, xcii.
32 Campbell, *Chief Justices*, v. 3, p. 94.
33 Quoted in Peter Campbell Scarlett, *A Memoir of the Rt. Honorable James, First Lord Abinger* (London: John Murray, 1877), p. 83.
34 Ellenborough to Wilberforce, *c.*1804, MS. Wilberforce c. 3, ff. 68–70, Bodleian Library.
35 The manuscript is found in the Ellenborough Papers at the Public Records Office at Kew, PRO 30/12, 17/9, f. 147.
36 Eldon to Wilberforce, *c.*1806, MS Wilberforce c. 3, f. 80.
37 John Lord Campbell, *The Lives of the Lord Chancellors and Keepers of the Great Seal of England, from the earliest times till the Reign of Queen Victoria* (New edition, Boston: Estes & Lauriat, 1875), v. 9, pp. 391ff.
38 Horace Twiss, *The Public and Private Life of Lord Chancellor Eldon, with Selections from his Correspondence* (London: John Murray, second edition, 1844), v. 3, p. 323.
39 See Wilberforce, *Life*, v. 5, pp. 341–2.
40 Hansard, v. 19, Appendix col. cxiii.
41 For a critical discussion of the King in Council, see V. A. C. Gatrell, *The Hanging Tree: Execution and the English People, 1770–1868* (Oxford University Press, 1994), pp. 543ff.
42 Twiss, v. 1, p. 398.
43 Twiss, v. 1, p. 399.
44 The importance of 'respectability' is underlined by recent scholarly debate; see F. M. L. Thompson, *The Rise of Respectability: a Social History of Victorian Britain, 1830–1900* (London: Fontana, 1988); Peter Linebaugh, *The London Hanged: Crime and Civil Society in the Eighteenth Century* (London: Penguin

Books, 1991); also Simon Cordery, 'Friendly Societies and the Discourse of Respectability in Britain, 1825–1875', *Journal of British Studies*, v. 34 (1995), pp. 35–58.

45 See Randall McGowen, 'A Powerful Sympathy: Terror, the Prison and Humanitarian Reform in Early Nineteenth-Century Britain', *Journal Of British Studies*, v. 25 (1986), pp. 312–34, and Gatrell, *The Hanging Tree*, especially pp 225–41

7 Mobilizing Opinion, 1811–18

1 See Thomas W. Lacquer, 'Crowds, Carnival and the State in English Executions, 1604–1868', in A. L. Beier, David Cannadine and James M. Rosenheim, eds, *The First Modern Society: Essays in English History in Honour of Lawrence Stone* (Cambridge University Press, 1989), pp. 305–55, and also V. A. C Gatrell, *The Hanging Tree: Execution and the English People, 1770–1868* (Oxford, 1994), especially pp. 56ff.

2 See Gatrell, pp. 225ff. See also Thomas Haskell, 'Capitalism and the Origins of the Humanitarian Sensibility', *American Historical Review*, v. 90 (1985), 339–61 and 547–66, and Randall McGowen, 'A Powerful Sympathy: Terror, the Prison, and Humanitarian Reform in Early Nineteenth-Century Britain', *Journal of British Studies*, v. 25 (July 1986), 312–34.

3 See Hansard, v. 18 (1811), col. 1263ff.

4 Hansard, v. 19 (1811), col. 106.

5 Letter to Lord Holland, BL Add. MS 51826, f. 150; and Sir Samuel Romilly, *Memoirs on the Life of Sir Samuel Romilly, written by himself; with a selection of his correspondence* (London: John Murray, 1840), v 2, p 367.

6 Hansard, v 19, col. 657

7 William Frankland, *The Speech of William Frankland in the House of Commons, . . . 29th of March 1811 on the second reading of several bills, brought in by Sir S. Romilly, for making alterations in the criminal law* (London, 1811)

8 Hansard, v 19, col. 645

9 Hansard, v. 19, cols. 651, 649, and 653, respectively.

10 See Hansard, v. 19, cols. 660–1, and cols. 743–5

11 Romilly to Lord Holland, 11 April 1811; BL Add. MS 51826 (Holland Papers), f 146.

12 Romilly to Lord Holland, 13 April 1811; BL Add. MS 51826, f 147.

13 Hansard, v 20 (1811), cols 296ff.

14 Hansard, v. 19, col 744.

15 See Hansard, v. 21 (1812), col. 701ff

16 Quoted in Romilly, *Memoirs*, v. 3, pp 19–20.

17 See Hansard, v. 21 (1812), col. 807ff.

18 Hansard, v. 21, col. 831ff.

19 Romilly, *Memoirs*, v. 3, p. 80

20 Hansard, v. 25 (1813), cols 389, and 524–6, respectively

21 Hansard, v. 38 (1818), col. 48.

22 Romilly, *Memoirs*, v. 3, p 334.

23 Hansard, v. 38, col 1185.

24 Hansard, v. 25, col. 526.

25 Hansard, v. 38, cols. 50–1.
26 See Leon Radzinowicz, *A History of the English Criminal Law and its Adminis-tration from 1750*, v. 1 (New York: Macmillan, 1948), pp. 517–18.
27 See Hansard, v. 26 (1813), cols. 301–4, and Romilly's *Memoirs*, v. 3, pp. 107–10.
28 Romilly, *Memoirs*, v. 2, p. 304–5.
29 *Monthly Review*, v. 61 (1810), p. 311; *European Magazine*, v. 57 (1810), pp. 211–12; *Quarterly Review*, v. 7 (1812), pp. 159–79; and *Monthly Magazine or British Register*, v. 31 (1811), p. 415.
30 *Anti-Jacobin Review*, v. 38 (1811), pp. 222–3.
31 *Edinburgh Review*, v. 19 (1812), p. 415
32 See Trowbridge H. Ford, 'English Criminal Law Reform During and After the Napoleonic Wars', *Anglo-American Law Review*, v. 7 (1978), pp. 243–70, which traces Brougham's efforts for penal and other areas of reform.
33 *Quarterly Review*, v. 7 (1812), p. 165.
34 *Eclectic Review*, v 6 (1810), p. 372.
35 *Eclectic Review*, v. 1 (1805), p. 2.
36 *Eclectic Review*, v. 5 (1809), p. 1152
37 *Eclectic Review*, v. 8 (1812), p. 87.
38 See *The Thought of the Evangelical Leaders: Notes of the Discussions of the Eclectic Society, London during the years 1798–1814* (Carlisle, PA: Banner of Truth, 1978 reprint of the first edition: London, 1856), John H. Pratt, ed., pp. 92–3.
39 *Christian Observer*, v. 9 (1810), p. 125.
40 See *Christian Observer*, v. 10 (1811), p. 389, on the criminal returns, and v. 15 (1816), p. 256, and v. 16 (1817), pp. 610 and 825.
41 *Monthly Repository*, v. 6 (1811), pp. 641–5 and 709–11.
42 *The Pamphleteer*, v. 3 (1814), pp. 115–54.
43 John William Polidori, 'On the Punishment of Death', *The Pamphleteer*, v. 8 (1816), p 283
44 Gatrell writes at length about the case of Eliza Fenning in *The Hanging Tree*, pp. 353–70.
45 See Romilly's *Memoirs*, v. 3, pp. 235–6.
46 *Examiner*, 13 August 1815; quoted in Gatrell, p. 363
47 William Hone and John Watkins, *The Important Results of an elaborate investigation into the mysterious case of Elizabeth Fenning* (London, 1815).
48 She even received an article in the *Dictionary of National Biography* (London: Oxford University Press, 1949), v. 6, pp. 1183–4.
49 Gatrell, p. 369
50 This was reflected in the shifting title for the society. See the accounts in *The Life of William Allen, with selections from his Correspondence*, in three volumes (London: Charles Gilpin, 1846), p 104, Hansard, v. 19 (1811), Appendix col. i, and Basil Montagu, *An Account of the Origin and Object of the Society for the Diffusion of Knowledge upon the Punishment of Death, and the Improvement of Prison Discipline* (London, 1812).
51 Radzinowicz, p. 348.
52 See Basil Montagu, *Thoughts upon the Abolition of the Penalty of Death in Cases of Bankruptcy* (London, 1821), p. 32, and *Thoughts on the Punishment of Death for Forgery* (London, 1830), p. 90.
53 Montagu, *Account*, pp. 3–7.
54 Allen, *Life*, v. 1, p. 92.

55   Allen, *Life*, v. 1, p. 104.
56   Allen, *Life*, v. 1, p. 106.
57   A list of subscribers appears at the end of Montagu's *Account*, pp. 14–15.
58   See *Memoirs of Sir Thomas Fowell Buxton, Bart.* (Third edition, London: John Murray, 1849; the first edition appeared in 1848), p. 27 On Wilberforce, see *The Dictionary of National Biography*, v. 1, pp. 322–3.
59   Allen, *Life*, v. 1, p. 178.
60   *The Opinions of Different Authors Upon the Punishment of Death*, selected by Basil Montagu (London, 1809).
61   Quoted in Montagu's *Account*, pp. 11–12.
62   *Opinions*, v. 2 (1812), p. 190.
63   Basil Montagu, *An Inquiry into the Aspersions upon the late Ordinary of Newgate* (London, 1815), pp. 3–4.
64   The exact size of the circulation of these tracts is unclear, but 2000 copies of numbers one and two were *reprinted* in 1818. Notes of the Subcommittee of the Society for Diffusing Information on the Punishment of Death, and Prison Discipline, January 23, 1818, Friends House Library (London) Temp. MS 4/5, p. 12b.
65   Tract no. 1: *Address of the Society for Diffusing Information on the Subject of Capital Punishment and Prison Discipline* (London, 1817), p. 4.
66   From Thomas Clarkson's *Memoirs of the Life of William Penn* quoted in Tract no. 1, p. 4.
67   Tract no. 2: *An Account of the Maison de Force at Ghent* (London, 1817), p. 12. The account originally appeared in *The Philanthropist*, v 7 (May 1817), pp. 31ff.
68   *On the Effects of Capital Punishment as applied to Forgery and Theft* (London, 1818), pp. 17–18.
69   Notes of the Subcommittee, 7 March 1818, Temp. MS 4/5, p. 14a.
70   Basil Montagu, *Some Inquiries respecting the Punishment of Death for Crimes without Violence* (London, 1818)
71   Montagu, *Some Inquiries*, p. 41.
72   See Jeremy Bentham's *Introduction to the Principles of Morals and Legislation*, chapter 3, sections 4–7 (p. 25 in the Hafner Press, New York, edition of 1948).
73   From 'On the Duty and Pleasure of Cultivating Benevolent Dispositions', *The Philanthropist*, v. 1 (1811), p. 2.
74   See Alexander Bain, *James Mill: a Biography* (London: Longmans, Green & Co., 1882), pp. 113ff.
75   *The Philanthropist*, v. 7 (1819), p. 152.
76   Notes of the Sub-Committee, 21 April 1817, Temp. MSS 4/5, Friends House Library, p. 6.
77   Notes of the Subcommittee, 5 May 1817, Temp. MS 4/5, p. 7.
78   A copy of the circular letter has been preserved with the Notes of the Sub-committee at Friends House Library, Temp. MS 4/5, p. 14b (15a). Five hundred copies of the circular were printed.
79   A sheet in the Ann Knight Papers at the Friends House Library (MS Box W2, 6/15) bears the title 'Authenticated facts &c. published *one at a time* in the Journals (Provincial) in England, without expense, being sent to the Editors as contributions'. It contains 27 sections ranging from parliamentary quotations to stories and statistics.

80 J. E. Bicheno, *Observations on the Philosophy of Criminal Jurisprudence, being an Investigation of the Principles necessary to be kept in View during the Revision of the Penal Code, with remarks on Penitentiary Prisons* (London, 1819).

81 Gatrell, pp. 403–8.

82 See Hansard, v. 37 (1818), cols. 603–6, and v. 38, cols. 271–84, 671–703.

83 See Romilly, *Memoirs*, v. 3, pp. 331–2, and *Christian Observer*, v. 17, p. 835, for other expressions of dissatisfaction with execution for those convicted of forgery.

84 T. F. Buxton, *An Inquiry Whether Crime and Misery are Produced or Prevented, by Our Present System of Prison Discipline* (London, 1818).

8 The Partnership: Mackintosh and Buxton, 1819–22

1 See John Fairburn, *Memoir of the Late Sir Samuel Romilly* (London, 1818), p 45. See also G. Smeeton, *Memoir of the Life of that Illustrious Patriot, Sir Samuel Romilly* (London, 1818).

2 Fairburn, p. 48.

3 Horace Twiss, *Life of Lord Chancellor Eldon* (London, 1844, second edition), v. 2, p. 324. The *Christian Observer* for November 1818 (v. 17, p. 768) recorded the story as evidence that Romilly was universally respected.

4 Stephen to Wilberforce, MS Wilberforce c. 50, f. 82, and Wilberforce to Stephen, MS Wilberforce d. 16, f. 105, Bodleian Library.

5 *Christian Observer*, v. 17 (1818), pp. 815–17.

6 Thomas Belsham, *Reflections upon the Death of Sir Samuel Romilly* (London, 1818) p. 1.

7 Quoted in C. G. Oakes, *Sir Samuel Romilly, 1757–1818: 'A Friend of the Oppressed': His Life and Times – His Work, His Family and His Friends* (London: George Allen & Unwin, Ltd., 1935), p. 377.

8 Fairburn, p. 49. Lord Holland took Romilly's children into his care.

9 See Hansard, v. 39 (1819), cols. 396–400.

10 Letter of 11 February 1819, quoted in Robert & Samuel Wilberforce, *The Life of William Wilberforce* (London: John Murray, 1838), p. 13.

11 Wilberforce to Simeon, 12 February 1819, quoted in full in the *Life*, v 5, p. 14.

12 Mackintosh to Lord Holland, 6 January 1819, BL Add. MS 51653, f. 79.

13 Mackintosh to Lord Holland, BL Add MS 51653, f. 79.

14 Mackintosh to Holland, 10 January 1819, BL Add MS 51653, f. 81.

15 Notes of the Subcommittee, 23 January 1818, Temp. MSS 4/5, p. 13b.

16 Favell later served as a member of the Dissenting Deputies as a representative of the Independents and would prompt the Common Council of London to petition for the repeal of the Test and Corporation Acts in 1828. See Guildhall Library, London, Minutes of the Dissenting Deputies, 3083, 6, pp. 177–9 (28 March 1827) and pp. 262–5 (25 January 1828).

17 Samuel Favell, *A Speech on the Propriety of Revising the Criminal Laws* (London, 1819), p. 27.

18 Favell, p. 26. See also the inscription, page iii.

19 For the London Petition, see the *Journals of the House of Commons*, v. 74, p. 33.

20 See Hansard, v. 19 (1811), Appendix cols. lxxiv–lxxvii, and *The Book of Common Prayer*, morning and evening prayers for absolution.

21   All are listed in the *Index of the Journals of the House of Commons, vols. 56–75* (London: Hansard & Sons, 1825), p. 732. See also v. 74 of the *Journals* (1818–19) under the various dates of their presentation

22   V. A. C. Gatrell's assertion that the Quakers initiated the 'petitioning wave in 1819' is unjustified, as is his comment that they had 'dictated' the 'terms' of the London petition. See V. A. C. Gatrell, *The Hanging Tree: Execution and the English People, 1770–1868* (Oxford: Oxford University Press, 1994), p. 401.

23   Hansard, v. 39, col. 399

24   See Mackintosh's 2 March speech, Hansard, v. 39 (1819), p. 799.

25   Diary entry for 9 February 1819, MS Wilberforce c. 37, f. 178, the letter to J. J. Gurney is quoted in John Pollock's *Wilberforce* (London: Constable, 1977), p. 264.

26   Charles C. F. Greville, *The Greville Memoirs: a Journal of the Reigns of King George IV and King William IV* (New York: Appleton and Co., 1875), v. 1, p. 14

27   Recorded in Wilberforce's diary, MS Wilberforce c. 37, f. 178.

28   Hansard, v. 39, col. 398.

29   On 22 January; see Hansard, v. 39, col. 71.

30   See Hansard, v. 39, cols. 645–49 for the Lords's debate, and cols. 740–59 for the Commons' discussion of Castlereagh's committee on prisons.

31   Prison reform is a full topic beyond the focus of this present study. Interested readers should begin with Michael Ignatieff's book *A Just Measure of Pain: the Penitentiary in the Industrial Revolution, 1750–1850* (London: Penguin Books, 1978) and David Taylor, *Crime, Policing and Punishment in England, 1750–1914* (New York: St. Martin's Press, 1998), especially pp. 141ff.

32   Mackintosh to Wilberforce, 28 February 1819, MS Wilberforce d 14, f 176.

33   Hansard, v. 39, cols. 776–7.

34   For the debate on Mackintosh's motion, see Hansard, v. 39, col. 777ff.

35   Mackintosh to Wilberforce, 28 February 1819, MS Wilberforce d. 14, f. 176.

36   Hansard, v. 39, col. 787.

37   Letter to J. J. Gurney, 25 February 1819, MSS Brit. Emp. s. 444, f 104.

38   Hansard, v. 39, cols. 807ff.

39   W. Smith to J. J Gurney, 3 March 1819, quoted in the Buxton *Memoirs*, p. 73.

40   *Christian Observer*, v. 18 (1819), p. 208.

41   *Edinburgh Review*, review of the *Returns of Prosecutions and Convictions for Forging Notes of the Bank of England*, v. 31 (December 1818 – March 1819), pp. 203–14; *Eclectic Review*, N S. v. 11 (January–June 1819), pp. 2–3.

42   William Roscoe, *Observations on Penal Jurisprudence and the Reformation of Criminals* (London, 1819), p. 38.

43   J. E. Bicheno, *Observations on the Philosophy of Criminal Jurisprudence, being an Investigation of the Principles necessary to be kept in View during the Revision of the Penal Code, with remarks on Penitentiary Prisons* (London, 1819), pp. 155–69

44   *Substance of the Speech of Thomas Fowell Buxton, Esq., M.P., in the House of Commons, March 2nd, 1819 ...* (London, 1819).

45   Hansard, v. 40 (1819), cols. 1518–36 *The Report of the Select Committee on the Criminal Laws* was ordered to be printed by the House of Commons, 8 July 1819.

46   Buxton, *Memoirs*, p. 74

47   Buxton to J. H. North, 19 April 1819, quoted in the Buxton *Memoirs*, p 76.

48 See Leon Radzinowicz, *A History of the English Criminal Law* (New York: Macmillan Company, 1948), v. 1, pp. 541–51, for a synopsis of the committee's methods and questions.
49 See the Appendices of the *Report*, pp. 124–270.
50 *Report*, p. 8.
51 Hansard, v 40, col. 1526.
52 John Miller, 'Report from the Select Committee on Criminal Laws', *Quarterly Review*, v. 24 (1820–21), p. 230.
53 Hansard, N.S. v. 5 (1821), cols. 893–5.
54 *Report*, p. 123.
55 *Report*, p. 116.
56 Witnesses from the CPS included Samuel Hoare, Basil Montagu, Thomas Furley Forster, Edward Forster, William Fry, Dr Stephen Lushington, Daniel Gurney (Buxton's brother-in-law), Sir Richard Philips and Richard Taylor; and from the PDS, William Evans and Isaac Lyon Goldsmid
57 See *Eclectic Review*, N S. v 12 (July–December 1819), p. 120
58 From the *Report*, p. 7:
      1) 1 & 2 Phi. and Mary c. 4. Egyptians (i.e., gypsies) remaining within the kingdom one month;
      2) 18 Charles II c. 3. Notorious Thieves in Cumberland and Northumberland;
      3) 9 Geo I c. 22. Being armed and disguised in any forest, Park &c.;
      4) _____ in any warren;
      5) _____ in any high road, open heath, common or down;
      6) _____ Unlawfully hunting, killing or stealing deer;
      7) _____ Robbing Warrens, &c.;
      8) _____ Stealing or taking any fish out of any river or pond, &c.;
      9) _____ Hunting in His Majesty's forests or chases;
      10) _____ Breaking down the head or mound of a fish pond;
      11) 9 Geo. I c. 28. Being disguised within the Mint;
      12) 12 Geo. II c. 29 Injuring Westminster Bridge, and other Bridges by other Acts.
59 From the *Report*, p. 7:
      1) 31 Eliz c. 9. Taking away any Maid, Widow, or Wife, &c.;
      2) 21 Jac I c. 26. Acknowledging or procuring any Find, Recovery, &c.;
      3) 4 Geo. I c. 11, s. 4. Helping to the recovery of stolen goods;
      4) 9 Geo. I c. 22 Maliciously killing or wounding cattle;
      5) _____ Cutting down or destroying trees, &c.;
      6) 5 Geo II c. 30. Bankrupts not surrendering, &c ;
      7) _____ Concealing or embezzling;
      8) 6 Geo. II c. 37. Cutting down the bank of any river;
      9) 8 Geo. II c 20. Destroying any fence, lock, sluice, &c.;
      10) 26 Geo. II c. 23. Making a false entry in a marriage register, & five related felonies;
      11) 27 Geo. II c. 15. Sending threatening letters;
      12) 27 Geo II c. 19. Destroying Bank, &c. Bedford Level;
      13) 3 Geo. III c. 16 Personating out pensioners of Greenwich Hospital;
      14) 22 Geo. III c 40. Maliciously cutting serges;

15) 24 Geo. III c. 47. Harbouring offenders against that (Revenue) Act, when returned from transportation.
60   *Report*, p. 15.
61   Hansard, v 40, col. 1534.
62   See the comments in the *Edinburgh Review*, v. 35, no. 70 (July 1821), pp. 314–353.
63   See Wilberforce, *Life*, v. 5, p 27.
64   Letter of 25 November 1819, MSS Brit. Emp s. 444, v. 2, f. 107.
65   Quoted in context in Pollock, *Wilberforce*, p. 269. W. R. Ward has described the aftermath of Peterloo as tying Evangelicalism into the developing class tensions, placing it on the side of the 'middle class' as against the 'lower orders'; *Religion and Society in England, 1790–1850* (London: B. T. Batsford, 1972), p. 105.
66   Journal entry for 10 January 1820, MSS Brit. Emp. s. 444, v. 4, f. 10.
67   On 9 May; see Hansard, N.S. v. 1 (1820), cols. 227–37.
68   On 19 May; see Hansard, N.S. v. 1, col. 480.
69   Hansard, N.S. v. 1, col. 1338.
70   See Hansard, N S. v. 2 (1820), cols. 491–6 and cols. 524–8 for the debates.
71   *Quarterly Review*, v. 24 (1820–21), p. 232.
72   Hansard, N.S. v. 2, col 496.
73   *The Times*, 7 August 1820.
74   Letter to H. Bankes, 11 November 1820, MS Wilberforce d. 16, f. 145, quoted in Pollock, p. 277.
75   Sixty-three are listed in the *Journals of the House of Commons*, v. 76 (1821).
76   Hansard, N.S v. 5 (1821), cols. 900ff
77   John Miller, *An Enquiry into the present state of the Statute and Criminal Law of England* (London, 1822), pp. v–vi.
78   *Christian Observer*, v. 20 (1821), no. 5 (May), p. 332.
79   See Wilberforce to Buxton, 24 May 1821, Anti-Slavery Papers, MSS Brit. Emp. s. 18, c. 106, f. 4.
80   See *Journals*, v. 76, p 411.
81   Hansard, N.S. v. 5, col. 1114
82   See the *Christian Observer*, v. 20, no. 6 (June), p. 398.
83   Basil Montagu, *Thoughts upon the Abolition of the Penalty of Death in Cases of Bankruptcy* (London, 1821), p. 32.
84   See Hansard, N.S v. 7 (1822), cols. 790–805.

9   Consolidation, Mitigation and Conclusions

1   Comprehensive descriptions of Peel's efforts can be found in Leon Radzinowicz, *A History of English Criminal Law from 1750* (New York: Macmillan, 1948), v. 1, pp. 567–90, and Norman Gash, *Mr. Secretary Peel* (London: Longmans, 1961), chapters 9 and 14 V. A. C. Gatrell reawakened the debate in *The Hanging Tree: Execution and the English People, 1770–1868* (Oxford· Oxford University Press, 1994); see especially chapters 20 and 21; partial responses include Boyd Hilton, 'The Gallows and Mr Peel', in *History and Biography: Essays in Honour of Derek Beales*, T. C. W. Blanning and David Cannadine, eds (Cambridge· Cambridge University Press, 1996), pp 88–112, and Simon

Devereaux, 'Robert Peel and the Conduct of Capital Punishment', in *Punishment, Pain, and Pardon*, Griffiths, ed. (forthcoming).

2 Peel to Liverpool, 12 October 1822, BL Add MS 38195, ff. 120–6.

3 See Hansard, N.S. v. 9 (1823), cols. 397ff.

4 On 27 May; see *Journals of the House of Commons*, v. 78 (1823), pp. 346–7

5 *Christian Observer*, v. 23 (1823), p. 400.

6 Eldon to Peel, BL Add. MS 40315, f. 83.

7 Peel to Eldon, 16 January 1823, BL Add. MS 40315, ff. 85–6

8 Hansard, Second Series, v. 10 (1824), cols. 1062–4.

9 See S. M. Waddams, *Law, Politics and the Church of England: the Career of Stephen Lushington, 1782–1873* (Cambridge: Cambridge University Press, 1992), pp. 25–34, for a summary of Lushington's views on crime and punishment.

10 *Journals of the House of Commons*, v. 79 (1824), p. 168.

11 See the *Report from the Select Committee on the Criminal Laws of England*, Parliamentary Papers, 1824, v. 4.

12 See Gash, pp. 321–6.

13 Eldon to Peel, September 1825, and 21 January 1826, BL Add. MS 40315, ff. 212 and 239.

14 See Hansard, N.S. v 14 (1836), col. 1218ff.

15 See Radzinowicz, p. 573, for a fuller description of its effects.

16 The bills became 7 & 8 Geo. IV c 27, the Criminal Statute Act; 7 & 8 Geo. IV c. 29, the Larceny Consolidation Act; and 7 & 8 Geo. IV c. 30, the Indemnity Act (affecting malicious injuries to property).

17 The act, 9 Geo. IV c. 31, was called Lord Lansdowne's Act, having been introduced by Lansdowne during the brief Canning/Goderich administration.

18 Hansard, N.S. v. 16 (1827), col 641, 22 February 1827

19 See his comment in 1826, Hansard, N.S. v 14, col. 1239; also, see Gash, pp. 336–7.

20 See *Christian Observer*, v. 26 (1826), p. 191, and v. 27, pp. 191 and 448.

21 *Seventh Report of the Society for the Improvement of Prison Discipline and for the Reformation of Juvenile Offenders* (London, 1827), pp. 5–6.

22 Quoted in the *Christian Observer*, v. 29 (1829), p. 318.

23 See Gash, pp. 478–85, for a fuller discussion of the Forgery Consolidation Act; see Scarlett to Peel, 13 August 1829, BL Add. MS 40399, f. 312; and Gregson to Peel, 7 November 1829, BL Add. MS 40399, f. 375.

24 See Hansard, N.S , v. 23 (1830), cols 1176ff

25 See Buxton to J. J. Gurney, 19 March 1830, quoted in Buxton *Memoirs*, p. 198. For evidence that Peel was working against entrenched opinion in the cabinet, see Edward Law, Lord Ellenborough, *A Political Diary, 1828–1830* (London: Bentley & Son, 1881), v 2, p. 195.

26 Peel had found information provided him by Buxton and Samuel Gurney insufficient to commute a death sentence pronounced on a young offender found guilty of stealing from a dwelling in 1826; see HO 17.76.20. See also Gatrell, pp. 566ff

27 Basil Montagu, *Thoughts on the Punishment of Death for Forgery* (London, 1830).

28 Hansard, N.S v 23, col. 710.

29   See Buxton, *Memoirs*, p. 199.
30   *Journals of the House of Commons*, v. 85 (1830), p. 463.
31   Hansard, N S. v. 24 (1830), col. 36.
32   *Journal of the House of Commons*, v. 85, p. 367.
33   Hansard, N.S. v. 25 (1830), cols. 51–2.
34   See Hansard, N.S. v. 24, cols. 1033ff.
35   Hansard, N S. v. 25, col. 77.
36   Lord Ellenborough, v. 2, pp. 271–3.
37   See Hansard, N S. v. 25, col. 856; Lord Holland attempted unsuccessfully to recommit the bill later; see cols. 1161–4.
38   Evidenced by some of his letters to his old tutor, Dr Charles Lloyd; see *Sir Robert Peel from his Private Papers*, edited by Charles Stuart Parker (London: John Murray, second edition, 1899), v 1, pp. 385–6
39   See Hilton, 'Gallows', p. 111.
40   Lord Ellenborough, v. 1, pp. 267–8; see also pp. 154–5.
41   See the King's letters to Peel in spring 1822 and summer 1823, BL Add MS 40 299, ff. 50, 67 and 70 and BL Add. MS 40300, ff. 241–8, and Gatrell's discussion of Peel and royal mercy, pp. 554ff.
42   See Lord Ellenborough, v. 2, p. 195.
43   For an outline of the Whig's measures, see Radzinowicz, pp. 600–7.
44   Hilton, 'Gallows', p 110.
45   See Gatrell, pp. 18–21.
46   See Williams James Forsythe, *The Reform of Prisoners, 1830–1900* (New York: St. Martin's Press, 1987), pp 15–39; see also Gatrell, pp. 578–9
47   Robert Hole, *Pulpit, Politics and Public Order in England, 1760–1830* (Cambridge: Cambridge University Press, 1989), p. 7.
48   Montagu, *Thoughts*, pp. 87–90.
49   Montagu's closing remarks, *Thoughts*, p. 201. Compare with the advice attributed to the Hebrew Rabbi Gamaliel recorded in the Book of Acts (5: 33–9).
50   See Gatrell, pp. 396–416.
51   See Buxton to Mackintosh, 30 November 1823, quoted in Buxton, *Memoirs*, pp. 118–9.
52   For a survey of the schisms, see David Bebbington, *Evangelicalism in Modern Britain: a History from the 1730s to the 1980s* (London: Unwin Hyman, 1989), pp. 75ff.
53   David Turley, *The Culture of English Antislavery, 1780–1860* (London: Routledge, 1991), p. 142.
54   See Turley, p. 154.
55   R K. Webb, *Modern England: from the Eighteenth Century to the Present*, second edition (New York, 1980), p. 180.

Bibliography

Primary sources

Manuscript sources

NOTE: References to British Library Additional Manuscripts are abbreviated as 'BL Add. MS', followed by the specific number and pages. The references below are shown by collection name, archive name, and the archive's reference numbers for the collection, which also serves as the style of reference in the body of this work.

Anti-Slavery Papers. Rhodes House Library, Oxford. MSS Brit. Emp. s. 18.
Auckland Papers. British Library. Add. MS 34458.
Bentham Papers. British Library. Add. MSS 33542–6
Bentham Papers. University College Library, London. By box and page number.
Brougham Papers. University College Library, London. By page number.
Sir Thomas Fowell Buxton Papers. Rhodes House Library, Oxford. MSS Brit. Emp s. 444.
Criminal Petitions. Public Records Office, Kew. PRO HO 17.
Cumberland Papers. British Library. Add. MS 36513
Ellenborough Papers Public Records Office, Kew. PRO 30/12.
Elizabeth Fry Papers. Library of the Society of Friends (LSF), Friends House, London. Portfolio 38; MS Vol. 261–4; and Temp. MSS 903/3.
Gladstone Papers. British Library. Add. MS 44356.
J. J. Gurney Papers. LSF. Gurney MSS, Temp. MSS 434 and MS Vols 181–3.
Judges' Reports. Public Records Office, Kew. PRO HO 47.
Hardwicke Papers. British Library. Add. MSS 35424, 35678, and 35691.
Holland Papers. British Library. Add. MSS 51520–957.
Ann Knight Papers LSF MS Box W2.
Liverpool Papers. British Library. Add MSS 38190–574.
Mackintosh Papers. British Library. Add. MSS 24487–34526, 51653–7, and 52436–53.
Peel Papers. British Library. Add. MSS 40181–617.
Perceval Papers. British Library. Add. MSS 49183, 49185.
Sir Samuel Romilly Manuscript. Lincoln's Inn Library. MS Misc. 246.
Society for Diffusing Information on the Subject of Capital Punishment & Prison Discipline: Notes of the Subcommittee. Friends House Library. Temp. MSS 4/5
James Stephen Papers. Cambridge University Library ADD 7349.
Henry Thornton Papers Cambridge University Library. ADD 7674.
William Wilberforce Papers. Bodleian Library, Oxford University. MS Wilberforce and MS Don e 164

Periodicals

The Christian Observer
The Eclectic Review

The Edinburgh Review
The Monthly Repository
The Pamphleteer
The Philanthropist
The Quarterly Review
The Times

Books and pamphlets

Allen, William. *Life of William Allen, with Selections from his Correspondence*, in three volumes. London: Charles Gilpin. 1846.

Anon. *A Letter on the Games Laws*. 'By a Country Gentleman ' London. 1815.

Anon. *Memoir of the Late Sir Samuel Romilly, M.P.* Printed by John Fairburn London. 1818.

Anon. *Memoirs of the Life of that Illustrious Patriot, Sir Samuel Romilly*. Printed by George Smeeton. London. 1818.

Anon 'Strictures on the Right, Expedience, and Indiscriminate Denunciation of Capital Punishment.' *The Pamphleteer*, v. 3 (1814), 115–54.

Belsham, Thomas. *Reflections upon the Death of Sir Samuel Romilly*. London. 1818.

Bentham, Jeremy. *A Comment on the Commentaries* and *A Fragment on Government*. Edited by J. H Burns and H. L. A. Hart London: The Athlone Press (University of London). 1977

———. *An Introduction to the Principles of Morals and Legislation*. Reprint of 1823 London edition. New York: Hafner Press. 1948.

———. *The Works of Jeremy Bentham*. Edited by John Bowring. New York: Russell & Russell, Inc 1962. Reproduced from the Bowring edition of 1838–43.

Bicheno, J. E. *Observations on the Philosophy of Criminal Jurisprudence, being an Investigation of the Principles necessary to be kept View in during the Revision of the Penal Code, with remarks on Penitentiary Prisons* London. 1819

Blackstone, William. *Commentaries on the Laws of England*, in four volumes Oxford. 1765–9.

Bowring, John. See Bentham, Jeremy. *The Works of Jeremy Bentham*.

Brougham, Henry Lord. *Historical Sketches of Statesmen who Flourished in the Time of George III*. Second edition. London. Charles Knight & Co 1839.

———. *Speeches of Henry Lord Brougham*, in two volumes. Edinburgh. Adam and Charles Black. 1838.

Burke, Edmund. *Reflections on the Revolution in France* London. 1790.

Burton, John Hill *Benthamania: or Select Extracts from the Works of Jeremy Bentham*. Edinburgh· William Tait. 1843.

Buxton, Thomas Fowell. *An Inquiry Whether Crime & Misery are Produced or Prevented, by Our Present System of Prison Discipline*. London 1818.

——— *Severity of Punishment· a Speech of Thomas Fowell Buxton, Esq. M.P. in the House of Commons . . . May 23rd, 1821*. London. 1821

———. *The Speech of Thomas Fowell Buxton, Esq. at the Egyptian Hall, on the 26th November, 1816, on the subject of the Distress in Spitalfields*. London. 1816.

———. *Substance of the Speech of Thos. Fowell Buxton, Esq. . . . March 2nd, 1819, on the Motion of Sir James Mackintosh, Bart*. London. 1819.

Chitty, Joseph. *A Practical Treatise on the Criminal Laws* London. 1816.

———. *A Treatise on the Game Laws and on Fisheries*. London 1812.

Clarkson, Thomas. *Memoirs of the Public and Private Life of William Penn.* Two British volumes in one American edition. Dover, N. H. 1827.

——. *Portraiture of Quakerism.* 1806.

Cobbett, William, ed. *Parliamentary History.* London: 1803.

Croker, (Miss) M. S. *A Tribute to the Memory of Sir Samuel Romilly.* London. 1818.

Favell, Samuel. *A Speech on the Propriety of Revising the Criminal Laws, Delivered Dec. 10, 1818, before the Corporation of the City of London.* London. 1819.

Fonblanque, Albany. *England Under Seven Administrations.* London. 1837

Frankland, William. *The Speech of Sir William Frankland in the House of Commons, on the 29th of March, 1811, on the second reading of several bills, brought in by Sir S. Romilly, for making Alterations in the criminal law.* London. 1811

Gisborne, Thomas. *The Principles of Moral Philosophy investigated, and briefly applied to the constitution of civil society: together with remarks on the principle assumed by Mr. Paley as the basis of all moral conclusions, and on other positions of the same author.* Second edition. London. 1790.

Greville, Charles C. F. *The Greville Memoirs: a Journal of the Reigns of King George IV and King William IV,* v. 1. New York: Appleton and Co. 1875.

Gurney, J. J. *Reminiscences of Chalmer, Simeon, Wilberforce, etc.* London. 1835

Hansard. See *Parliamentary Debates.*

Harrison, George. *Education Respectfully Proposed as the Surest Means within the Power of Government to Diminish the Frequency of Crimes.* London. 1803.

Hoare, Samuel, Jr. *Rules Proposed for the Government of Gaols, Houses of Correction, and Penitentiaries.* Published by the Society for the Improvement of Prison Discipline, and for the Reformation of Juvenile Offenders. London. 1820

Hobhouse, Henry. *The Diary of Henry Hobhouse (1820–1827).* Edited by Arthur Aspinall. London: Home & Vanthal. 1947.

Holford, George. *Thoughts on the Criminal Prisons in the Country.* London. 1821.

Horner, Francis. *Memoirs and Correspondence of Francis Horner, M.P,* in two volumes. Edited by his brother, Leonard Horner, Esq. Boston: Little, Brown and Co. 1853. (London edition, 1843)

Journals of the House of Commons. London. 1772–1830.

La Rocque, André Jean de. *The State of the Laws, Tribunals, Bar, Morality & Constitution of Great Britain.* London. 1808.

Law, Edward, Second Baron / First Earl Ellenborough. *A Political Diary, 1828–1830.* Edited by Lord Colchester. London: Bentley & Sons. 1881.

Mackintosh, James, Sir. *Debate Upon Sir James Mackintosh's Motion for Abolishing the Punishment of Death in certain cases of Forgery.* London 1830.

Madan, Martin. *Thoughts on Executive Justice, with respect to our Criminal Laws, particularly on the Circuits.* London. 1785.

Mill, John Stuart. *Utilitarianism and Other Essays.* London: Penguin Books. 1987.

Miller, John. *An Inquiry into the Present State of the Statute and Criminal Law of England.* London: John Murray. 1822.

Mitford, J. Freeman, 1st Baron Redesdale. *Observations occasioned by a Pamphlet entitled 'Objections to the Project of creating a Vice-Chancellor of England'.* London. 1813.

Montagu, Basil. *An Account of the Origin and Object of the Society for the Diffusion of Knowledge upon the Punishment of Death, and the Improvement of Prison Discipline.* London. 1812.

——. *Hanging not Punishment Enough.* Reprinted by Basil Montague. London. 1812 (1701).

—— *An Inquiry into the Aspersions upon the Late Ordinary of Newgate, with some Observations upon Newgate and upon the Punishment of Death.* London 1815

—— *The Opinions of Different Authors Upon the Punishment of Death,* in three volumes. Collected by Basil Montagu. London. 1809–13.

——. *Some Inquiries respecting the Punishment of Death for Crimes without Violence.* London. 1818.

——. *Some Thoughts upon the Liberty and the Rights of Englishmen.* London. 1819.

——. *Thoughts on the Punishment of Death for Forgery.* London. 1830.

——. *Thoughts upon the Abolition of the Penalty of Death in Cases of Bankruptcy.* London. 1821

More, Hannah. *Thoughts on the Importance of the Manners of the Great to General Society* and *An Estimate of the Religion of the Fashionable World.* Published together in a new edition. London. 1809

Paley, William. *The Principles of Moral and Political Philosophy.* Seventh American edition Boston. 1811

Parliamentary Debates. Edited by W Cobbett and T. Hansard (after 1812 by Hansard alone). London. 1803–20, in 41 volumes *New Series.* Edited by T. Hansard. 1820–30, in 25 volumes.

Parr, Rev Dr Samuel. *Characters of the Late Charles James Fox* (by 'Philopatris Varvicensis'), in two volumes. London. 1809.

Peel, Robert. *Sir Robert Peel from his Private Papers.* In three volumes edited by Charles Stuart Parker. Second edition. London John Murray. 1899.

Phillips, Sir Richard. *Golden Rules for Jurymen* London. 1820.

Pratt, John H. *The Thought of the Evangelical Leaders: Notes of the Discussions of the Eclectic Society, London during the years 1798–1814.* Based on notes taken by the Rev. Josiah Pratt. Reprint of first London edition of 1856. Carlisle, PA: Banner of Truth Trust. 1978.

Report of the Select Committee on the Criminal Laws, 1819 and *Report of the Select Committee on the Criminal Laws, 1824.* Fascimile edition in the *Irish University Press Series of British Parliamentary Papers: Legal Administration: Criminal Law,* vols 1–2. Shannon, Ireland. 1968.

Romilly, Sir Samuel. *Letters, containing an account of the late Revolution in France, and observations on the Constitution, Laws, Manners and Institutions of the English; written during the Author's residence at Paris, Versailles and London   translated from the German of Henry Frederic Groenvelt* London. 1792

——. *Memoirs on the Life of Sir Samuel Romilly, written by himself; with a selection of his correspondence.* Edited by his sons In three volumes. London: John Murray. 1840

——. *Objections to the Project of Creating a Vice-Chancellor of England.* The second edition, to which is added 'A Letter from the Author to a Noble Lord' London. 1813. (First edition came out in 1812.)

——. *Observations on a Late Publication intituled Thoughts on Executive Justice to which is added, a Letter containing remarks on the same work* London. 1786

——. *Observations on the Criminal Law of England as it Relates to Capital Punishments, and on the mode in which it is Administered.* London. 1810

——. 'Review of Bentham on Codification'. *Edinburgh Review,* v 29. 217–37.

—— *The Speeches of Sir Samuel Romilly in the House of Commons.* London. 1820.

———. *Thoughts on the Probable Influence of the French Revolution on Great Britain.* London. 1790.

Roscoe, William. *Observations on Penal Jurisprudence and the Reformation of Criminals.* London. 1819.

Scarlett, James, First Lord Abinger. *A Memoir of The Right Honorable James, First Lord Abinger, Chief Baron of Her Majesty's Court of Exchequer.* Edited by his son, Peter Campbell Scarlett, C. B. London· John Murray. 1877.

Society for Diffusing Information on the Subject of Capital Punishment and Prison Discipline. *Address of the Society... with an account of a Visit to Warwick Gaol.* (Tract no. 1) London. 1817.

——— *An Account of the Maison de Force at Ghent.* (Tract no. 2) London. 1817.

——— *On the Effects of Capital Punishment as Applied to Forgery and Theft.* (Tract no. 3) London. 1818.

Society for the Improvement of Prison Discipline, and for the Reformation of Juvenile Offenders. *Inquiries Relative to Prison Discipline.* First edition. London 1818.

———. *Reports of the Committee of the Society for the Improvement of Prison Discipline, and for the Reformation of Juvenile Offenders.* London. 1818–32

Stephen, James. *Dangers of the Country.* London. 1807.

Stockdale, (Miss) M. R. *A Shroud for Sir Samuel Romilly: an Elegy.* London: 1818.

Vaughan, Thomas. *The Scriptural Character of Civil Punishments Vindicated.* Oxford. 1830.

Venn, Henry. *The Complete Duty of Man: or, a System of Doctrinal and Practical Christianity.* Seventh edition. Bath. 1803

Wakefield, Edward Gibbon. *Facts Relating to the Punishment of Death in the Metropolis.* London: James Ridgeway. 1832.

Wilberforce, A. M. *Private Papers of William Wilberforce* London. 1897.

Wilberforce, Robert Isaac and Samuel *The Life of William Wilberforce,* in five volumes. London: John Murray. 1838.

Wilberforce, William. *The Correspondence of William Wilberforce,* in two volumes. Edited by his sons. Philadelphia: Henry Perkins. 1841.

———. *A Practical View of the Prevailing Religious Systems of Professed Christians, in the Higher and Middle Classes in this Country, Contrasted with Real Christianity.* London. 1797

Worsley, Israel. *Some Thoughts on Christian Stoicism, an antidote against the Evils of Life: A Sermon preached at Plymouth on Sunday, November 15, 1818, in Consequence of the Much-lamented Death of Sir Samuel Romilly.* London. 1818.

Secondary sources

Unpublished theses

Bradley, Ian. 'The Politics of Godliness: Evangelicals in Parliament, 1784–1832'. Unpublished D. Phil. Thesis, Oxford University. 1974.

Rendall, Jane. 'The Political Ideas & Activities of Sir James Mackintosh (1765–1832): A Study in Whiggism Between 1789 and 1832'. Ph.D. thesis, University of London. 1972.

Stuart, F. C. 'A Critical Edition of the Correspondence of Sir Thomas Fowell Buxton, Bart., with an account of his career to 1823'. MA thesis, University of London. 1957.

Published books and articles

Allen, C. J. W. *The Law of Evidence in Victorian England*. Cambridge: Cambridge University Press. 1997

Anstey, Roger *The Atlantic Slave Trade and British Abolition, 1760–1810*. Atlantic Highlands, NJ: Humanities Press. 1975.

Atkinson, Charles Milner, assisted by John Edwin Mitchell. *An Account of the Life and Principles of Sir Samuel Romilly, K.C., M.P., H.M. Solicitor General, 1806–1807*. Derby· Hobson & Son, Ltd. 1920.

Bain, Alexander. *James Mill: a Biography* London: Longmans, Green, and Co. 1882.

Baker, J. H. *An Introduction to English Legal History*. Third edition. London: Butterworths. 1990.

Beattie, J. M. *Crime and the Courts in England, 1660–1800*. Princeton: Princeton University Press. 1986.

Bebbington, David. *Evangelicalism in Modern Britain: a History from the 1730s to the 1980s*. London: Unwin Hyman. 1989.

——. 'Revival and Enlightenment in Eighteenth-Century England'. *Modern Christian Revivals* Edith Blumhofer and Robert Balmer, eds. Urbana: University of Illinois Press. 1993.

Beynon, Helen 'Mighty Bentham' *Journal of Legal History*, 2 (1981), 62–76.

Bradley, Ian. *Call to Seriousness: the Evangelical Impact on the Victorians*. London: Jonathan Cape. 1976.

Brown, Ford K. *Fathers of the Victorians: the Age of Wilberforce* Cambridge University Press. 1961.

Burrow, J. W. *Whigs and Liberals: Continuity and Change in English Political Thought*. Oxford. Clarendon Press. 1988.

Burton, John Hill. *Benthamania: or Select Extracts from the Works of Jeremy Bentham*. Edinburgh: William Tait 1843.

Buxton, Charles, ed. *Memoirs of Sir Thomas Fowell Buxton, Bart*. London: John Murray 1849.

Campbell, John Lord *The Lives of the Chief Justices of England, from the Norman Conquest till the death of Lord Tenterden*, in three volumes London. John Murray. 1857

——. *The Lives of the Lord Chancellors and Keepers of the Great Seal of England, from the earliest times till the Reign of Queen Victoria*. New edition. Boston: Estes & Lauriat. 1875.

Chadwick, Owen. *Victorian Miniature* Cambridge: Cambridge University Press. 1991.

Cockburn, J S., and T A Green, eds. *Twelve Good Men and True: the Criminal Trial Jury in England, 1200–1800*. Princeton: Princeton University Press. 1988.

Cohen, Stanley and Andrew Scull, eds. *Social Control and the State*. New York. St Martin's Press. 1983

Colley, Linda *Britons: Forging the Nation 1707–1837*. New Haven: Yale University Press. 1992.

Collins, Sir William J. *The Life and Work of Sir Samuel Romilly*. London. 1908. (Reprinted from the Transactions of the Huguenot Society, 1908).

—— *Some Notes on Sir Samuel Romilly and Etienne Dumont* London. 1924. (Reprinted from the Proceedings of the Huguenot Society, v. 12, no. 6.)

Cooper, David D. *The Lesson of the Scaffold* London: Allen Lane 1974

Cordery, Simon. 'Friendly Societies and the Discourse of Respectability in Britain, 1825-1875.' *Journal of British Studies*, 34 (1995), 35-58.

Cornish, W. R. and Clark, G. de N. *Law and Society in England, 1750-1950*. London: Sweet & Maxwell. 1989.

Cosgrove, Richard A. *Scholars of the Law: English Jurisprudence from Blackstone to Hart*. New York: New York University Press. 1996.

Coupland, Sir Reginald. *Wilberforce*. London: Collins. 1945 (1923).

Crimmins, J. E. 'Strictures on Paley's Net: Capital Punishment and the Power to Pardon'. *The Bentham Newsletter* (publication of the Bentham Project, University College, London), no. 11 (June 1987), 23-34.

Devereaux, Simon. 'The City and the Sessions Paper: "Public Justice" in London, 1770-1800'. *Journal of British Studies*, 35 (1996), 466-503.

——. 'The Criminal Branch of the Home Office, 1782-1830'. *Criminal Justice in the Old World and the New*. Greg T. Smith, Allyson N. May and Simon Devereaux, eds Toronto: University of Toronto Press. 1998. Pp. 270-308.

——. 'Robert Peel and the Conduct of Capital Punishment'. *Punishment, Pain, and Pardon*, Griffiths, ed. Forthcoming.

Dicey, A. V. *Lectures on the Relation Between Law and Public Opinion in England During the Nineteenth Century*. London: Macmillan and Co., Ltd. 1952 (first edition in 1905).

Dictionary of National Biography. London: Oxford University Press. 1949-50.

Dictionary of Quaker Biography. Unpublished, typed manuscript in loose-leaf binders at Friends House Library, London.

Dinwiddy, John *Bentham*. Oxford: Oxford University Press. 1989.

Emsley, Clive. *British Society and the French Wars, 1793-1815*. Totowa, NJ: Rowman and Littlefield. 1979.

——. *Crime and Society in England 1750-1900*. London: Longman. 1987

Fiering, Norman S. 'Irresistible Compassion: an Aspect of Eighteenth-Century Sympathy and Humanitarianism'. *Journal of the History of Ideas*, 37 (1976), 195-218.

Fifoot, C. H. S. *Law and History in the Nineteenth Century* (a Seldon Society Lecture). London: Bernard Quaritch. 1956.

Ford, Trowbridge H. 'English Criminal Law Reform During and After the Napoleonic Wars'. *Anglo-American Law Review*, 7 (1978), 243-70.

Forster, E. M. *Marianne Thornton: a Domestic Biography, 1787-1887*. New York: Harcourt, Brace and Co 1956.

Forsythe, William James. *The Reform of Prisoners, 1830-1900*. New York: St Martin's Press. 1987.

Foucault, Michel. *Discipline and Punish: the Birth of the Prison*. Translated from the French, *Surveiller et punir: naissance de la prison* (Paris, 1975). New York: Vintage Books. 1979.

Fry, Katherine and Creswell, Rachel Elizabeth. *Memoir of the Life of Elizabeth Fry, with Extracts from her Journal and Letters*. (Reprinted from the second edition, 1848.) Two volumes in one. Montclair, NJ: Patterson Smith. 1974.

Furneaux, Robin. *William Wilberforce*. London: Hamish Hamilton. 1974.

Gash, Norman. *Aristocracy and People: Britain 1815-65*. Cambridge, MA: Harvard University Press. 1979.

——. *Mr. Secretary Peel: the Life of Sir Robert Peel to 1830*. London: Longmans, Green and Co. 1961.

Gatrell, V. A. C. 'Crime, Authority and the Policeman State'. *The Cambridge Social History of Britain 1750–1950*, v. 3. F. M. L. Thompson, ed. Cambridge Cambridge University Press. 1990. Pp. 243–310.

——. *The Hanging Tree: Execution and the English People, 1770–1868*. Oxford: Oxford University Press. 1994.

Green, Thomas Andrew. *Verdict According to Conscience: Perspectives on the Criminal Trial Jury, 1200–1800*. Chicago: University of Chicago Press. 1985.

Halévy, Elie. *The Growth of Philosophical Radicalism*. Translated from the French by Mary Morris. London· Faber & Faber Limited. 1948 (originally published in French, 1901–4; first English translation in 1928).

——. *A History of the English People in the Nineteenth Century*, v. 1. *England in 1815*. Translated by E. I Watkin and D. A. Barker. New York: Barnes & Noble Inc 1961.

——. *A History of the English People in the Nineteenth Century*, v. 2. *The Liberal Awakening, 1815–1830*. Translated from the French by E. I. Watkin New York· Barnes & Noble Inc. 1961.

Hart, H. L. A. *Essays on Bentham: Jurisprudence and Political Theory*. Oxford· Clarendon Press (Oxford University Press). 1982

Haskell, Thomas. 'Capitalism and the Origins of the Humanitarian Sensibility', parts 1 and 2. *American Historical Review*, 90 (1985), 339–61 and 547–66

Hay, Douglas, et al. *Albion's Fatal Tree: Crime and Society in Eighteenth-Century England*. New York: Pantheon Books. 1975.

Heasman, Kathleen. *Evangelicals in Action· an Appraisal of their Social Work in the Victorian Era*. Geoffrey Bles. 1962.

Hempton, David. *Methodism and Politics in British Society, 1750–1850* London· Hutchinson. 1984.

Hilton, Boyd. *The Age of Atonement: the Influence of Evangelicalism on Social and Economic Thought, 1795–1865*. Oxford: Clarendon Press. 1988.

——. 'The Gallows and Mr. Peel.' *History and Biography: Essays in Honour of Derek Beales*. T. C. W. Blanning and David Cannadine, eds Cambridge· Cambridge University Press. 1996. Pp. 88–112.

Hindmarsh, D. Bruce. *John Newton and the English Evangelical Tradition*. Oxford: Clarendon Press. 1996.

Holdsworth, Sir William. *A History of English Law* (in sixteen volumes) V. 13, edited by A. L Goodworth and H. G. Hanbury. London: Methuen & Co., Ltd. 1952.

Hole, Robert. *Pulpit, Politics and Public Order in England, 1760–1830* Cambridge· Cambridge University Press. 1989.

Hostettler, John. *The Politics of Criminal Law Reform in the Nineteenth Century*. Chichester: Barry Rose Law Publishers Ltd. 1992.

Howse, Ernest Marshall. *Saints in Politics: the 'Clapham Sect' and the Growth of Freedom*. Toronto: University of Toronto Press. 1952.

Hume, L. J. *Bentham and Bureaucracy*. Cambridge· Cambridge University Press 1981.

Ignatieff, Michael *A Just Measure of Pain: the Penitentiary in the Industrial Revolution, 1750–1850*. London: Penguin Books. 1978.

——. 'State, Civil Society and Total Institutions: a Critique of Recent Social Histories of Punishment' *Social Control and the State*. Stanley Cohen and Andrew Scull, eds. New York: St Martin's Press. 1983. Pp. 75–101.

Innes, Joanna and John Styles. 'The Crime Wave: Recent Writing on Crime and Criminal Justice in Eighteenth-Century England'. *Rethinking Social History: English Society 1570–1920 and its Interpretation.* Manchester: Manchester University Press. 1993.

Jay, Elisabeth *The Religion of the Heart: Anglican Evangelicalism and the Nineteenth-Century Novel.* Oxford: Clarendon Press. 1979.

Jupp, Peter J. 'The Landed Elite and Political Authority in Britain, ca. 1760–1850'. *Journal of British Studies,* 29 (January 1990), 53–79.

Keeton, George W. and Georg Schwarzenberger, eds. *Jeremy Bentham and the Law: a Symposium.* London: Stevens & Sons Ltd. 1948

Kirby, Chester. 'English Game Law Reform'. *Essays in Modern English History in Honor of Wilbur Cortez Abbot.* Port Washington, NY: Kennikat Press. 1971 (reissue of 1941 original). Pp. 345–80.

Kriegel, Abraham D. 'A Convergence of Ethics: Saints and Whigs in British Antislavery'. *Journal of British Studies,* 26 (1987), 423–50.

Laquer, Thomas W 'Crowds, Carnival and the State in English Executions, 1604–1868'. *The First Modern Society: Essays in English History in Honour of Lawrence Stone.* A. L. Beier, David Cannadine and James M. Rosenheim, eds. Cambridge University Press. 1989. Pp. 303–55.

Lean, Garth. *God's Politician: William Wilberforce's Struggle* London: Darton, Longman & Todd. 1980.

Lemahieu, D. L. *The Mind of William Paley: a Philosopher and his Age.* Lincoln, NE: University of Nebraska Press. 1976.

Lieberman, David. 'From Bentham to Benthamism'. *The Historical Journal,* 28 (1985), 199–224.

——. *The Province of Legislation Determined: Legal Theory in Eighteenth-century Britain.* Cambridge. Cambridge University Press. 1989.

Lobban, Michael. *The Common Law and English Jurisprudence, 1760–1850* Oxford: Clarendon Press. 1991.

McGowen, Randall. 'The Body and Punishment in Eighteenth Century England' *The Journal of Modern History,* 59 (1987), 651–79.

——. 'The Changing Face of God's Justice· the Debate over Divine and Human Punishment in Eighteenth Century England'. *Criminal Justice History,* 9 (1988), 63–98.

——. 'Civilizing Punishment: the End of Public Execution in England'. *Journal of British Studies,* 33 (1994), 257–82

——. 'He Beareth Not the Sword in Vain: Religion and the Criminal Law in Eighteenth-Century England'. *Eighteenth-Century Studies,* 21 (1987–88), 192–211.

——. 'The Image of Justice and the Reform of the Criminal Law in Early Nineteenth-Century England'. *Buffalo Law Review,* 32 (1983), 89–125

——. 'A Powerful Sympathy: Terror, the Prison and Humanitarian Reform in Early Nineteenth-Century Britain'. *Journal of British Studies,* 25 (1986), 312–34.

——. 'Punishing Violence, Sentencing Crime'. *The Violence of Representation: Literature and the History of Violence.* Nancy Armstrong and Leonard Tennenhouse, eds London: Routledge. 1989

Mackintosh, Robert James. *Memoirs of the Life of Right Honorable Sir James Mackintosh,* in two volumes Boston: Little, Brown & Co. 1853.

McLynn, Frank. *Crime and Punishment in Eighteenth Century England.* Oxford University Press. 1989.

Maine, Sir Henry Sumner. *Lectures on the Early History of English Institutions*. New York: Kennikat Press. 1966. This is a facsimile reprint of the seventh edition of 1914.

Manning, D. J. *The Mind of Jeremy Bentham*. London: Longmans 1968.

Martineau, Harriet. *A History of the Thirty Years Peace, 1816–1846*. Shannon, Ireland: Irish University Press. Fascimile of third edition (London, 1877–8). 1971

Matthews, Nancy L. *William Sheppard, Cromwell's Law Reformer*. New York: Cambridge University Press. 1984.

Meacham, Standish *Henry Thornton of Clapham, 1760–1815*. Cambridge, MA: Harvard University Press. 1964

Medd, Patrick. *Romilly: a Life of Sir Samuel Romilly, Lawyer and Reformer*. London: Collins. 1968.

Mill, John Stuart. *Utilitarianism and Other Essays*. London: Penguin Books. 1987

Oakes, C. G. *Sir Samuel Romilly, 1757–1818· 'A Friend of the Oppressed': His Life and Times – His Work, His Family and His Friends*. London: George Allen & Unwin, Ltd. 1935.

Odgers, W Blake. 'Changes in Procedures and the Law of Evidence'. *A Century of Law Reform: Twelve Lectures on the Changes in the Law of England During the Nineteenth Century*. London· Macmillan. 1901.

Palmer, J. 'Evils Merely Prohibited'. *British Journal of Law and Society*, 3 (1976), 1–16.

Palmer, Stanley H. *Police and Protest in England and Ireland, 1780–1850*. New York: Cambridge University Press. 1988.

Philips, David. *Crime and Authority in Victorian England, 1835–1860*. London: Croom Helm. 1977

——. 'A Just Measure of Crime, Authority, Hunters and Blue Locusts'· The "Revisionist" Social History of Crime and the Law in Britain, 1780–1850'. *Social Control and the State*. Stanley Cohen and Andrew Scull, eds. New York: St. Martin's Press 1983. Pp 50–68.

Pollock, John. *Wilberforce* London. Constable. 1977.

Porter, Roy and Teich, Mikulas, eds. *The Enlightenment in National Context*. Cambridge: Cambridge University Press. 1981.

Postema, Gerald J *Bentham and the Common Law Tradition*. Oxford: Clarendon Press 1986.

Potter, Henry *Hanging in Judgment: Religion and the Death Penalty in England*. New York: Continuum. 1993.

Radzinowicz, Leon. *A History of the English Criminal Law and its Administration from 1750*, v. 1. *The Movement for Reform, 1750–1833*. New York: Macmillan Company. 1948

Roberts, M. J. D. 'The Society for the Suppression of Vice and Its Early Critics, 1802–1812'. *The Historical Journal*, 26, 1 (1983), 159–76.

Rosen, F *Bentham, Byron and Greece· Constitutionalism, Nationalism, and Early Liberal Political Thought*. Oxford: Clarendon Press. 1992.

—— 'Utilitarianism and the Reform of the Criminal Law' (draft). *Cambridge History of Eighteenth Century Political Thought*. Forthcoming.

Schofield, T. P. 'A Comparison of the Moral Theories of William Paley and Jeremy Bentham' *The Bentham Newsletter*, no. 11 (June 1987), 4–22

Selth, Jefferson P. *Firm Heart and Capacious Mind: the Life and Friends of Etienne Dumont*. Lanham, MD: University Press of America. 1977

Semple, Janet. *Bentham's Prison: a Study of the Panopticon Penitentiary*. Oxford: Clarendon Press. 1993.

Stephen, Sir James. *Essays in Ecclesiastical Biography*, in two volumes. Second edition. London. Longman. 1850.

Stephen, Sir James Fitzjames. *A History of the Criminal Law of England*, in three volumes. London: Macmillan. 1883.

Sugarman, David, ed. *Legality, Ideology and the State*. New York: Academic Press. 1983.

Taylor, David. *Crime, Policing and Punishment in England, 1750–1914*. New York: St Martin's Press. 1998.

Thallack, William. *Peter Bedford, the Spitalfields Philanthropist*. London. 1865.

Thomas, William. *The Philosophic Radicals: Nine Studies in Theory and Practice 1817–1841*. Oxford: Clarendon Press. 1979.

Thompson, E. P. *The Making of the English Working Class*. New York: Pantheon Books. 1963.

——. *Whigs and Hunters: the Origin of the Black Act*. New York: Pantheon Books (Random House). 1975.

Thompson, F. M. L., ed. *The Cambridge Social History of Britain 1750–1950*. Cambridge: Cambridge University Press. 1990.

Thorne, R. G. *History of Parliament: the House of Commons, 1790–1820*, in five volumes. London: Secker & Warburg. 1986.

Tobias, J. J. *Crime and Industrial Society in the 19th Century*. New York: Schoken Books. 1967.

Todd, Janet. *Sensibility: an Introduction*. New York: Methuen. 1986.

Turley, David *The Culture of English Antislavery, 1780–1860*. London: Routledge. 1991

Twiss, Horace. *The Public and Private Life of Lord Chancellor Eldon, with Selections from his Correspondence*. Second edition. London: John Murray. 1844.

Waddams, S. M. *Law, Politics and the Church of England: the Career of Stephen Lushington, 1782–1873*. Cambridge: Cambridge University Press. 1992.

Wagner, Henry. *Some Romilly Notes*. London. 1909. (Reprinted from the Transactions of the Huguenot Society, 1909.)

Walsh, J. D. 'Origins of the Evangelical Revival'. *Essays in Modern English Church History, in Memory of Norman Sykes*. G. V. Bennett and J. D. Walsh, eds. New York: Oxford University Press. 1966. Pp. 132–62.

Ward, W. R. *Religion and Society in England, 1790–1850*. London: B. T. Batsford Ltd. 1972.

Watts, Michael R. *The Dissenters; Volume II: The Expansion of Evangelical Nonconformity*. Oxford: Clarendon Press. 1995.

Wiener, Martin J. 'The March of Penal Progress'. *Journal of British Studies*, 26 (1987), 83–96.

——. *Reconstructing the Criminal: Culture, Law, and Policy in England, 1830–1914*. Cambridge: Cambridge University Press. 1990.

——. 'The Unloved State: Twentieth-Century Politics in the Writing of Nineteenth-Century History'. *Journal of British Studies*, 33, 3 (July 1994), 283–308.

Wilberforce, Robert Isaac and Samuel. *The Life of William Wilberforce*, in five volumes. London: John Murray. 1838.

Williford, Miriam. *Jeremy Bentham on Spanish America: an Account of His Letters and Proposals to the New World*. Baton Rouge: Louisiana State University Press. 1980.

Zaller, Robert. 'The Debate on Capital Punishment during the English Revolution'. *American Journal of Legal History*, 31 (1987), 126–44.

Index

Printed in the United States
29039LVS00001B/53